In Search of Woman's Passionate Soul

Caitlín Matthews has written over 25 books and is an internationally renowned expert on the Celtic and Goddess traditions. She teaches worldwide on practical spirituality, the Celtic tradition and shamanism, and has a shamanic practice in Oxford, England.

by the same author

The Elements of the Celtic Tradition
The Elements of the Goddess
The Little Book of Celtic Wisdom
The Little Book of Celtic Blessings
Singing the Soul Back Home
The Celtic Tradition
The Encyclopaedia of Celtic Wisdom

In Search of WOMAN'S Passionate Soul

REVEALING THE DAIMON LOVER WITHIN

Caitlín Matthews

ELEMENT

Shaftesbury, Dorset • Rockport, Massachusetts • Brisbane, Queensland

© Element Books Limited 1997
Text © Caitlín Matthews 1997

First published in Great Britain in 1997 by
Element Books Limited
Shaftesbury, Dorset SP7 8BP

Published in the USA in 1997 by
Element Books, Inc.
PO Box 830, Rockport, MA 01966

Published in Australia in 1997 by
Element Books Limited
for Jacaranda Wiley Limited
33 Park Road, Milton, Brisbane 4064

Cover design by Mark Slader
Text design by Roger Lightfoot
Typeset by ABM Typographics Limited, Hull
Printed and bound in Great Britain by
J W Arrowsmith, Bristol

British Library cataloguing in Publication
data available

Library of Congress Cataloging in Publication
data available

ISBN 1-85230-942-3

Cover illustration
'Cupid and Psyche' by Sir Edward Burne-Jones (1833–1898)
(reproduced by permission of the Trustees, the Cecil Higgins Art
Gallery, Bedford, England)

Contents

List of Plate Illustrations

Picture Credits

The author and publishers would like to thank the following for permission to use illustrations: 1, 14, 15 Deborah Koff-Chapin, The Centre for Touch Drawing, Langey, Wa, USA; 2 Rex Features Limited, London (Liam Neeson, Mel Gibson, Keanu Reeves, Johnny Depp); 3, 7 *The Rider Wait Tarot*, Random Century Hutchinson, London; 4 'The Baleful Head' by Sir Edward Burne-Jones, Southampton City Art Gallery and The Bridgeman Art Library, London; 5 André Paulvé Productions, The Ronald Grant Archive; 6 CBS, The Kobal Collection; 8 BBC Film Productions, The Ronald Grant Archive; 9 American Zoetrope, The Kobal Collection; 10 Geffen Pictures, The Kobal Collection; 11 'Green Man' by Chesca Potter; 12 reproduced by kind permission of Tharpa Publications, York, UK © Andy Weber & Tharpa Publications. 13 Deutsches Archäologisches Institut, Rome and The Trustees, The Cecil Higgins Art Gallery, Bedford, England. Every effort has been made to trace all the copyright holders but if any have been inadvertently overlooked the publishers will be pleased to make the necessary arrangement at the first opportunity.

Dedication

In honour of the eternally creative motion of the Daimons and Muses.

> Nunc nunc beatur artes   per vos vigil decensque
> quas sic sacratis ambo   nus mentis ima complet,
> ut dent meare caelo,   per vos probata lingua
> reserent caducis astra   fert glorias per aeuum.
> Ac lucida usque ad aethram   vos disciplinas omnes
> pia subvolare vota,   ac nos sacrate musas.

Now are the Arts blest, for together you so sanctify them that they grant access to heaven, open the stellar regions to mortal beings, and let faithful prayers ascend even to the bright ether. Through your observation and articulation, understanding fills the expanses of the mind. Through you, well-tempered language attains eternal honour. Bestow your sacred power upon all the Arts, and upon us ...

Martianus Capella *De Nuptiis Philologiae et Mercurii*

Acknowledgements

To all the women who contributed their experiences to this book I am deeply indebted: as pioneer explorers of the spiritual landscape and its inhabitants, you have named and recognized the unexplored dimensions of the soul for the benefit of generations of women after you.

To my husband, John, for putting up with 'the other man' in my life: many thanks for not bringing a co-respondency suit!

To Pat Kemsley who believed in this book and whose faith enabled it to come to light.

Many thanks to Kathleen Raine for permission to quote her daimonic poems and to Anne Lister for the verses of her songs: the words of the heart are the pathways of true soul-finding.

Preface

A savage place! as holy and enchanted
As e'er beneath a waning moon was haunted
By woman wailing for her demon-lover!

SAMUEL TAYLOR COLERIDGE, *Kubla Khan*

This book was conceived many years ago at a time when I was hardly courageous enough to talk about this subject even to my closest friend. It was always a pending project, never a top-of-the-list priority, for reasons of sheer professional panic.

The reason for this reticence (and those who know me would normally not call me shy!) was that throughout my life I have had a fulfilling relationship with my life's creative genius: my daimon. The process whereby I came to understand this masculine figure which filled my dreams, my sexual awakening and my creative and spiritual life was a complex one. The definitions I have drawn in this book were hard-won – wrought out of confusion and self-doubt, and despite the unhelpful attitudes and conventions of society which happily accord man a muse but disallow woman any such creative helpmeet.

Because this subject is so little discussed and rarely defined, I felt that it was essential to gather raw material from the horse's mouth, from women themselves. The rare books which deal with, or rather, skirt about, this subject are normally written by psychoanalysts who have formed professional Jungian explanations of their clients' experiences. I wanted the experiences of women to speak for themselves and the reader to be able to view this subject from a wider perspective.

The main method by which I gathered this material was through questionnaires and by personal interview. Over a hundred women from various countries were approached, drawn from a range of ages, occupations and backgrounds. They were not randomly selected but chosen because, for the most part, they were actively engaged in the creative exploration of their spiritual and creative frontiers. Some were known to me as friends, some I had never met. Most were in middle life. All were offered the chance to contribute their experiences under their own first names or under pseudonyms, since this subject is both intimate and potentially soul-exposing. Many women had never before considered this topic in a reflective way: it was only comprehensible to them through their emotional experience. Some declined to answer, saying that in order to respond in a coherent way they needed to read this book first. I hope that their daimonic exploration can now begin!

The respondents (as the women answering the questionnaire have been called throughout this book) have helped me descend, via an ever-extending stairway, into the abyss of the inner beloved. Although there were times when that stair became Escher-like in its dimensional complexity, when I found myself ascending and descending a series of nesting boxes, one within the other, I could not have written this book without the respondents' help.

Any conclusions I've made are not necessarily for all women to accept. The major problem when chasing the daimon is his transformational ability; he shape-shifts in sequences which are different in each individual. It isn't possible to generalize or provide models for each experience.

The whole question of the daimon has been camouflaged behind a load of psychoanalytical jargon. Books dealing with the Jungian perception of the daimon as 'animus' speak almost entirely about classical archetypes, as though there were no nearer examples in our own society. So I have tried to exemplify the daimon more locally and contemporaneously by allowing the reports of my respondents to speak for themselves. Such myths and stories as I have used are sometimes of only fragmentary usefulness since many delineate the juvenile phase of young womanhood. I hope that the respondents' material will be seen as a framework for more in-depth stories about the mature phases of womanhood.

A daimon is the inner inspirer of many woman. He usually takes the shape of a male figure who appears in women's dreams, fantasies and reflections, and has a significant role in shaping and guiding their outer lives. The daimon is frequently projected upon a human man and reflections of him are found in performers, singers and other inspirers.

When I first began to go through the experiences that women had sent me I was both delighted and alarmed – delighted that so many had responded so enthusiastically and alarmed at the responsibility attached to using this material with due respect. It soon became clear that many of the respondents were under the impression *that they were alone in experiencing such things*; most had no idea that the daimonic relationship was common to others.

Women's experience of the daimon strikes on many levels, at different times and seasons. It doesn't have a common developmental curve in all women and, for this reason, the reader should be aware that her own personal experience cannot be measured against any kind of 'norm' or standard. Whatever she experiences is 'normal' for her. Some women are highly conscious of the daimon while others are largely unaware of him; some experience clues, suggestions and hints of his presence in a vague kind of way, while some may feel ashamed, guilty or worried that something is out of the ordinary, something that cannot be explained or discussed with others.

The respondents' reports reveal all shades and levels of this. Some have been working to clarify the daimon for years and have a deep spiritual resourcefulness to support their exploration; some have been theoretically aware of the daimon but uncertain of how their own experience is to be understood and accepted; some have been bemused or confounded by the daimon, struggling in deep waters with overwhelming emotion and confusion; yet others have quietly accepted that they are companioned by the daimon and have continued their lives accordingly, without reference to any outside authority, only to their own experience. All these ways are commonplace.

Jung, the first to discuss the interior masculine as 'animus', was certainly right in his assessment of how contrasexual images are received and understood.

> They mobilize prejudice and become taboo like everything else that is unexpected ... They are felt to be fascinating and numinous ... surrounded by an atmosphere of sensitivity, touchy reserve, secretiveness, painful intimacy ...[28]

This very truth has made this a difficult book to write, since the women who contributed to it have had to reveal these areas of painful intimacy through personal confrontation with what had hitherto lain secret and taboo. To bring shape to the work has been a correspondingly complex task.

This book will examine the ways in which the daimon can be transformed from a sometimes negative and suppressed image into an empowering and creatively inspiring figure who can access the passionate creative nature of the female soul. It hopes to show how that daimon lover can open the pathway to physical ecstasy, creative passion and spiritual fulfilment, accessing women's hidden yearnings and releasing a deep, spiritual potency.

Women have a passionate soul which has been shrouded, veiled and obscured in myriads of ways. The social and historical reasons for the loss of our passionate soul are obvious to all: the long denigration of women and of female ways of perception is a legacy from which we are going to be recovering for many generations. Women have either quietly covered their passion or become demented (privately or publically) with frustration at not expressing it over the centuries.

When something so vital has been abused for so long, it is sometimes hard to coax it back. By seeking out our souls, honouring them and allowing the passion to reinhabit them, we enable the discovery of our authentic selves. To seek out our passion, we need to ask what it is we most desire, and then follow our chosen pathway in company with the daimon – the masculine soul-image who will not betray, demean or denigrate our quest.

I am privileged to have been able to read other women's accounts of their struggles; their extraordinary revelations and spontaneous responses have been very moving. Many women used the questionnaire as a springboard for self-exploration, so that their realizations arrived as newly-minted soul-currency for other women to recognize and spend within themselves.

Producing this book has changed me, both by the process of dwelling upon its subject and by considering the illuminating answers of other women. It has caused my own daimonic relationship to shift into another, more subtle, mode. I await further revelations with great interest.

Throughout I have tried to use the language of the heart to address women and the secret which women share, bringing it into the sphere of normality. 'What do women most desire?' was frequently the subject of medieval folklore: this book pursues that question and attempts to answer it. My regret is that for reasons of space I have had to leave out so much material from the reports themselves, as well as a full overview of the daimon in literature and history.

At the end of each chapter are questions, reflections, tasks and suggestions to help the reader to explore her own sacred symbolic landscape and her relationship with the daimon. Please use these creatively and remember 'to live the question' rather than strive for a narrow definition or quick explanation. My intention in this book has been to define clearly the role of the daimon, with the help of other women's insights. I hope that the reader will be enabled to find pointers, clues and support for her own daimonic relationship and that, by addressing her personal daimon, her own sexual, creative and spiritual life may be greatly enriched.

Caitlín Matthews

Note

I would ask readers to be aware that, in most women's experience, the daimon is not an incarnate man, although his image can be projected on to one. The daimon is, rather, a spirit or messenger who appears in many male guises and who may be an ambassador or representative of Love itself. It is therefore important for the reader to note that the daimon is not 'a man' or, indeed, 'men at large' but the 'spirit of the divine and inspirational masculine'.

For clarity, it is also important to note that the Jungian 'animus' wears masks which are derived from our social conditioning; although it often doubles as the true daimon, swanning about in many guises, it is mostly illusory. The daimon, on the other hand, is the true soul-companion of women. His appearance may derive from our mythic culture, but his innate quality is that of helper.

In these pages, I shall be using the term 'daimon' to represent the true soul-companion, and 'masked or unemergent daimon' when referring to the projections which can block our clear sight of the true daimon. Many of the respondents use the term 'animus' in the general sense of the 'inner beloved' or the masculine presence in their soul; I have retained this usage when quoting the questionnaires.

I have attempted to keep technical language to a minimum; terms I have coined appear in the Glossary on p233. The numbers in the text refer to the Sources on p237.

CHAPTER 1

The Masks of the Daimon

In the unconscious of every man there is hidden a feminine personality, and in that of every woman a masculine personality.

C G Jung *The Archetypes of the Collective Unconscious*

THE BURNING GLASS

A woman's soul is like a magical container which is bigger and more capacious inside than it appears outside. It holds treasures and wonders, terrors and monsters, desires and passions. Many of us never look inside because we fear the soul holds scary and unusual things; we're not quite sure how we feel about its contents. Those who *have* peeped within soon realize that a lifetime's exploration awaits them. Those who are familiar with the contents of the soul discover, and are enabled to use, precious gifts of power, delight, creativity, passion and that most rare jewel – the authentic self.

The discovery of the authentic self is a long business for human beings. For women it is lengthened by society's disabling expectations and projections upon women at large. In the search for the authentic self we make many mistakes and take many wrong turnings, we read books (both unhelpful and supportive), take other people's advice (or ignore it), look in every place but the right one. We need light, direction and motivation to find ourselves, as well as passion to sustain our search.

In this book I'm suggesting that that light and passion may well come from a source we had never before considered: from an inhabitant of our soul who most often assumes a male guise – the figure of the daimon. The world *daimon* (pronounced dymone) comes from the Greek meaning 'a spirit who bridges the divine and the human state'.

Wherever we look in world mythology and folklore, we find a mysterious male figure who is intimate with women, one who inhabits the country of the soul and who reveals deep wisdom, bringing resolution through his searching light. We may experience him as the beloved of our heart, as an apparition or ghostly being who haunts our dreams, as a fearful monster who seeks transformation, or as the patriarch who preaches stern duty in a remorseless, charismatic way. All these images and more are the masks of the daimon.

He doesn't always get a good press, nor are his qualities always recognized or employed by the women who experience him. Women have run away from him shrieking rape, murder or trickery! Others have cursed him and his cleverness, spurned his suggestions and spat upon his proffered love. Others have waited patiently and tried to understand him and his ways, while some have sought him desperately, seeing him in every male face, in every relationship. Still others, weary with victimhood, have remained chained to outworn projections, while he has raged at them to have some self-respect.

Then there are those of the passionate sisterhood who have run and welcomed him with open arms and run wild with him on the mountains. There are the women who have opened their souls to share their gifts generously to all, after the example of the Good Giver and Friend who has helped them find their inner treasure. There are those who have succumbed to ecstasy and whose whole lives are an orgasm of delight, shared with the daimon. There are the quiet women of confidence whose calm exterior curtains a passionate tumble of entwined limbs. There are the creators who bring forth the children of their daimon-lovers as poetry, music, painting and craft. There are the spiritually-devoted women whose praise and prayer are a love-making gift to the universe.

The daimon is not exclusive to one kind of woman: be she old, young, rich, poor, healthy or ill, he stands ready to cherish and support as her soul-partner if she will only say 'yes'. Until that moment of assent, the daimon may be hard to get to know. We shall spend some chapters exploring his ways and how we react to them, with the help of women like you and me.

The daimon of this book is central to women's sexuality, creativity and spirituality. He is the inner inspirer of women: one who appears in male shape in their dreams, fantasies and meditations and plays a significant part in guiding and shaping their outer lives.

The soul of every human being is encoded with an image of desire. In men, the image usually appears as female; in women, as male. Throughout adolescence, the influence of this image intensifies like a burning glass, heightening sexual desire. In later years, this image exercises a strong influence in many areas of life when its features and characteristics are sought in sexual partners, in intellectual colleagues, in objects of spiritual veneration, and in creative inspiration and artistic fulfilment.

In the classical world, the word *daimon* was used to mean 'the inspirational spirit-companion or genius of a human being'. Similar to the Roman *genius*, the daimon was the spirit which was believed to be present at one's birth and which guided and protected one's soul.

The word *daimon* later fell into disrepute in medieval Christian terminology where it was diminished to 'demon', meaning 'an evil spirit' or 'little god' – a definition which is retained in modern usage. However, the angelic and beneficent aspects of the daimon have yet to be identified and reclaimed by society at large. Throughout this book, I shall be using *daimon* in the particular sense of 'the male soul-image of women'.

Throughout the Middle Ages, the usual term for a male spirit interested in women was *incubus*, a night-visiting demon who slept with women and gave them erotic dreams. (Men were visited by the *succubus*, a female spirit who caused them to ejaculate during sleep and who stole their seed.) In tales describing the conception of Merlin, his mother was visited by an otherworldly spirit whose identity remained a mystery, even to her. Such stories were salaciously related and decried by churchmen.

Women's sexuality was surrounded by myths and legends, telling of otherworldly assignations, abductions by fairy lovers, and men enchanted into bestial shapes seeking congress with women. Folk songs abound relating the adventures of ghostly and demonic lovers who cross the boundaries between the worlds to reclaim their brides, to win sweethearts back from mortal husbands. Such oral stories diminish as time wears on, or else are incorporated into the tide of literature. But whether we look to the folk song of the House Carpenter who returns for his bride or to the wild love of Heathcliff for his Catherine in Emily Brontë's *Wuthering Heights*, the daimon lover is clearly distinguishable.

Side by side with these written traditions are spiritual practices which are not so well recorded. In the native shamanic traditions of every culture, the female shaman has her spirit husband; in the mystical literature of the world, women have discovered the sexual-spiritual union with the divine as nuns, priestesses or mystics. In myths such as *Cupid and Psyche* the female search for the face of the daimon – for the unknown, inner beloved – is portrayed as a transcendent spiritual quest rather than a sordid or supernatural drama.

At the same time as these stories were being told, usually to the detriment of women, it was a male convention to claim an other-worldly female inspirer or muse. No comparable tradition was vouchsafed to women, since they were not socially accepted as creators or artists. This unequal view passed directly and unconsciously into the work of C G Jung, who defined the contrasexual image of the female soul as male, as the *animus*, taken from the Latin for 'soul'. He also held that a man's contra-sexual image was female, defined as the *anima*. Jung's theory was considerably coloured by his own generation's view of women as inferior to men. While he presented the anima, the inner ideal woman who appears in the psyche of men, as something desirable and helpful, he treated the animus with less partiality, seeing it as something doubtful and necessitating self-control on a woman's part.

Despite the findings of Jung and his followers, the daimon is still largely undefined within modern culture. However, when women speak of their experience of the daimon, other women immediately understand, recognizing him from their own experience. Many of the respondents who had read Jung remarked that his definitions still left them confused and dissatisfied since 'the animus' was not what they experienced. The daimon abides in the fantasy life of women and is a dynamic influence on the way they experience and relate to sexual partners and on their creative vocation and spiritual needs.

Because the daimon is often unconscious or submerged in the female psyche, it has been only covertly acknowledged and seldom understood. He frequently loiters in the feminine psyche as a dark figure, analogous to the Beast in folk story, and as such he is conjured afresh in films such as *Interview with a Vampire* (based on Anne Rice's book), with its legend of 'drink from me and live forever'. Women continue to seek for ways to 'unenchant' or manifest the object of their fantasy life, to transform the obscure Beast into the handsome Prince, or to throw over the traces of humdrum lives and run off with the wild outlaw.

The truth of the matter is, the demon lover, the incubus, the daimon, the animus – whatever we call him – has not gone away. He is still among us in many guises. One woman's beloved can be another's demon or angel. Like the men with whom we choose to live our lives, he may be anything from abusive to angelic, depending upon our experience.

How does the daimon function in everyday life? The relationship with the inner beloved is different from that which a woman has with her physical lover. It has a subtle dynamic which is hard to crack or understand. It is often misunderstood in terms of a physical relationship; also the reflection of the daimonic image upon human men can become a real problem for many women. How does the daimon manifest in woman's experience?

- She may be aware of referring life events to an internalized masculine figure who sometimes 'answers' her.
- She may experience the masculine in herself but project it upon the human men around her.
- She may identify entirely with the authority and strength of the internal masculine in herself, embracing it as part of herself.
- She may purposely ignore the presence of an accompanying male figure in her soul, only to struggle with it in dreams or daily life situations where she may similarly ignore or deny her own power.
- She may be always dreaming of a masculine figure whom she understands as a potential lover, continually fantasizing new scenarios where they are together.
- She may accept and welcome an internalized male figure as a friend and vigilantly watch with interest where he leads her, in dreams, dialogues, meditations, etc.

Do all women experience the daimon? Most heterosexual women have some glimpse of him but women who are innately lesbian, as opposed to women who have chosen a lesbian life-style, sometimes experience a female rather than a male figure in their soul-life. Do men have similar experiences? Men experience a parallel internalized relationship with their contrasexual other, the muse or anima, but such a study is outside the scope of this book.

When do women first experience the daimon? From the questionnaires, 75 per cent of the respondents reported that their first experience took place at puberty or during childhood; for the remaining 25 per cent it was in their twenties, thirties and forties. We will be looking at this initiatory experience in Chapter 2.

What is it like, this relationship with the daimon? Here is Suzanne's account of awakening to her daimon in her forties, which was sparked off by an encounter with a real life musician, Jeff. After she had distinguished between the human man and the man within, she was able to relate to her daimon as 'a guide, guardian angel, healer, visitor, friend, lover, protector, inspirer, companion, refuge, saviour and anything else you can name'. She goes on to describe her experience of the daimon.

> When I meditate he speaks to me, in the centre of my brain. Sometimes he says a few words, sometimes we have a long conversation on a deserted beach. Since I've been doing healing visualizations for my shoulder, he's appeared and drawn several hot pokers from my arm and cast them into a cool stream, after which my pain disappeared and I slept well.
>
> Sometimes when I can't sleep, he holds me till I fall asleep. He isn't there, yet I can feel his breath on my neck. It's like being enfolded in the wings of an angel, I feel so safe. I live in an attic and sometimes when it's raining, I sit listening to the rain falling on the roof and he talks to me through the language of the raindrops' pattern.
>
> Before I met him I wasn't alive. I was sitting in the dark and he led me into the light. I most often describe him as 'my beloved angel'. Without him, I was like an unlit lamp. The real Jeff is happily married, and I don't wish to spoil that. I relate to him on a different level. What I feel for the daimon is *absolute, unconditional love*, which I've never experienced before. I'd do anything for him. I talk to [him] all the time. He's always with me. *It's such a relief to write about this!*

Note the need to define this experience. The questionnaire was greeted with almost universal relief by respondents, most of whom had never had an opportunity to express their experiences before. Many women are frequently so locked into patterns of secrecy and self-concealment that they are unaware of their own motivations and desires, out of touch with their passion. Denial of our dynamic nature imprisons us, like a princess in a tower waiting to be released by a disenchanting prince. The daimon seeks to liberate our dynamic and authentic nature, awakening it to passion.

Passion signifies our 'total engagement' in something – self-identification with the object of passion, whether it be a cause, a person or a task. There is a strong vocational element to passion: we respond to the quality which is already strong within us. But passion is powerful and so our society is fearful of it because it implies lack of control. The passion I speak of here includes sexual desire and the creative current, as well as the ecstasy of spiritual experience. Passion is a soul-sign, just as imagination is a faculty of the soul. Passion changes us and bids us find authority deep within. If a woman attempts to liberate her authority through passion, she is seen as mad, bad and danger-ous! But we cannot connect with the mainspring of our authentic and dynamic nature without passion.

The first step along the path to our true selves is to find the thread of our passion and follow it to the source. Since the dai-mon's primary task seems to be to awaken our passion, let us first try to find him.

DEFINING THE INDEFINABLE

How do women explain the daimon to themselves? Significantly, it is men who have most commonly defined the daimonic experi-ence down the ages, usually in unhelpful ways, but it is now time to tell the story from women's point of view. When there is no standard definition of what we experience, great confusion can arise, especially when we encounter definitions which don't seem to fit our actual circumstances. The definitions which follow have arisen from respondents' personal reflections rather than from study. They represent the recurrent categories in which women define the daimon.

- a twin-soul
- the image of a destined partner
- a past incarnational memory of self or partner
- a psychological part of the self

- a spirit
- the completion of the androgynous self
- a soul-companion
- inspirer or guide

In their quest for the most fitting definition, some of the respondents have accepted and rejected several of the above in their lifetimes; each of these definitions is held to be true and actual until our experience shows us otherwise.

The explanation of the daimon as a twin-soul is an old definition. Melissa writes, 'This meeting with the daimon who brings the sense of wonder, should not be restricted to some but should be extended to all women who reach out for the other half of their souls.'

Human beings naturally symbolize things in relative dualities because that is how life appears: male/female, day/night, Yin/Yang, etc. But there is also a human longing for unity, wholeness and completion. This unity is partially experienced in childhood but, at puberty, strong sexual differentiation takes place and we each move into the sphere of the gender into which we were born, experiencing separation from the unity of childhood. Thereafter, the dance of relationships seeks out that unity once more.

Lairdearg writes:

> He shows us the power of our sexuality as women, and helps us to see that, as women, we can be powerful beings in our own right, not trying to be powerful in the way men are, not being afraid of our power. *Without my daimon I am literally emasculated; I am only half of myself.* He is the stake supporting the tree, enabling, assisting, advising.

This sense of mirroring and reflecting the daimon as a means of self-completion is strongly expressed throughout the respondents.

It is not surprising that many women experience the daimon as twin-soul, for it is an ancient myth. In Plato's *Symposium*,[56] Socrates tells the following myth, which explains why men and women forever seek after each other. Once there were three sexes: men, women and hermaphrodites who were like two people – male and female – joined together, with one head, two faces, and four arms and legs. But when the hermaphrodites aspired to divinity, Zeus caused them to be sliced in two halves so that each became the half of what once had been whole. 'This love ... is always trying to make two into one and to bridge the gulf between one human being and another.'[56] This myth also explains homosexuality: 'the woman who is a slice of the original female is attracted by women rather than by men ... while men who are slices of the male (hermaphrodite) are followers of the male.' Socrates concludes that the happiness of the whole human race, women no less than men, is to be found in the consummation of our love, and in 'the healing of our dissevered nature by finding each his proper mate'.

The theory of twin souls is also substantiated in mystical Jewish belief.

> The world rests upon the union of the male and the female principle. That form in which we do not find both the male and the female principle is neither a complete nor superior form. Before coming to this earth, each soul and each spirit is composed of a man and a woman, united in one single being. On coming down to earth, the two halves are separated and sent to animate two different bodies.'[50]

The Jewish 'soul-half' is the male *basheirt* or the female *basheirta* , a kind of destined partner.

Many respondents have spoken in terms of the daimon as the soul's counterpart in some way, as guide or inspirer. Some, like Meg, feel a sense of predestined meeting.

> I felt that my soul was already in touch with his on another plane and that one day our orbits would cross down here on earth too and that we would both know and become one. I was always convinced that it was the spirit of a real man I had inside me, not just another part of me.

Pat thought of her experience as

> a premonition of the man I was to marry, but he didn't manifest physically. Within three months I met a dark-haired man with whom I had a two-year relationship.

The past-incarnation assumption is one made by many women when defining their daimon. Fionnula, a young Irishwoman who consulted me recently said, 'I think I'm being haunted by a lover from a past incarnation,' and then went on to describe what appeared to be a very straightforward case of daimon-visitation. Fionnula had no prior frame of reference to explain her experience and, to compound matters, she had recently met a man who corresponded in most regards to her daimon.

I myself spent a confused period trying to understand my daimon as a past incarnation of my own, since he would very potently and physically manifest through my body to the extent that I could understand things from his viewpoint entirely. I now understand this phenomenon as a direct embodiment of the daimon's spiritual power, but at the time it was very confusing and I was on the verge of believing that I had been 'born in the wrong body', so strong was the physicality of this experience.

The sense of haunting occurred to Anna, who thought that she was 'imagining the spirit of a poet who had lived in the same locality some time before'. And Pat now sees her daimon in terms of reincarnation.

> I feel he and I were in a past life in North America. This time he has chosen not to incarnate and so works with me on the other side. He comes into consciousness unexpectedly and the feeling of joy and love are quite profound. I keep having the sense my true love is not on earth for me this time. This aspect of him comes as Buffalo Medicine Man, as my protector, lover and partner.

Elizabeth has followed many daimonic themes.

> I wasn't aware of [the daimon] as within but as another thing: in pop stars, actors who I fantazied about. One particular figure had a strong inner relationship with me and appeared as a prince to my princess. I felt strongly at the time that this was a past-life scenario, inspired by this person playing a particular role on TV and awakening memory within me. The relationship was a sexual one, but also had a strong brother-sister element – 'you and me against the world' – with a doomed-love side, which I've had to overcome falling into in life.

For Anne,

> The scenario that rationalizes it for me is that we were lovers in a past life, connected with the French Resistance in the Second World War. It doesn't explain everything but it makes a certain amount of sense.

With Suzanne, the sense of familiarity was experienced in reincarnational terms.

> For three years I lived with a seemingly impossible scenario about meeting my daimon, and having met him, I simply want to meet him again. In my visions he is breath-taking, but his presence is like a blessing. I feel I've always known him.

In my shamanic practice, many people ask me how much of my memory is genetic and ancestral, and how much is reincarnational. This is hard to define, for we take in information in such subtle and subliminal ways. With some women, the sense of being accompanied by the daimon through many lives is very strong. This is reinforced by his appearances in various historical guises in their dreams and visions. The theme of 'undying love' which follows us down the ages is likewise marked.

For those who are uncomfortable with lives after death, or with notions of spiritual realities beyond the earthly realm, the definition of daimon as a psychological part of the self is commonly acceptable. Many respondents were very happy with the Jungian view of the animus as part of the soul, and we shall explore this in more detail below. They were unwilling to perceive the daimon as having a life of his own.

Susanna spoke of a trend which was strongly marked in most of the American respondents.

> My background in counselling encouraged me to analyse and explain things in psychological terms, overlooking the spiritual aspects ... Despite a life-long interest in Jung, I find that I'm still confused, in my personal life, about the difference between the shadow and the animus. It seems to me that my shadow is my animus is my daimon.

Miriam says:

> As an adult and writer, I did some work with the Inner Critic. In my late twenties or so, I was aware that my male fantasy images were an aspect of myself.

The methods by which we express our intimate and mystical experience have very much been affected by psychological terminology. For some women, this is helpful and supportive, while others find it disorienting and undermining to their innate understanding of the spiritual cosmos.

Some respondents were totally at home with the idea of the daimon as a god or spirit which visited them. Many had close personal alliances with gods and spirits and drew parallels between these and the daimon. The daimon as spirit can be experienced in every shade from divine to demonic – we shall examine the full range in Chapters 5 and 6.

Janet and Meg both speak of their childhood, when they experienced the beginning of a symbiotic relationship with their daimon which has become transformative. Janet writes:

> I was never alone. My companion was in the form of a fairy who comforted and played with me. I think I came to recognize this spirit as taking on different appearances later.

Meg says that she was

> always aware of invisible spirits in the woods where we used to play: these were tree spirits and flower fairies and I used to imagine being with them and talking to them: they were very much an outdoor thing. I think these spirits evolved into my daimon since he was, at first, half human and half spirit.

Meg's last statement is very interesting in the light of the original classical definition of the daimon as a spirit mid-way between divine and human realms.

The explanation of daimon as spirit is very rarely given in psychological studies, which most often speak of the animus as an internalization of external masculine factors in a woman's life, but it is the one which is most common among the respondents: a sense of the daimon as a being close to hand, but separate from themselves. I suspect that this explanation seldom comes to light due to the social constraints on admitting to belief in spirits, to a fear of encouraging fantasies or to a universal anxiety about possession by spirits.

The many respondents who spoke of the daimon in spirit terms betrayed none of this anxiety, but wrote pragmatically about their daimons as close and intimate friends of their souls. Gwen, for example, says:

> My daimon is a companion unlike any other friend I've ever had: it doesn't compete with or compensate for human relationships. It is different and special.

And Melissa writes:

> I would use the term 'very colourful, loving friendship', meaning that we are very good friends and soul-mates. Usually I meet him in my meditations at the end of the day and we chat about the meaningful events that happened to me; I also come to him in times of need, and then ask him for clues, signs, teachings that will lead me to find the best course of action to take. I also contact him when I'm happy to share the bubbly feelings with him.

The daimon as soul-friend is taken for granted and is very often an experience which directly extends out of the childhood secret companion.

Some women have experienced the simultaneity of their own femininity with their daimon as a fusion of sexes, feeling themselves as an alchemical syzygy or being of male and female characteristics. In some girls entering womanhood we can see the onset of eating disorders which are connected to the desire to revert to a childlike androgyny of body, so that the physical confusion of puberty, the awakening sexuality and the responsibilities of adulthood are differentiated.

This study has not sought to exclude lesbian women but, unsurprisingly, very few responded to my questionnaire. In the psychic circuitry of homosexual people the inner beloved of a lesbian is *more likely to be female*, and that of a gay man to be male. The polarities of homosexual people are still balanced, however, for if the biological female body is experienced as 'male', the contrasexual soul image will appear as female. The same follows for gay men who are biologically male, but who perceive in a female manner: their inner beloved may be correspondingly male. But the many shades and variations of sexual orientation cannot be so generally defined in this very subtle area.

'It is the animus who stands behind female homosexuality', writes Jung in a very sweeping generalization that will affront many true lesbians.[70] Although there are many women who are born lesbian, there are also a good many heterosexual women who live lesbian life-styles, and here we may see some truth in Jung's statement. Some women *choose* a lesbian life-style in order to find more harmonious relationships than those they have had with men. Often, sexual transitions made for this reason are seldom fruitful since something essential is not being confronted and the nature of any human relationship is bound to bring it to the surface again. If there is internal confusion and self-identification with the masculine aspects presented by the daimon, then it is possible that a radical urge to change the gender we present will lead us to explore a lesbian life-style. If we stare transfixed in the mirror of soul-image long enough, we may come to believe it to be a true reflection.

The lesbian and bisexual women who responded made it clear that their experience cannot be so easily generalized. Annie says:

I've experienced enormous shifts in sexual energy, switching from heterosexual to lesbian relationships. I experienced sex with men as disempowering and myself as passive. Sex with women has been for me far more powerful, with a sense of being self-determining. I am also able to enjoy sex for its own sake. This has brought changes of style in the way I dress and present myself. My shape has even changed in that I think my shoulders have got broader.

Frances speaks of her early disenchantment with men:

When I was living as a lesbian, sexually my daimon was still very much present – and male. The emptiness I experienced when I pushed him away, when learning to understand my personal and cultural fury with men, was infinite and I was distinctly out of balance. A woman ignores or cuts off her daimon at her peril.

The major reason that so few lesbians returned their questionnaires was simply because the questions were totally irrelevant to them. Eve, alone of the respondents, has written of her contra-sexual other as female.

She has been with me since childhood in many forms, but her perfume and presence have never varied. I have painted her and sought her image in my relationships. In myself I recognize some of the male characteristics you refer to in the questionnaire, but my inner image remains wholly feminine.

The stories of how a man attains and relates to his muse are legion, the stories of how woman encounters her daimon as inspirer are seldom told. Lauren writes:

For me the role of the daimon is to lend inspiration and inner spark. Like the pilot light of a woman's personal inner world, the daimon is there to spark the fire of creativity, sensuality and spirit. I also think a well-functioning daimon can help us live a feminine existence with some masculine fortitude.

Melissa points to the disparity of the inspirational other.

It is taken for granted that male artists will have a Muse; because almost nothing has been written about the daimon from women's standpoint, this has been a hidden, private experience of some who dared to meet him, but unfortunately unknown to other sisters.

Sheila defines the daimon in a way which includes many of the foregoing definitions.

In each woman there exists a male counterpart: a kind of twin self. He makes himself known to us in dreams and sexual fantasies. We see his face in the faces of lovers, pop stars and actors. To some of us, he has a hand in our creative life, helping us to form the words of a poem, keeping us focused in our work. He knows us intimately, and wants us to bring all our inner riches into the daylight of the everyday world. He shows us the way to fulfil our potential.

Making sense of and coming to terms with this experience of the daimon is one of the most difficult things in our society. While it is considered normal and beneficial for a man to rejoice in a muse, an inner spiritual inspirer, it is not similarly acceptable for a woman to have a daimon.

All these definitions are attempts to reveal the truth as it is experienced by the respondents. They represent only the tip of the iceberg where women's experience is concerned because so little research has been undertaken in this area, and what little information we have has been gleaned from a predominantly psychological point of view, excluding these many aspects from the full picture.

Human beings crave definition and diagnosis to help give shape to their experiences. The first thing a patient wants to know is, 'Doctor, what have I got?' Significantly, when women seek therapy to understand their daimonic experience, both they and the therapist often treat their problem as an illness or flaw which needs correction. Rather than seeing the daimon as a drawback, we need encouragement to see him as a helper who can co-operate with us to find better ways of living.

But if you have no correlation or definition for a very powerful experience you are having, if there is no social framework for discussing your emotional or spiritual life, it is little wonder that many women feel like freaks. Where there is no positive daimonic model, there is a corresponding assumption of oddity. Thirty per cent of the respondents to my questionnaire were bewildered but delighted to learn that other women experienced the same thing as themselves, that they were not alone, mad or possessed. This conspiracy of silence must surely end!

We can look back down the centuries and catch glimpses of the cover-up – in women whose daimonic fervour's sole expression was through spiritual devotion, through domestic busyness, through immersion in romantic fiction, through the creation of handicrafts. If we look even casually, we can understand why women locked themselves into solitary states of passionate fulfilment. For them there was no other outlet – and no relief in the comparison or mutual sharing of experience.

Why women's long silence on this subject? Is it the fear of ridicule or exorcism, as here in the novel *Troytown Dances*,[43] where the heroine, Miranda, is pondering the nature of the daimonic relationships she is powerfully experiencing.

> She feels the first stirrings of the panic that rises from the isolation of strangeness, of otherness. Her rational brain tells her that she should seek expert help. Her heart tells her another story: help with what? She is not ill, she is not mad, she is not harming anyone. She has lived through two or three years of this obsessional haunting and not failed as mother or wife.
>
> She dismisses the idea of involving a professional other, fearing that her joy would be interned like an illegal alien. She lives in a world that only accepts conventional ideas from the here and now as the rightful citizens of society. Any creative idea, any other-worldly visitant might be purged, mocked or exterminated from her life. It would be like witnessing the torture and destruction of her own child.

Only a very few of the respondents have undertaken Jungian analysis in order to understand their experiences. Many respondents have expressed to me their fear of being thought mad or possessed, and their horror at the thought of unguardedly telling any other person about their often powerful, ecstatic or overwhelming experiences. The last thing they wanted was to seek out a therapist who might prescribe drugs or incarceration in a mental institution, or who might, by subtle psychological means, vacuum their precious experience out of their souls. Since the majority of the respondents are from Britain where it is still uncommon for people to visit a psychologist or analyst of any kind, this attitude is not surprising. Respondents from America were happy to express their experiences in psychological language though they generally felt no less vulnerable when speaking about their daimonic relationships.

Sheila comments that denial of the daimon

> means that women are cut off from a richness which is part of the fabric of womanhood. It is generally understood that men have their Muses, but not that women have a male counterpart. However, it's only in comparatively recent times that women have

had the opportunity and freedom to have creative lives.

Women are now impatient to understand themselves in ways that will aid the reintegration of women and the feminine into a society that has signally ignored the contribution of both for hundreds of years. The work of every woman is to rediscover the ancient spiritual wisdom of self-knowledge in contemporary ways, to seek out the bridges into the soul's treasury.

THE JUNGIAN DIMENSION

In the breaking of the long silence surrounding the contrasexual other, homage must be paid to the psychologist C G Jung, who explored the contrasexual soul-image of men and women. He held that all human beings have the ability to project and dramatize the common, primordial elements of human experience or 'the collective unconscious', and that these elements tend to take on the characteristics of the opposite sex. Simply put, human beings use their soul as a mirror: a man's soul-mirror would show to him a female image or 'anima', while a woman's soul-mirror would show her a male image or 'animus'. Jung held that these contrasexual images arose unconsciously and that they were 'projected onto' or embodied in the shapes of those about us.

As the anima represents a collective view of woman as she has appeared down the ages of human experience *in relation to man*, so the animus represents the collective view of man as he has appeared down the ages of human experience *in relation to woman*. It is therefore critically important that both sexes sort out their projections from the reality of human experience. In this book, we shall be examining only the female experience of the contrasexual.

The value of Jung's influence cannot be underestimated, but his grasp of the animus in women was a theoretical rather than a subjective one; being a man, he focused predominantly upon the anima – the female image which shines in the soul-mirror of men. His assessment of the animus' role in the female soul was coloured by his generation's prevailing attitude to women.

Before the contrasexual image is integrated, Jung held that it often partakes of the worst traits of its sexual counterpart: thus, the unintegrated anima can behave in a bitchy, emotional and fickle way, while the animus can behave in a dogmatic, argumentative and domineering way. Jung believed that these negative manifestations could be dissolved and integrated if the contents of the contrasexual image were resolved, but he did not believe it possible to dissolve the anima and animus archetypes themselves. Part of the Jungian psychoanalytic process concerns discovering how much the contrasexual image is coloured by our actual relationships with the opposite sex and the subsequent clarification and integration of the anima or animus.

Part of the problem that many women have found with this otherwise helpful concept is that it fails to express the many-textured experience of the contrasexual from the personal point of view. Too often, the anima or animus are seen as theoretical abstractions, explicable mostly by reference to human family relationships or to idealized spiritual definitions. Also, if definitions of 'domineering, argumentative and dogmatic' are applied 'to women who are already anxious about their intellectual capacities, a woman can feel defeated from the outset'.[82]

In his exploration of the psyche, Jung defines the Ego as our conscious being. What lies outside of the conscious part of our lives he terms the Shadow. He speaks of the anima and animus as existing under the penumbra of the Shadow in early life, until experience brings them into perspective. Thus a woman is born with female sexual characteristics with a female ego that is Anima: her Shadow is termed Animus. In order to consciously relate to the Animus, a woman must deal with the Shadow. However, the Animus is the go-between who bridges woman's Ego and Shadow. And, as Anne Deloon McNeely says, a woman's conscious ego can often have more of the Animus than the Anima about it.[49]

'If the encounter with the Shadow is the apprentice-piece in the individual's development, then that with the anima/us is the "master-piece".'[28] Jung saw the exploration and integration of the contrasexual image as the work of middle life. And indeed this is usually the case with daimon. Only in middle life do we move away from habitual patterns and dependencies inculcated by our upbringing and reach the true ground of our being. Thus, men tend to 'shift from the active style of "mastery" in early life to a more passive style of "accommodation" in later life', while women shift from accommodation in early life to mastery in later life.

It is important to identify and helpfully define the daimon as early in middle life as possible, especially if the daimonic relationship is fraught with strife or confusion. Although a young woman may be aware of the daimon, she is seldom self-possessed enough to analyse her condition. It is often enough to recognize the hand-holds on this ascent to discover the authentic self – hand-holds which begin in childhood and grow clearer in adolescence.

The goal of Jung's psychological system is to reach 'individuation', the point at which we become aware of the whole of Being – often an overwhelming experience in which the inner voice of personal destiny calls the individual to follow its path. This goal is achieved by creative collaboration between the conscious and unconscious aspects of the personality, rather than by the overall domination of the personality by the ego. This process is subtle and cannot be forced or intellectually instituted without the co-operation of the soul.

The Jungian animus is confusingly understood both as a *complex* and as an *archetype*. A complex is described as 'a collection of images, ideas, feelings and habitual actions that is compelling or motivating in a nonrational way'. An archetype is described as 'a universal tendency to respond to a typical human situation of instinctual-emotional arousal by forming affective images'. The animus is described as 'a psychological complex comprising the excluded aspects of female gender identity: images, ideas, feelings and action patterns which are associated with the opposite sex'.[83]

What does all this mean? According to Jungian theory, a complex is built up of particular collections of ideas and images garnered during a woman's upbringing, and characterized as male by the subject; but an archetype is something universally experienced by people of many conditions and therefore purposefully present and operative.

So what is the relationship between the animus and the daimon? The term animus is most often used to describe the problematic features of 'the excluded masculine aspects' in women, which have to be clarified. The daimon, as I define it, is much more than a complex which can be explained away as resultant from our upbringing and culture or analysed into good behaviour. It is nearer to Jung's notion of an archetype.

I hold that the daimon is a universally experienced phenomenon appearing individually among women world-wide, with active power to inspire, support and companion them. I further hold that the true daimon may be hidden by masks and appearances of the masculine deriving from women's social background and upbringing. This series of masks may indeed be termed 'the animus', but the daimon is women's true, universal experience of the masculine, which becomes clear when women begin to the live from the ground of their authentic selves.

The finding and claiming of our authentic selves can be likened to the Jungian goal of individuation, the unification of all aspects of the self. This process may sound like a selfish or nirvana-seeking aim, impossible to achieve or maintain; however, it is only the establishment of a practical framework for living *which must be habitually practised and returned to*. Living from our authentic selves is not an end which we achieve, but an ongoing practice of referring to our innate truth, beauty and intrinsic worth as women. We will be exploring ways of uncovering the daimon and finding our authentic selves as we go along.

Jung's attempt to map the soul-images of men and women reflected the gender stereotypes of his generation. With the rise of female consciousness, much of his work has to be reappreciated. It is now recognized among post-Jungian feminist analysts that there is a tendency for women to accept personal blame for 'the animus complex' if the analytical process is poorly handled or conducted in a strictly classical Jungian manner. So much has changed in the area of feminine consciousness that a completely new approach to the animus has evolved: this was started by the work of M Esther Harding, Irene Claremont de Castillejo and Emma Jung, and continued in the work of Polly Eisendrath-Young, Marion Woodman, and Ann and Barry Ulanov, among others.

I must report that the evidence of the respondents who have shared their daimonic experience is significantly more lively, authentic and experiential than much of the Jungian writings on the animus, which are often cerebral, theoretical and lacking in charge. The respondents' answers have all the delight of engagement, all the passion of women responding to ecstasy.

The daimon can be experienced in many different ways (*see* plate illustration 1). But if we assess the respondents' experience of the daimon, we find that they fall into five loose categories:

1 *Primal Forms*
invisible friend
animal
toy
a feature of nature such as a rock, tree, hill

Primal forms occur mainly, but not exclusively, in childhood. They represent our first exploration of otherness, mutuality and loving nurture. This is a deep, symbiotic relationship which prepares girls for life in the wider world; it is recapitulated when mature integration of the daimon happens in later life.

2 *Obstructing Forms*
raptor
soul-thief
criminal
outlaw
provoker of strife

Obstructing forms occur in girls and women who have not identified with their own female self and potentialities, who experience guilt or shame rather than self-respect, who struggle with the conformities of society and their place within it. The obstructing daimon personifies danger and charisma and both represents and seeks to highlight obstructions in the free flow of life through fear and repression of personal power. This is a relationship based on attraction/repulsion, wherein the unknown masculine beckons but whose forbidden or alien aspects terrorize.

3 *Patriarchal Forms*
critic
judge
watcher
authority figure

Patriarchal forms occur in adolescent girls and women who distrust their innate female authority and potentialities, and who may also demonstrate depression, self-sabotage or self-sacrifice. These forms represent the basilisk attention of the patriarchal world which can stultify personal growth and erode or restrict female self-esteem. This is a relationship based on perfection and appeasement wherein the masculine is 'out there watching us somewhere'.

4 *Complementary Forms*
lover

partner
beloved
spouse

Complementary forms occur from adolescence onwards and can vary at different stages of maturity – from the pin-up to the internalized beloved of the soul. These forms represent the exploration of eros, the desire for completion and fulfilment, and can include elements of obsessive dependency and unhealthy self-effacement, as well as loving support and self-respect. This is a relationship based on mutual regard (at its best) or projected idealism (at its worst). Here the masculine is experienced as compensatory, or as complementary in more mature modes.

5 Inspiriting Forms
inspirer
deity
spirit-companion
initiator

Inspiriting forms occur from childhood onwards, usually growing in intensity and usefulness as a woman matures, and often replacing earlier forms. These forms represent the maturation of the soul, of female selfhood and creative motivation. The relationship is based on the balance of true daimon with authentic self, often having a nuptial or spiritual marriage as its symbol. Here the masculine is included in the circle of the authentic self.

Women of all ages and backgrounds may continue to experience one or more of these daimonic forms. Readers should be careful not to judge themselves by these categories, for we have all experienced some part of each of them. We should especially be careful not to take on blame, shame or guilt, but rather to consider that all women at this time in our society are in the process of transformation from disempowerment to creative authority.

What has become clear from writing this book is the unique subtlety of every woman's experience. The daimon is multi-form, with many roles and functions; each woman experiences the daimon in her own way, at different levels of understanding, through her life. And, although woman may integrate and absorb the daimon's teachings into her conscious understanding, it is most significant that, in the fullest integration, the daimon still remains – not a man, not the male aspect of a woman, but something beyond the Jungian viewpoint.

Seeking 'the parts that are missing' – to go off in search of the 'inner child' or the 'wise elder', for men to seek their 'inner woman' and women their 'inner man' – has become the post-Jungian pastime. What is the significance of this? We need to define exactly the word 'inner'. It is frequently used to describe psychological states or conditions present within the psyche or soul. It is often, imprecisely, used to mean 'of the spiritual realms'. Throughout this book I avoid use of 'inner' since it implies a psychological state. The quest for 'the parts that are missing' is in fact a *spiritual*, not a psychological, search.

The quest for spiritual wholeness is what underlies Jung's own work, although some post-Jungians have reduced this search to a psychological rat-maze. The study of psychology should be representative of its meaning – the study of the soul (the mapping of which was Jung's life vocation). But maps are only tools for deeper exploration: we do not reverently enshrine them in glass-cases with little 'you are here' notices stuck on them.

If we see the daimon as a spiritual reality, which I believe we should, we remove the strain upon personal blame and responsibility but we set up a dynamic which is currently difficult for society to accept: the reality of the contrasexual soul-image as something independent of ourselves and with a reality of its own. Psychology has tended to keep us at a safe remove from this power-point, isolating us from passion by speaking of archetypes, complexes and internalized states which seem mistily distant. The actual experience of meeting archetypes is skated over by reference to alchemical images or to mystical experiences of long-dead people.

For women who are swimming strongly in the tide of their personal daimonic experience, there is no such safe distance. Everything is raw, immediate and passionate. They are moving through the soul-map, often at speed; the inhabitants of that map are experienced as real, not imaginary, not wrought of fantasy, not explainable away as archetypes.

This is not to deny the helpful nature of Jungian analysis, which has aided many people to cope with overwhelming experiences resulting from their soul journey. I wish to stress the importance of *personally engaging with* and *personally recording* the points in our progress where soul experience is powerful, moving and passionately inspiring. In the land of the soul, *we are each* the real explorers; we do not always need the interpretive anthropologist to define our progress.

Jung spoke of the unconscious soul as a museum which has 'no history outside its individual manifestations', going back to the pre-historic roots of being.[50] The natural history of the daimon cannot be told in one place, in neat, sequential unfoldings. It can only unfold in each woman's life and experience. Each of us creates a contour map from our life experience which alters all the time. Some regions of experience will be well mapped, others may be fearfully neglected. Every time a new piece of information is received, the contour lines, dimensions, distances and appearances also change.

If each lifetime is a time corridor in which we experience many things, in which we recognize and reject helpful and unhelpful experience, and if it is only at the end of our lives that we have an overview of our soul's progress, then it stands to reason that full knowledge will be difficult to gain. Speaking about and sharing our daimonic experience is but one facet of what, for women, is a collective process of definition.

Women's collective silence and lack of perspective do not have to remain a yawning chasm. Although self-depreciation, self-doubt and lack of self-esteem are still widespread, the collective move towards self-definition and perspective can now be seen in the spiritual side of the women's movement. Feminism has involved some abrasive confrontations with received and habitual social patterns. The response to women's struggle towards self-definition and recognition has ranged from outrage to shocked acceptance. An uneasy political correctness has emerged at this troubled time of truce as a method of social politeness. This political correctness is becoming endemic within feminism and unfortunately threatens one of the major routes to female authority. It involves a neglect and disregard of the masculine, the projection of a patriarchal shadow upon the entire male population past and present, and a refusal to contemplate anything other than the female and feminine in relation to women.

For some women, it may be a scary or outrageous notion that in some hidden part of their femininity lurks an undefined masculinity that is not biological, not wholly psychological, and perhaps of spiritual origin. Some reject the male in any form, including any psychological or spiritual form, as Miriam states clearly, 'I don't want to be told what to do by a man – even, especially, an inner man!' Due to such conflicts, some women reject the possibility of a helpful daimon, seeing it as a kind of poisonous residue of patriarchal culture which must be purged away.

The quick-set cement of political correctness which strives to encase difficult concepts in a uniform grey blandness is mischievously poised to encase women's issues on all sides. It is essential to clarify here and now that the inner masculine figure in women's souls cannot be dismissed as a patriarchal ploy to keep women down, or the obsessional concern of a few middle-class women. The daimon, and our relationship with it, may tell us much about the gender misunderstandings between women and men and the development of women's consciousness, but it transcends politically-correct boundaries by its sheer wild ubiquity. As Meg says, 'If I was told that it was wrong for me to have the feeling of a male side within me, they may as well tell me not to have a heart or soul.'

Barbara Hannah has defined the goal of woman as 'to find the "inherited collective image" of the spirit or mind which she has always projected onto man'.[22] The daimon is not a secret agent of the patriarchy sitting in a woman's soul and reporting back to a disapproving multitude of men. The role of the daimon is quite different from the men and male values which surround each woman; rather, like a messenger from the deep unexplored soul-country, he asks her to listen to the messages of her authentic self, deflecting attention from himself onto the message itself.

The deep wounding of women is twofold: not only have social conditions been monstrously unbalanced but also, and worse, there has been silence about what goes on in women's souls, and women's own inability to access and understand this. The professional and psychological response which formally classifies certain essential soul-features as 'dangerous or life-threatening terrain' to women has not helped. A resident daimon does not have to be met with pest-control methods.

The exclusion of male aspects from women's soul experience cannot long endure, for it delays the return of women's authority. If the daimon can be welcomed back, he will illuminate places of power and passion that will release women from prisons of fear and stultification, and that will in turn release women's ability to bridge impasses in the gender war and to rebalance our world.

It is saddening to realize that although, collectively, women have the answers to the puzzle of the daimon, the only way their experience is being assessed for general understanding is through the psychological approach. It is *women who are the true authorities* in this neglected field of understanding, not those commentators who observe from the side-lines. And it is only by returning to the source-text – women's experience itself – rather than criticism of the text, that we learn about the daimon. So let us begin at the beginning and return to our childhood to find where his track begins.

Questions

1 What male figures and images inform or relate to your experience?
2 Which experiences give you a feeling of wholeness and completion?

Actions

Draw the features of the daimonic figure which preoccupies you at this moment. If his features are unclear, focus upon his overall 'feel' or impression.

Reflection

Reflect on the ways in which you 'make love' with life, on the avenues and channels of your passion and power.

Exploring the Ideal Masculine

If the daimon is dormant or unclear to you, take a sheet of paper and map out your impressions and experiences of the masculine in your own life. Jot down words, pictures, phrases, people, etc. How do they connect? Answer these questions:

• What qualities does the ideal masculine have in your opinion?
• What qualities of the ideal masculine appear in men around you?
• At what moments in your life has your soul been touched by these qualities?

- What does your ideal man look like in your ideas, impressions, heart of hearts?
- How do you respond *as a woman* to the ideal masculine – as a concept, within your experience, within men you know, within men or male figures in the world of history?

CHAPTER 2

In Search of the Beloved

He came out of the blue.
He didn't ask, he brought nothing,
And I don't know his name,
I just know he wants me.
For he simply lay down on my bed
and called me Woman.
He came out of the very blue
And before I said no,
He set himself up as a squatter
within my very heart.

Song by Francisco Buarque de Holanda
(translated by Melissa)

INVISIBLE FRIENDSHIPS

The path of the daimon often starts in childhood, in the invisible companions and secret friends who guide our play. I am fortunate in being able to consciously trace the development of my own daimon from early childhood. From my earliest memory of being a baby and for many years afterwards, I would lie for many hours in communion with what I called 'the Shapers'. These appeared to me as the geometric shapes which shift kaleidoscopically across the field of vision when we close our eyes or stare at a bright light. The Shapers had colour, shape and quality and would associate together in different dances which conveyed meaning, knowledge and story to me. It wasn't until I was about four that the individual molecules of the Shapers began to take on personality, forming companions who were invisible to others. These companions included a fallen tree I used to play upon and the chalk downs where I walked, as well as anthropomorphic figures.

My first invisible companion was called Sysgrin and she was female. In character, she was like the Robber Maid from Hans Christian Andersen's *The Snow Queen,* or like an older bossy sister. Under her influence, I formed a gang of girls who roamed the playground in wild games and met secretly in our den, an earthy hollow in the bushes. In relation to Sysgrin, I experienced myself as male to her female.

At the menarche she changed, as a caterpillar changes in its chrysalis into a butterfly, from female into male, even as my body changed from child to woman. The period of transition was accompanied by dreams and visions of great violence in which faceless raptors, groups of tribesmen or torturers appeared. When the 'interference' of puberty subsided, the figure which emerged was a male companion: a dark-haired pirate and seafarer with whom daring deeds upon the high seas got pretty mixed up with adolescent sexual awakening.

During this period of transition the childhood games which I'd acted out alone and with other children began to internalize as I reached my teenage years, becoming scenarios which I would ponder over as I walked, or sometimes write down as stories. I was well aware that 'the invisible friend' syndrome was considered to be a thing of childhood, to be abandoned when people 'grew up'. I very consciously never relinquished this link, wilfully retaining it, continuing to dialogue with my inner friends and seek their advice, using them as sounding-boards and mentors for my ideas and problems.

Even as early as 13, I was aware of the spiritual marriage between myself and the daimon, recognizing that beyond the pirate and the other forms lay a far truer image which life was preparing me for. I knew that unless I attended to my life's vocational direction, I would never fully achieve this union. But even when we know something is true and good for us, we still find ways of ignoring the truth, of straying from the way and cultivating habits which impede us: I am no different from any other mortal in that respect.

The pirate companion lasted through until I was about 20 when he began to change again. My immersion in his swashbuckling, outlaw qualities was partially responsible for leading me into marriage with a real outcast, a man who had put himself beyond the boundaries of society and was living on the streets when I first met him. This marriage was an attempt to reclaim, tame and transform the outlaw, but it did not work. I became enmeshed: my health and creative functions were dragged into the dust, not to recover until I left the marriage.[44]

The pirate departed and was replaced by an ancient Irish poet who has guided and overseen my creative life as a true daimon up to the present moment. This has been a rewarding relationship which has had direct results in the poetry, music, and writing I have produced as well as in the maturing of my soul. Although the Shapers continue to lend their molecules to many shapes and companions, I recognize the thread of the daimon through my life as a constant musical theme sounding true above the welter and bombast of life's orchestra. I know that to steer true, I must ever listen for that beloved theme and play with it, sing with it.

The threshold of adulthood is sadly a time when we cease to play, sing, dance and engage in the game with the same vigour that we had in childhood. If we totally sever the bridge to our playful and passionate nature, our lives can become prisons of frustration and confusion. Here are some of the respondents' own childhood experiences, each very different.

For Frances and Amanda, the daimon was triggered by hospitalization and the need for a friend. At six and a half, after the painful re-setting of a knee-cap bone, Frances recalls sitting in the beech grove in the garden and meeting the first of her 'childhood folk':

> The Green Man emerged from two beech trees that I was most fond of, picked me up and walked about with me sitting on his shoulders. He seemed to be part of the trees, resolving into a gentle giant of a man. When I first saw a picture of Green Man, when I was about eight or nine, I felt a tremendous rush of friendship or kinship and relief that he had been real all the time.

Amanda was seven when hospitalized for tonsillectomy.

> The night before surgery, I was alone and afraid. I was staring at the snowy night through the window, listening to Sesame Street as the presenter began to sing 'You've Got A Friend'. I began to cry, wanting to have someone there with me. Then I became aware of a male presence in the room, very near to me. I felt embraced and comforted by this presence and stopped crying. I saw no one but the space was charged with love.

Ioho was aware of 'many people in my childhood that nobody else could see'. Between the ages of 7 and 13, in South America, she came into contact with people with whom she felt she had a shared experience of such vision.

> The Indians who guided through the rainforest in Venezuela, the old guys who led us across the desert plains, they seemed to have a vision which was familiar to me. I had one constant companion who was, and who I feel is, aligned to the daimon: One Feather. He seemed very much stronger, bigger than my father. To me he was my *real* father and, as I myself resembled a little Indian child, this seemed to make sense to me – I believed he was my real family and was there to watch over me.

Ioho was also aware of chaotic presences whom she called the Black Elves.

> I grew to believe what I thought they had told me: that I was evil, that I had done great wrong in a different realm (I had no understanding of past lives and believed these things had occurred in a separate world), that I had to do what they told me; yet at the same time I had more power than them and was destined to become something I later thought of as a great black witch.

Most children's experience is not this traumatic, although childhood terrors should perhaps be treated with more gravity and respect and less dismissal. Although their understanding and reasoning may not be mature, children have powerful experiences of realities which adults cannot perceive so clearly. The adult who says 'there's nothing there' is keen to dismiss 'imaginary' terrors; such an attitude similarly dismisses the 'imaginary' companion who is often the child's best protector.

For most children, the world of play and the enactment of heroic roles is the school of life. Allegra recalls how she and her secret friend 'would ride horses, climb and jump streams, go to Africa and hunt wild animals'. Diana and Fiona also rode invisible horses. Fiona writes:

> My companions as a child were toy animals. Between eight and ten, I had an invisible black horse, whom I rode around the playground as me and my friends enacted the adventures of Storm. Storm is related to my animus, who appears in his most positive form as the horseman.

Diana had 'crushes on literary figures such a D'Artagnan and

Sherlock Holmes' while Hue remembers the

> sort of hazy boundary between my 'self' and certain favourite images, a sort of strange familiarity or identification with certain heroes. I can remember wanting to *be* Tarzan, Errol Flynn's pirates, Roy Rogers or Robin Hood.

The exploration of or identification with male figures is common in girlhood, as Sheila relates.

> Rather than an awareness of an inner male presence, I assumed the character of a boy in dressing-up games with school friends in primary school. As a ten-year-old, my favourite role was that of a 'jungle boy' who featured in one of the comics of those times.

Clothes-wars between girls and mothers figure large in the reports. Between the 1940s and 1960s children were generally not free to choose their own clothes or what they wore on a particular day. Allegra writes of her secret friend:

> John is who I would have been if I had been a boy ... we had telepathic communication. I imagined him within me, especially when my mother made me do Shirley Temple stuff. I wanted to be dressed in khaki shorts just like John.

Annie also recalls that:

> Although I had an invisible dog as a very young child, I remember no particular invisible companion. From the ages of five to eight, I desperately wanted to be a boy. One reason was that I wanted to be a cowboy when I grew up. My longing to be male was quite profound: I told my friends I didn't play with dolls, but part of me wanted to. Most of my dolls were female and came with dresses on. But one was androgynous with short hair, and I dressed him as a boy in blue and called him Michael.

Accepting a female body and all that being a woman entails is a hard task: the advantages seem disproportionately outweighed by the disadvantages. Girls resent that most of the fun is had by boys, although this is not so bad now as during my schooling in the fifties. I remember a class where we were directed by the teacher to enact Stone Age people doing their daily work to some music. After five minutes of vigorous hunting, I was pulled out of the activity and told by my teacher to go and pick berries with the other girls – hunting was a boy's activity!

The tomboy emerges from the prevailing social signal that

womanhood is a disadvantaged condition that excludes us from the rewards and advantages of manhood.

The roots of the daimon, the soul's companion, begin in childhood. I believe that our childhood play is formative in our sacred symbolic landscaping, that we plant seeds at this time which we will harvest in later life. The reciprocal exchange between ourselves and invisible friends creates a symbiosis which can mature into a fully-fledged daimonic experience. But, before that, there are many further stages on which the daimon will audition.

THE AWAKENING

The first images of the masculine that we experience in our games in youth provide a template for the daimon. They are sometimes immature images, but they carry with them the essence of what may mature. They are most often characterized by feelings of freedom, spontaneity, trust, devotion, love and longing.

The following accounts bridge the evolution of eros from child to early adolescence. Gwen speaks of her pre-sexual intimation of the daimon:

> I had several 'imaginary' childhood companions, some of whom are still 'good friends'. One in particular has evolved into my daimon but it wasn't for many years that I realized my daimon had been foreshadowed by and was in fact my childhood friend. When I was three or four I remember lying in bed and seeing the sleeping form of a man beside me. He was my 'husband in a dream' and I just thought it was my husband, either in the future or in the past. I loved him very much (rather like my teddy) with no sexual feelings. I just felt like a big lady with her man and always the warm feeling or afterglow, contentment. I never saw him awake and it just felt right that he should be there. Later, as an adult, I realized that this feeling was not non-sexual but post-coital. He looked very much like my present husband, but I realized when older that he was a figure from the historical past.

Janet recalls how, at 10–12:

> I became aware of the inner male presence. As I was falling asleep I was aware I wasn't alone. Someone very wonderful, masculine was with me, not unlike the romantic knights I'd read about. The major difference in this experience was that my body actually

reacted physically – I didn't understand what was happening, yet I remember thinking how these strange feelings were so wonderful. I felt special, cherished, like a princess of myth. This recurred infrequently, usually in the hypnogogic pre-dream state.

The full awakening of eros begins when puberty triggers physical response. It is then that girls begin to project the image of their daimon upon the male figures who excite sexual response in them. When teenagers cover their bedroom walls with pop-idols, they are not just 'going through a phase', they are seriously 'studying form'. These are relationships which cannot be reciprocated but they provide the safe distance at which the emotional turmoil of sexual arousal and the excitement of first love can be experienced.

It is commonly thought that, unlike men, women are not aroused by visual stimulus, but it is true to say that the sight of male beauty does have its effect, and that it is not confined to the bedrooms of adolescents! The respondents made it clear that actors, singers, writers, dancers, and other public figures still communicated the genuine daimonic charge of excitement for them. As Fiona comments: 'The sight of the Scottish Rugby Union Captain, Gavin Hastings, without a shirt, was a tremendous and totally unexpected turn-on!'

Jocelyn recalls the pin-ups of her adolescence:

> ... the young Elvis Presley and young Cliff Richard, who both seem to have once embodied a kind of spiritual sexuality that just poured through them, especially Elvis. James Dean was a favourite image of sulky teenage rebellion, but also with a streak of cruelty. I've also been drawn to older male artists, like Picasso, spiritual teachers like Ram Das, and political leaders on the left like Yassar Arafat and Gorbachev, Che Guevara and Castro. More recently I've been attracted to young angst-ridden wounded men like River Phoenix, Keanu Reeves and male models in the Gaultier ads.

'Pin-ups' continue to inspire women (*see* plate illustration 2 for a selection of current favourites). The following is a role-call of those whom the respondents found inspiring:

Actors: Alan Rickman, Liam Neeson, Daniel Day-Lewis, Nicol Williamson, Richard Burton, Dustin Hoffman, Jack Nicholson, Alec Guinness, Sean Connery, Mel Gibson, Kevin Costner.

Actors in Specific Roles: Michael Praed as Robin Hood in *Robin of Sherwood*; Peter O'Toole in *Lawrence of Arabia*; John Thaw as Inspector Morse, the intellectual detective; Patrick Stewart as Captain Picard in *Star Trek Next Generation*; Keanu Reeves as Siddhartha in *Little Buddha*; Brad Pitt in *Legends of the Fall*.

Singers: John Lennon, Bob Dylan, Peter Gabriel, Paul McCartney, Neil Diamond, Freddie Star, Leonard Cohen, Sting.

Sheila favours 'men with a sense of mystery: aloofness is very attractive to me, for instance, the actor Charles Dance, and Colin Firth as Mr Darcy in *Pride and Prejudice*'. Frances looks for men who 'have presence, wisdom and a great sense of humour; the ones who are talented, eccentric and well weathered'. Hue is moved by 'the outsiders, clever, dignified, strong, invincible, at home in nature but also with an air of sweetness about them'.

Meg is attracted to singer/song writers such as Roy Harper, John Martyn and Peter Gabriel through their songs and spiritual ideas.

> They are men I feel a strong spiritual link with and this is more attractive to me than what they look like. They have the ability to touch my soul with their songs.

Ioho is drawn to

> the gentle, musical and slightly weird men; to David Bowie for his sensitivity, and the unworldly quality which attracts that part of me which isn't at all human, the lonely part which believes home is out there across the galaxy. I wonder if what I love is the *change* that comes over these men when they make love, as the daimon, the power of the masculine, enters them?

The pin-up is an important phase in which the features of the daimon are pored over. Meg writes:

> I suspect that most women, like me, never considered their daimon as anything but an outlet for their sexual-emotional fantasies, an ideal man or Mr Right who you created when you were a teenager but who then sticks around. Most women then find a man in public life to pin these feelings on to: a pop star, a film star, etc, and then all their daimonic energies are focused on to fantasizing about their unattainable figure.

This unattainability factor is important because it allows the raw sexual current to emerge without danger. It is a factor we will consider in depth in Chapter 3. The kindling of women's passion was once traditionally part of the old-fashioned courting rituals which preceded union. Today's young woman has a different scenario to contend with: usually an urgent boyfriend demanding sex on the first date. Women need to be kindled – not only to sexual passion but also to emotional and psychic openness.

For a modern woman to discover her own eros and explore its potential is a less easy business. We no longer have the ancient arbiters of the sexual experience at hand to help us. Most young women have only the handbook of a women's magazine or the romantic novel or their giggling peers' first sexual attempts to educate them – usually a sad travesty of the sacred sexual experience.

Upon the virgin pages of a young woman's soul is written a promise of ecstatic fulfilment and abandonment which the first sexual encounter seldom validates. The sacred dimension of awakening sexuality is often mislaid in snatched embraces or sordid tumbling, only to be discovered again when maturity within equal and committed partnerships has grown.

But long before the first lover approaches, the daimon comes as the unknown, unseen lover, a preparer of the way, to initiate the girl into womanhood and all that active sexuality implies. Without that awakening, a woman may founder on the first foothills of human relationship, as does Deborah Southernwood in Mary Webb's *The Golden Arrow*.[73] Importuned by her sweetheart for his first kiss, Deborah suddenly meets her own unpreparedness:

> Passion was new, terrible. She had not realized the feelings involved in it. She had thought of herself as a wife, with the same emotions, the same poise, as she had in her maidenhood. To many women marriage is only this ... a physical change impinging on their ordinary nature, leaving their mentality untouched, their self-possession intact. They are not burnt by even the red fire of passion – far less by the white fire of love. For this last Deborah was prepared ... But when Stephen kissed her in the wood, a new self awoke in her. She was horrified; she needed time to fuse the two fires ...

This adolescent period of preparation is absolutely essential, which is why the rape of pre-pubescent girls is so horrific: since they have not yet been touched by the fire of physical passion, their rape is an even deeper violation than that of unwilling but mature women.

Responsibility for inciting sexual passion was once taught to men and women in traditional societies; it is there in the chorus of the *Song of Songs* ('do not stir up love til he please'), which the Semitic and Mesopotamian cultures both understood. 'If we eat the fruit of the tree before it is ready, eating it may leave us with only a sour, bitter taste or an empty feeling.'[66] This is often the experience of those who go straight to sex without the ripening of relationship.

The image of The Lovers in the Waite/Colman Smith tarot deck (plate illustration 3) shows this graphically: the daimon as initiator into sexual activity spreads his angelic wings over the woman's horizon; as she stares upon him she receives his teaching about how desire is roused; standing beside the woman is a man who gazes upon only her. Does the man wait to initiate the woman into sexual experience, or does he wait to receive the ancient knowledge which was once taught by gifted women who were in touch with their daimons and knew how to initiate men into the sacred dimensions of sexuality?

The Indian *devadasi* and Mediterranean hierodule have both been misleadingly described as 'sacred prostitutes', but the sacred service of the body to the divine masculine was at the root of this custom. In this way, all men were as the god to the hierodule; and to each male client, the hierodule was as the goddess. Herodotus writes of the custom in Babylon where, at least once in their lives, women were expected to serve their term at the temple of the Goddess Mylitta. A woman undergoing her sacred service sat in the temple precincts until a man threw a coin into her lap in the name of Mylitta, whereat she was obliged to lie with him. After this service, women then went home to continue their lives.[26]

Hinduism retains a straightforward and unembarrassed attitude to the service of the divine male and female principles in the veneration of the *lingum* (phallus) – which is adorned and anointed as symbolic of the Divine Masculine, the power or *purusha* of Shiva – and the sacred *yoni* (vulva), symbolic of the Divine Feminine. Hindu and Buddhist art commonly depicts the union of male and female divinities.

In the West, it is considered prurient to even mention the phallus, although this was not the case in ancient Greece, where herms, phallic-headed images of Hermes (Mercury), were everywhere displayed for good luck, and comic actors wore huge phalli. Grossly over-endowed images have continued this tradition in buffoonery – for example, Punch's phallus in *Commedia dell'arte*. In the Eleusinian mysteries, phalloi (phalluses) were borne in procession in baskets and may have been part of the inner contemplation of the mystery. In the mysteries of the god Dionysos, women also carried symbolic phalloi.

The veneration of the phallus was commonplace in ancient Greece and still is in modern India – a balanced and accepted way of saluting the Divine Masculine principle. Such rites are discounted by some modern women as revelling unhealthily in the male. The importance of the phallus as a core symbol for women has been misrepresented by Freud's concept of 'phallus envy'. Envy is not the issue here: it is the generative and connective bridge of the daimon that is desired.

The image of the daimon as awakener is seen in the Central American figure of Kokopelli, the well-endowed wanderer with his flute; it is also seen in the beloved image of Krishna (who also comes with a flute) in his sporting with the Gopis; it is apparent in the Greek god Dionysos, in whose service respectable women became inspired to bacchic frenzy. Euripides wrote in his play *The Bacchae*, 'He who leads the throngs becomes Dionysos'; for whoever awakens our female passion is indeed our Dionysos.

These images are resonant with adolescent sexual awakenings which set up tremendous emotional tides. For some people, first love is experienced as a physical illness or disturbance, and they are unable to recognize the pull as attraction. Once an object of desire has appeared in a young woman's life, her whole life can become a holocaust of longing for the beloved.

The young woman's first exploration of her own body and female identity at puberty is often constellated about the figure of the bride. Melanie, the heroine of Angela Carter's novel *The Magic Toyshop*,[8] spends hours posing in front of the mirror, 'exploring the whole of herself'; swathed in net-curtaining 'she gift-wrapped herself for a phantom bridegroom'. This kind of fantasy-play with the daimon is a rehearsal for physical relationships, arriving organically out of our childhood ability for pretend-play. The daimon allows the game of make-believe, extending childhood play into a preparation for adult relationships. The world of men is an unknown territory to young women, whose only ambassador is the daimon.

The Roman ceremony of preparation for marriage involved the betrothed young woman in a visit to the temple of Vesta, there to leave her childhood toys and dolls before she donned the saffron veil of a bride. The awakening of sexual desire still involves the putting away of childhood things: the doll is no longer needed when the doll's owner is about to step into the world of adult relationships. In our society, this initiation into adult relationships also involves the giving up of many cherished things we were never intended to give up. When the Little Mermaid attempts to live as a mortal woman with her prince, she leaves behind forever the realms of faery; she sacrifices her swimming tail in return for feet, her singing voice for silence. Every step upon those feet pains her as if she were treading on knives, yet she endures all for her lover who fickly chooses another.[4] The lot of many women who enter into adult partnerships is the consignment of virgin integrity to the far shores of memory, along with the playful power to discern with imagination.

Young women soon learn how to access the power of the feminine as they grow up, often harnessing it for their own controlling ends. The sexual cat-and-mouse games that mature women play with men have their roots here, sometimes transmuting young women into sorceresses who taunt and manipulate. The cruelty of young women who have come into their sexual power early and without control is proverbial.

> We know her first
>   when the slaking of desire bites:
> then is she hard and cruel,
>   testing her teeth.
>   In the young
> it is called love,
>   but beasts know better this first Spring:
> the bitter shoots that pierce sleep,
>   the unslaked flank.[40]

Learning how to temper this early power with sufficient control, compassion and self-respect is difficult when there is no rite of passage to oversee the physical awakening. Ioho gives a full picture of her experience, beginning with the chaotic power which emanated from 'the Black Elves'.

> They tripped me up, knocked me out, sent me spinning. By the time I was six or seven they were convincing me to wreak havoc. Gradually I took control in that I wouldn't necessarily do what they said, but continued to use their energy. It wasn't until I began

the process of my healing sincerely, sanely, at about 21, that I stopped this destructive way of living. This experience had been a good teacher, though I don't believe I had a clear understanding of social ethics, of what was acceptable until my early twenties. They had over-ridden much of what my parents presumably tried to instill in me: I listened to the force which had the most power.

During the transition point, when my active acceptance of the power transformed from the negative into the positive of the Horned God, the confusion was at times fairly acute. I couldn't use the power of my Lord as I had done with that of the elves, yet it was slippery ground, at times leaving me beaten up and extremely vulnerable (which in itself was a great healer, of course).

I recall, rather stoned, picking up a man in a bar. He was a piano-player and as I'd got increasingly stoned, I had found myself weaving energy threads around him with the elves drawing him in. In his apartment, something triggered me back to my need to stop playing these destructive games – I'm not sure what it was, an old jazz record he played, I think. The control disappeared in a sickening flash. I remember so well the feeling, standing by the window, a lost child alone in the apartment of a strange man twice my age. Total vulnerability. A spirit guide, one who had been with me over the change, took my hand and led me out, without saying a word, back into the street, the musician shouting after me. I threw up in the gutter, slept in a cemetery till dawn.

Ioho's unsparing self-portrait of coming to terms with the chaotic power unleashed within her, gives us a glimpse into the dynamic of passion whirling out of control. Lauren writes:

There were times in the past when both my sexual and creative daimons edged into the dangerous or the irresponsible. But I also see that those were times in which I barely acknowledged their existence, let alone honoured their presence in my life, and these incidents were attempts to gain my attention. Part of my dealing with my sexual daimon is coming to terms with the issue of manipulative charm. Because, so often, sex was made into a game of control in the relationship, I've shied away from sexual relationships until I could discern within my self what was genuine and what was manipulative. I coped with this by initially removing myself from the situation, then going through the individual aspects and intuitively determining if it was genuine or not. When I finally felt able to sincerely be part of a sexual relationship, it felt much lighter.

Both Ioho and Lauren have striven with the manipulative elements of the awakening period and overcome them as they matured. But for many women another problem emerges when the daimonic experience has been so beautiful that it floods human relationships. Meg admits:

> I have expected too much from men I am close to. I half expect them to understand me instantly the way my daimon does and then become disappointed by the lack of spiritual bonding. My daimon also points out to me what aspects of him are missing in the man I'm with at the time. I find it hard to accept someone for what they are straight away because this little voice says, 'he doesn't like the same music as you' or 'he doesn't believe in God', so I find it hard to concentrate on the good things. After a while, I silence the voice inside but he flares up with 'I told you so' if it all goes wrong.

Pat speaks to all young women of the daimon: 'Enjoy his gifts, the doors he opens to yourself, to your soul and creativity, to your sexuality.' But she also warns that caution is needed, that 'distorted aspects of the daimon may manifest as a product of cultural, social and religious conditioning over generations.' A woman 'may carry a soul-wound in her psyche that is a collective one' and the daimon 'can be the mirror of outer patriarchy and the inner oppressor perpetuating women's victim role'. We will be examining those distortions in Chapter 5. In the meantime, Pat reminds us that it is important for 'a young woman to realize that she is not a failure, has not done anything wrong'.

It is from the daimon that we learn sexual response, but this process also has its problems. The image of the daimon may become so rigidly fixed in place that we are not content until we have found his likeness faithfully reproduced in a human man. It is supremely difficult for young women to differentiate daimon from human lover, but it is equally difficult for young men in search of the idealized muse – who is just as easily transposed upon a human woman.

POWER AND PROJECTION

Jane Austen's exploration of late 18th-century sexuality in her novels *Pride and Prejudice* and *Sense and Sensibility* centres on partnerships between men and women whose respective soul-images are appropriately reciprocal. If she were writing now, her book might be entitled *Power and Projection*, for Austen would undoubtedly draw upon the most up-to-date psychological language to define her lovers and their motivations.

Once the capacity for sexual love is awakened, desire and passion often lead the way. This is the state of adolescent girl, seeking for her lover amid an array of young men. She may be led by the image of her daimon to find a man who corresponds in many respects to her needs; she herself may feature in a similar projection on the part of a man who sees his anima in her.

When the daimon is projected on to a man, so that he is cloaked in the mantle of the beloved, he can usually no longer be seen as separate from the beloved. This intensifies the strain on the relationship, since the human lover's own identity and qualities are submerged in those of the daimon.

Linda Leonard writes of her own erotic projection of the daimon on to the creative architect Howard Roark: at the first opportunity, she met and fell in love with a married architect who seemed to correspond to this archetype.[32] This kind of projection of the daimon or pin-up on to the actual lover was described as 'disastrous' by most of the respondents when I asked if any had ever chosen a sexual partner because of some resemblance to their daimon. Here are some of their responses.

Lauren writes:

> When I've chosen an infatuation because of my sexual daimon, I've found it difficult to dissect the real person from the ideal vision. In these cases I found myself expecting the person to be more spiritually and emotionally evolved than they were in reality. As a friend put it, 'I thought he was so deep, but it was just another minnow pool.'

Ioho relates:

> It's always proved such an absolute disaster that I learnt my lesson. I did it in two ways. First I used to be attracted by rough, tough powerful men with shining eyes. I never found one who wasn't so soft on the inside that I couldn't wipe him out or terrify him. The tougher the man, the more he wants to be mothered, however implicitly, and that isn't a role I care to take on. The other thing

I've done is fall for someone who both reminded me of One Feather and had that otherworldly quality. It was an extraordinary relationship, entirely overwhelming and entirely surreal. We lived in a spiritual wonderland, floating through life in this exhilarating magnetic force field, cut off from the world and everyone else. When we eventually grounded, we crashed in an explosion of rage and resentment. If I were male, I would have been him, I realize. He mirrored for me every aspect of my animus that I detested, as I did the anima for him. We loved each other with a passion that felt like survival. We held on to each other and ran like hell, then we let go and ran like hell in opposite directions.

Gwen says laconically,

When you're looking for a cross between Christ and Shiva, you don't run into a lot. When I did find anyone they were either real bastards, didn't fancy me, or both!

Anne puts her finger on the button that has detonated many relationships: 'I think my anger with the man for not being the daimon was probably the main cause why the relationship failed.'

Miriam writes, 'I think that in the past my sexual partners were often aspects of the destructive daimon that I was playing out in my life.' This phase of daimonic projection seems to last longest in women who haven't married, as though it was still necessary to measure the frequency of any lover against that of the daimon. Melissa says, 'I've always chosen my sexual partners based on an ideal figure of the Lover in my dreams.' Meg's current partner is

the only one man who resembled my daimon. We have been together for nearly four months and my daimon spirit is still flying. The more I get to know him, the more this is intensifying. You never know, perhaps our souls have joined the same orbit at last!

But we do not just project our desires and soul-images onto others, we also *accept* the projections of others and wear them ourselves. This is especially so for women living now in a society that has vaunted the ideal feminine and placed it on a pedestal of perfection. The inventors of this ideal feminine have been the male designers who have projected immature versions of their muse upon all women; and in this projection women have been arch-collaborators. The tyranny of the fashion magazines overshadows the teenager whose figure is still maturing and who is sometimes driven to feats of desperate self-sabotage in order to pare her shape down to fashionable proportions. The fashion houses continue to dictate how women should appear to others in the coming season and many obligingly reciprocate.

The visual mediums dictate messages to both men and women, feeding upon our anxieties and fuelling false expectations. The tyrannical perfection of celluloid overshadows our physical relationships as we 'watch handsome, perfectly-proportioned, naked lovers make perfect love in front of our eyes'.[66] Our own intimacies are not so perfect because we don't have the opportunity to shoot a dozen 'takes' for each of our actions in bed. These false expectations are engineered by our background and society, underscoring our perceived human imperfections in withering relief. However, these are projections which we accept for ourselves: they do not belong to us.

In every partnership there are two sets of couples: the woman and man, and their contrasexual soul-images. A man brings his muse, under wraps as the anima; a woman brings her daimon, disguised under veils of the animus. Add to every relationship its own hidden agendas, needs, compulsions and stories and you have the perfect explosive dynamite of projection and power, inadequacy and compensation. Here are a few of the scenarios which human beings play out with each other: we may recognize aspects of these in our own or others', relationships.

Need/Compulsion	Partner chosen as compensation
meal-ticket	over-achieving bread-winner
rescue	decisive hero/ine
no self-worth	strongly-opinionated
lack of self-identity	strong personality
overbearing identity	weak personality
abused	abuser
lonely	gregarious
wants child to confirm own existence	surrogate father/mother, boy/girl-next-door
assurance and approval	father-, mother- or authority-figure
power-trip	wimp
victim	power-tripper
manipulator	mother's boy/father's little girl
loyal	faithless

The variations spiral beyond this very generalized list, in lesser or greater gradations. Some scenarios of projection and power also seem to reflect themselves in successive generations, creating

inherited patterns which are hard to escape or break. These partnership attractions are, we must remember, mutual projections
which bind opposites together. They are roles played by men as
well as women. The conflict of the hidden agendas involved in
them strongly colours such relationships.

As human beings, we seek what makes us whole, but we tend
to be very lazy: we leave undeveloped tendencies and abilities
within ourselves, seeking their completion or compensation in a
partner. Many relationships are based upon habitual laziness
rather than loving respect. If one partner challenges this laziness,
the relationship may falter unless both work hard to supply their
own deficiency. If the other partner refuses to change, that person is suddenly faced with his or her own inadequacy and lack of
self-definition.

If women defer self-identification at the critical last stage of
adolescence because they pair off with their first partner of
choice, the daimon cannot become a supportive ally until they
have undertaken the important work of self-exploration. Dealing
with each of the daimon's appearances can only be done if we are
true to our self, without acting a part, without projecting our
inadequacies upon each facet.

A prime example of this syndrome is seen in Dorothea Brooke,
the bookish heroine of George Eliot's *Middlemarch*. This high-
minded yet naive young woman is drawn to a particular daimonic mirror; she reflects, 'The really delightful marriage must be that
where your husband was a sort of father, and could teach you
even Hebrew, if you wished it.' She does indeed find such a man
in the middle-aged and inadequate clergyman, Casaubon, whom
she marries so that she can aid him in his life-task of writing a *Key
to All Mythologies*. Casaubon's study is an arid sham with no
manifest result, but such is Dorothea's enthusiasm for his great
work that he briefly believes himself to be capable of finishing it.
For him, 'she filled up all the blanks with unmanifested perfec-
tions, interpreting him as she interpreted the works of Providence,
and accounting for seeming discords by her own deafness to the
higher harmonies'. Dorothea's marriage is based on her projections, which give her an actress's ability for rhetoric but little else.
The relationship goes to the wall when another more dynamic
man comes into their introverted orbit.[14]

Seeking validation and approval from lovers and partners,
young women often relinquish the maturing of their own

identity, merging instead into the compensations of a complacent relationship. Such a relationship ultimately becomes very disappointing, especially if it is built upon such dependencies and projections. Such couples do not 'live happily ever after'. The magical ring of romance and marriage is *not* a charmed circle of completion, but an arena of safety wherein men and women need to *continue working* at their relationship and attaining maturity. Partnerships cannot remain in an adolescent time-warp.

TRUE LOVE FOREVER?

Let us be in no doubt, the daimon is a powerful current in a woman's life, as potent as lightning. If *sufficient* characteristics of the daimon are found in a satisfying sexual partner, then the daimonic relationship seems to be well integrated – most of the women I have spoken to continue to enjoy a relationship with their daimons as well as with their husbands and lovers. Even accounting for the feminine skill of dealing with several agendas at once, what does this continuing dialogue with the daimon denote? Does it seek to undermine stable human relationships?

Let us look first at the daimonic relationship. The daimon appears in as many different ways as there are individuals and relationships. A woman may experience the daimon in her soul as follows:

- a single figure who doesn't change
- a single figure who evolves, sequentially, into other figures
- a main figure with a series of companion figures
- a chorus of figures whose joint contribution produces a coherent song

But this is precisely the same model which we recognize from human relationships:

- a stable partnership with one man
- a sequential series of relationships with one man after another
- a stable relationship supplemented by relationships or friendships with other men
- no current relationship, but a series of male relationships of a broad social kind

Within these frameworks women seek out their daimonic and human partners, according to their needs and circumstances. Younger women may tend towards multi-relationships with men, but perhaps have a stable daimonic figure; older women may tend towards a stable male relationship but enjoy a series of daimonic figures. There are many varieties of experience: there is no 'right' one.

A women must walk the path which the daimon – the true soulmate or companion upon the quest for passion – has opened to her, trying not to project him onto a man except where the reflection can help clarify latent aspects of her lover.

The woman who is inspired by the ideal of her daimon – and, equally the man who is inspired by his anima – may find her chosen partner wanting in many respects if that has been the major criterion of their union. Love is not always reciprocal. Unequal or unrequited love is always difficult to handle, whether one is the object or subject. During these periods of unequal human response, women will be drawn more deeply into the fulfilment of the daimonic dance. During periods of equal response, the contrasexual image will be less dominant. The daimonic relationship is not normally cause for a co-respondency suit!

Absorbing the projections of one's partner may be part of first love's enchantment. There may even be times when this role is a very necessary reciprocation, a kind of 'make-believe' which has its own appropriate seasons in love-making or when the partner is feeling needy or below par. But *retaining these projections* long term is no basis for a healthy relationship.

In plate illustration 4 the human couple seem to be regarding each other, but in actuality each is relating not to the real partner but to the projections which have been given to or absorbed by the other.

The emptiness of partnerships is reflected in many folk-stories. *The Goose Girl* by the Brothers Grimm[20] tells how a Princess and her maid change places because the Princess takes the line of least resistance. The maid becomes the Princess and is married to the destined Prince, but she is *the false bride*. It is only when the real Princess becomes a Goose girl and her helpful male friend, Conrad, discovers who she really is, that the false bride is recognized as such and is taken out and killed.[20]

Men and women frequently marry 'the wrong partner'; they marry with the false bride or bridegroom, the immature projection, not the real partner. It is extraordinary how many people speak of their suspicion, the night before the wedding, that they may indeed have made the wrong choice. Threat of mismating usually causes the contrasexual image to prompt these suspicions, sometimes sending dreams of great anguish and confusion. The role of the daimon and muse is to support, companion and guide the authentic self: anything which betrays the authentic self prompts such a reaction. Unfortunately, very few people are courageous enough to act upon these dream warnings or to admit their mistake at the eleventh hour.

Here we are beginning to distinguish between the many subtle influences which are present within a relationship:

- the attractiveness of the human partner
- the surface projections of gender which are given to or absorbed by the partner
- the contrasexual figure of muse or daimon

We note that in the 'night before the wedding dream', as in the story of the Goose Girl, it is the contrasexual figure who emerges to warn of disaster. Why should the muse or daimon do such a thing if the contrasexual figure were not a true friend? The truth is, it is *not* the contrasexual figure itself which causes the difficulty in relationships but *the immature social projections* which we accept as belonging to ourselves and which represent the false bride or bridegroom. The friendship of the contrasexual figure does not intrude upon the human partnership any more than do the human friendships of either partner before their union.

The immature social projections which surround the contrasexual soul-image happen in both men and women. Both partners may realize 'this is not the person I married' when the first flush of desire has died down. Physical intimacy with another human being upon whom the soul-image has been immaturely projected erodes any illusions very quickly: the notion that the beloved is perfect, has no gross bodily functions, does not make mistakes and is always kind and considerate, soon melts in the noon-day sun of real life. As Marge Piercy writes in her poem, 'A Story Wet as Tears':[55]

> Though courtship turns frogs into princes,
> marriage turns them quietly back.

When the projection upon the lover fades, when the glamour of first love or infatuation dissolves, the beloved appears in such a mundane light that rejection is almost inevitable.

'True love' has become so clichéd that it is hard to use that phrase; it has become endowed with encrustations of expectation and projection. However, the authentic love which arises from the being's core and bedews every facet of a relationship is not the same as projection. Plato's *Phaedrus* defines true love in strangely resonant, daimonic terms:

> Every lover is fain that his beloved should be of a nature like to his own god ... his every act is aimed at bringing the beloved to be every whit like unto himself and unto the god of their worship.[56]

This sounds remarkably like simple projection at first glance, but Plato touches something more profound here.

Marriage is a contract whereby each soul commits to the other, as the Elizabethan soldier-poet Sir Philip Sidney wrote, 'My true love hath my heart and I have his.' This formal exchange between lovers may be formally ratified by legal witnesses or blessed by religion, but it remains a mutual sacrament of reciprocation wherein hearts and souls are exchanged in a meaningful sense. Any marriage or stable partnership goes through many stages, of which the first is mutual infatuation. Over time, any residue of immature projection is washed out in the washing machine of daily married life, but sometimes disillusionment can set in. At this point the marriage is not unsavable, but both partners have to recognize what has happened and reapply themselves to the next phase.

If, at this juncture, both partners can transcend this disillusion and seek out the wise guidance of their contrasexual friend, they may herald the next phase of deeper mutuality in which the partnership becomes a true marriage. Here, partners take back the immature projections they have bestowed upon the other and return to the ground of their authentic selves so that they may accept each other as the true bride and groom. In this phase, the contrasexual figure of each acts as match-maker, and the partners' contrasexual friends become deeply acquainted, giving another dimension to the relationship.

Very many people do not attempt to bring their partnership to this conclusion, for it takes patience and forbearance. If at the end of a process of readjustment, both partners find themselves strangers, with no shared shred of love or mutuality, there seems little point in prolonging the agony. A high proportion of divorces in the West are due to an incompatibility or immaturity of soul.

Both men and women ricochet from partner to partner, seeking the *image* rather than the reality of love. But unless they find it first within themselves, they will most certainly not find it elsewhere. The pursuit of the image can be seen in the way in which ageing husbands reject their middle-aged wives in favour of younger women. Rejected when her surface beauty retreats, the wife no longer embodies her husband's immature anima projection in any regard and his eye is quickly engaged by a younger woman who reflects his anima perfectly. But this is not a pursuit for men only – women also play this game. Very often it would appear that a woman should leave her partner if he reflects her own damaged masculine image. But this is no solution since, 'her own damaged masculinity will seek out and find his double' in another partner.[79]

Women who are able to relate well to their daimon find deep wells of help and support. The increased confidence they receive may freak out some men, who may feel threatened and seek out less challenging new partners. This risk may unconsciously deter some women from making the attempt.

It is important to note that though immature projections upon partners are inherent in most relationships 'they are not the fault of personal reality'.[82] We need to lift blame from the self, parents, partners and men at large and squarely recognize, by neutral assessment, just how much projection comes from these quarters and how much from our own side. The process of unmasking our projections in our relationships with men is almost always extremely painful and self-revealing. Treasure those realizations, collect them and piece together the many-sharded mirror into an image – and you will find yourself.

It is only when we give up such projections upon partners that our partners can be free to be themselves and not move, marionette-like, to our string-pulling. The way to free oneself from such projection is to *return to the ground of one's authentic self* and always speak and act from that basis.

In every meeting between man and woman, the essential harmony of the universe is potentially present, although not necessarily manifest. We react to each other on a variety of levels and sometimes 'fail to meet' at all.[10] Reasons for such failures are given by Claremont de Castillejo as:

- being on a different levels of awareness
- one or other is playing host to a role or archetypal aspect
- one is not listening to the other

The different responses and priorities of men and women keep us in separate countries. Men are rarely raised to value feeling or to take notice of it in their planning. Women are generally encouraged to value their feelings as good indicators. Yet many women have schooled themselves to react in a male way, with calm and rational reserve, when their feelings beneath are incandescent with reaction. Any form of emotional dishonesty or repression inevitably stores up trouble that will erupt later. Ignoring feelings in a relationship can cause great rifts; simultaneous reactions to partner-projections can lead to a crippling sense of being unable to meet on any level. Communication then breaks down before it can be established. This inability to meet on equal ground is usually a cause of separation.

Stable partnerships are becoming more and more rare: the media including every women's journal on the news-stand proclaim the message of unfaithfulness as a resort for unsatisfactory partners, in tit-for-tat vendettas. It takes frequent reassessment by both partners for a partnership to remain functional on all levels, and a recognition that the momentum of the relationship will alter over the years.

Sheila speaks of the attraction of opposites, which for her keeps her marriage in balance:

> My current partner reflects my daimon in that he is very self-contained and has hidden depths. I fell in love with him because he was different; he fell for me because he found me mysterious.

The neglect of the daimon has meant the diminishing of this mystery, for he can still lead us into the garden of sacred sexuality wherein both partners find the deepening of their union.

The *Book of Proverbs* asked where the perfect wife, whose price was above rubies, might be found. The question most women ask today is: 'A considerate man, where is he to be found?' A good man is hard to find, but Janet speaks thus of her husband:

> I'm blessed to have a jewel of a spouse who is everything that everyone dreams of. My friends tell me that if I could clone him, I'd be rich! In any case he is gentle, supportive, caring, loving, a

great listener, generous and a wonderful skilled lover. I couldn't ask for more. I dream and he helps me manifest my dream into reality.

The sense of a true balance between male and female, or between subject and contrasexual other is not solely the domain of heterosexual people. That same sense of balance may be experienced by homosexual men and women also, as Ioho relates.

> I'm heterosexual, but have had brief relationships with women. When I've been with a woman, the feminine in me is stronger as if, with the balance of the polarity sheering from the centre region over to the feminine, my acknowledgement and response to the animus, as expressed through the other woman, is to shift further too. However, I've encountered the shift from animus to anima, but in a heterosexual relationship. This has happened only as glimpses, flashes across the face and form of the man I'm with, and most often in sacred ritual with one particular man whose gentleness is extraordinary. His faith is deeply focused upon his Goddess and only recently, since beginning magical work with me, has he begun to work with the God energy, allowing that to rise up through him consciously, empowering him.

Here Ioho touches upon the inner mystery of sacred sexuality towards which the contrasexual other will lead both men and women, if they so allow. This is the 'mating on all the planes', which esotericist Dion Fortune wrote about, wherein man and woman, male and female, masculine and feminine are united on human, contrasexual and divine levels.[15]

From the first ecstatic call of the daimon onwards, through raw sexual awakening to stable relationship, each woman descends into the unknown depths of a relationship, whether with the daimon or with a sexual partner, with a sense of ignorance or inexperience. Love is not wholly pleasurable, but neither should it be wholly painful. The bittersweet mixture is part of love's nature – a truth which is often forgotten in this age of instant gratification. In 'Demeter's Daughter' by songwriter Anne Lister,[85] the older Persephone speaks of her experience in a positive and retrospective way; she speaks not of rape and unwillingness, but of the reality which every woman experiences as the daimon leads her into the depths of the unknown by opening the doorway of her sexuality:

They say he forced me but that's not true
Of my own free will I followed him down.
To his dark place beneath the hills
To his dark palace below the ground.
And there he loved me and I loved him
Though all the world there was icy dark
We never noticed the light was dim
With the bright lights inside our hearts...

The fairest flower that ever grows
Grows far deep inside a bush of thorns
And happiness then is like the rose
For without pain nothing good is born
To know the daylight you must know the dark
To know the flowers you must know weeds
You cannot meet again unless you part
Nor eat a pomegranate without seeds.

Many women have asked me anxiously whether the daimon should be ignored when women reach sexual maturity and have physical relationships with a man. I know from where their anxiety emanates: they do not want to hurt the man they love, but neither do they want to cut off the bridge to their soul.

The true daimon does not intrude upon our mature human relationships as a piggy-in-the-middle. It is his task to guide us aright, to lead us to where our souls will be happy and fulfilled. We must regard the daimon as a frequency, colour or quality which turns up whenever our souls are on track. We may find his frequency is partially shared by the human men who attract us, but we must not confuse the two.

The search for understanding of the daimonic relationship is often a long quest, as difficult as understanding our human relationships. But while human relationships may come and go, love does go on forever.

This is portrayed movingly in Anthony Minghella's extraordinarily subtle film, *Truly, Madly, Deeply.*[90] When Nina's husband Jamie, a concert cellist, dies untimely of a trivial ailment, Nina enters the isolation of bereavement in a creative way. Like any woman with her daimon, she talks to Jamie all the time, especially when she is alone walking. He tells her to lock the back door and to walk in the middle of dark streets at night for safety. In their rat-infested flat, she feels accompanied by him when she plays a Bach sonata upon the piano, humming the cello part herself. The cello itself stands in the corner, a mute representative of the dead Jamie: a fact that is underscored when Nina's sister asks for its loan for her son's cello lessons. Nina's over-reaction to the suggestion tells us that, for her, the cello *is* Jamie.

Then, one day, when she is playing the Bach sonata, she actually hears his cello accompanying her: Jamie is physically present with her in the room, to her shocked delight. He is a very tangible and mundane ghost, and their relationship very quickly settles into the gentle bicker of married life. She notices that the rats have gone from the flat: her handyman remarks that rats don't like ghosts. She speaks to her therapist – in whose presence she has previously expressed her bitter anger at Jamie's leaving of her – to get a reality check about her new experience of Jamie's ghost, but it is from her language student, Maura, that she receives the reassurance that spirits 'are everywhere, walking here with us'. It is with Maura, that she meets a new friend, Mark, a psychologist who attempts to date her. Nina is unable to reciprocate or to tell him the reasons why she is unwilling to see him.

Returning from work one night, she finds that Jamie has invited other ghosts back to their flat. They are all male musicians with a great capacity for watching old movies, which they do round the clock to Nina's aggravation. The flat is no longer rat- but ghost-infested. They particularly enjoy *Brief Encounter*, a film in which a woman teeters on the brink of leaving her husband for a romantic liaison. The closing dialogue between the woman and her husband after she has decided to abort the affair is particularly poignant in view of Nina's circumstances. It is handled with tremendous English under-statement.

The husband in the film, who knows nothing certain but has his suspicions, says, 'Whatever your dream was, it wasn't a very happy one was it? Is there anything I can do for you?' The wife responds, alluding to her secret assignations, 'The trips helped.' The husband speaks with understanding and appreciation, 'You've been a long way away – thank you for having married me.'

The ghosts gently chorus this last dialogue by heart, as if to convey its meaning to Nina. After he has attempted to restructure and decorate the flat to his own taste, Jamie says to her, 'You can tell me to just go', as Nina finally loses her temper with him, the furniture moving making her feel that she has been burgled every time she comes home.

But it is not until Nina attends the birth of Maura's baby that she is able to emerge from the indecision of bereavement. She makes a firm arrangement to see Mark and ends up sleeping with him. In choosing life, she unwittingly says goodbye to Jamie, who appears to her no more. We see her place the cello into its case as reverently as a body in a coffin, ready to give to her nephew, as a bold rat stalks the mantelpiece. When Mark comes to collect her for their next date, Jamie stands at the window with his companion ghosts, who all comfort him with supportive pats as the tears of farewell slip down his face. He has seen how well she is loved by Mark and departs.

This wonderful film was mentioned by several of the respondents as representative of their own daimonic experience. In it we see the wondrous relay of love which underpins Nina's life. Her relationship with Jamie does not end at death, but continues, along with her other male and female relationships with living people. She shows no awe or reverence to the ghosts, only a matter-of-fact acceptance and sometimes annoyance. We also note that Jamie does not come to monopolize her or insist on former rights and privileges, but in order to support and enable her over the bridge of separation. His forbearance and acceptance of Nina's ongoing love is as important as Nina's ability to emerge from bereavement and find a new partner.

In our human relationships, our prior love of the daimon is similarly submerged and integrated, for love – wherever and however we experience it – is never forgotten or wholly overlaid. It is the perfume, frequency or colour that saturates our whole experience. We are not therefore asked to give up the daimon, for love does not demand forgetfulness. Its sole command is that we take up the relay torch of love and run with it. For in love's realm there is no death or separation, only rejoicing that love continues to burn with passion.

Questions

1 Did you have a secret/invisible childhood companion? Did this companion evolve into your daimon?
2 What qualities do you project upon partners?

Actions

List your adolescent pin-ups and the kinds of men who inspire you now. What qualities attract you? How are these qualities linked with your daimon?

Reflection

Reflect upon these words of the poet, Rumi:

> Lovers don't finally meet somewhere:
> They're in each other all along

Meeting the Daimon

Close your eyes and visualize a doorway ahead of you. When it is clear to you, ask your daimon to come to the door and meet you. See the door opening and the figure who stands there. Do not be alarmed or disturbed by your first impression, just record it: it may well change now or later.

Ask the figure, 'Are you my daimon?' Be attentive to the answer: this may come in words, in heart-to-heart communication, or you may feel as though it arises from within you. Let be whatever happens and record this afterwards.

If dialogue is easy, then dialogue with the daimon.

If dialogue is difficult, then be content with a first meeting. Other sessions can help develop communication.

To finish, say goodbye to the daimon and visualize him turning and closing the door behind him.

CHAPTER 3

Stories in the Soul

Who is this Singer that sends his voice through the dark forest, and inhabits us with ageless and immortal music, and sets the long echoes rolling for evermore?

Mary Webb, *Gone to Earth*

ROMANCING THE HERO

When we are visited by our daimon – whether in dream, reverie or recognized within a man – we are thrown into a deep place which most often manifests itself as a story. This story may be a simple scenario which replays like a tape-loop, or may evolve into a complex of sequences, finally becoming a nearly-completed story. For most women, this story will be subliminally spun out over many years, evolving and transmuting, but sending out a frequency of desire and passion. We respond to this frequency wherever we meet it, perhaps incorporating new scenes into our ongoing story.

We see a re-triggering of the daimonic image in C S Lewis's novel, *That Hideous Strength*,[33] where Jane Studdock meets the extraordinary figure of Dr Ransom, a man who has walked with planetary spirits and who exemplifies the Wounded King.

> She had long since forgotten the imagined Arthur of her childhood – and the imagined Solomon too. Solomon – for the first time in many years the bright solar blend of king and lover and magician which hangs about that name stole back upon her mind.[33]

Until this meeting, she had striven to be 'a modern woman', pouring herself into the mould of patriarchal appeasement, cool, efficient yet totally at sea with her husband. Meeting Ransom causes her to revert to her true female self: a painful encounter which makes her simultaneously confront the core meaning of the masculine, which she has been avoiding. As Ransom notes:

> The male you could have escaped, for it exists only on the biological level. But the masculine none of us can escape.

The daimon has always been the leading man in the stories which women chose to read and tell; he mirrors and complements their role as leading lady. Although these stories have been dismissed as mere wish-fulfilling fantasies, this is not always true. Stories about the daimon are nearly always stories about *the woman herself*: male and female roles within our story need to be examined carefully to see what levels are being explored and ignored.

Human beings have always turned to story-telling to express deep truths experienced within them. This understanding now fuels a whole industry of psychoanalysis, story-therapy and self-exploratory workshops. But for most of us, the story which revolves in our soul is not so obvious, nor is its meaning clear to us. We unconsciously pursue our own story in other forms, in novels, TV series, songs and legends.

Ioho recalls listening to the stories told by her daimon, One Feather, or those

> read from a book, or related by someone around a Circle sacred fire: so the little child is evoked in me. I look up into the face of the story-teller, tiptoeing after his every word, catching each one, breathing it into my soul.

That is what we do when we track the story of ourselves and the daimon.

The romantic hero has provided many guises for the daimon over the years, in many different genres – from chivalric heroes like Lancelot and Prince Charming, through the poets and artists of the romantic era such as Lord Byron (the pin-up of his generation) to the masterful, but sometimes manipulative characters of Charlotte Brontë's Mr Rochester or Austen's Mr Darcy. Modern archetypes also include the anti-heroic figures such as the 'Bit of Rough', the Toy Boy, the Rambo and the Drop-Out who feature in dramas of social realism, but these are rarely so attractive to women as the romantic hero, although women addicted to excitement and to a charismatic, masked daimon, may find these anti-heroic types appealing. We shall examine the rogue forms in Chapter 5.

The female preoccupation with true romance has been much scorned: stories of 'true lerve' are the stuff of women's magazines, pulp novellas and teen-zeens, avidly read by women in desperate or compensatory ways. Many women read these novels in order to contact their own daimon, which is conceived of as the ideal bed-mate, the exciting lover, someone who is dangerous, irrational and inspiring. To spend a few quiet hours in his company is all they seek. Men rarely tolerate this level of romance in themselves and see it as a form of female weakness. They prefer action to reading about the action.

The average romantic pulp novel caters for the woman who longs for a perfect partner. The men in these novels are usually well-heeled, in exotic or attractive professions, are desired by another woman, are sometimes temperamentally difficult or have a fascinating if romantically flawed personality, but are usually decent enough at the core. They are pictured as rescuers from economic straits, as men committed to wider social concerns or with fulfilling caring careers. In short, they are Prince Charming in modern dress.

The women in these novels are usually disadvantaged in major ways: with little experience of the world, in difficult jobs or manipulative relationships, or in recovery from them. These are heroines who crave 'lerve' in romantic block capitals, and so are those who read their stories. In romantic novellas, we rarely read of women who have 'real life' problems such as children from previous marriages! For that we have to turn to romantic social realism, which portrays a heroine who is normally very poor, pretty and inexperienced, surviving appalling affronts to her womanhood, harassment at work or other hassles. The majority of TV soaps rarely rise above standards of wish-fulfilling social realism. They both reflect and refute real life, without giving us the mythic depths of romance.

As Anna writes:

> The tendency of teenage literature to romanticize and sentimentalize daimons leaves women very naive and vulnerable, unable to draw out the strengths of their inner self, and prey to possessions

by fragmented and suppressed aspects of themselves which are then projected on to their lovers.

But where teen-zines and true romance magazines concentrate on the vicarious satisfactions of union with the pin-up and the hunk, the pulp novellas and romances are normally geared to middle-aged women facing up to the disillusions of married or single life.

These nodes of disillusion occur at significant stages of female development in our society; some may become doorways of opportunity for the daimon to reassert himself in conscious or less conscious ways. They are associated with the loss or relinquishing of:

- the secret childhood companion
- the ideal of 'true, perfect love' during teens or twenties to a harsher reality
- a job or career during child-bearing years or through unemployment and redundancy
- the ideal of marriage or no partnership to the reality of unequal labour for little reward or lack of companionship
- maternal identity when children leave home
- youthful attractiveness at menopause
- social status as an old or unemployed woman

These seven nodes are associated with projections relating to identity, status and self-worth, and all women will recognize them as flash-points of emotional discomfort, hardship or pain. If we peel away the social projections, we can perhaps acknowledge these nodes as opportunities for initiatory change and look for helpful stories and scenarios within ourselves as to how we can make these transformations come about rather than sinking into despair.

It is often at these points that women seek out the heroic and inspiring aspects of their daimons in stories, myths, dreams, reveries and fantasies. These modes of story-telling and listening all have distinct functions, which we should clarify here.

- *Romance*: a story with a wish-fulfilling conclusion with which we can identify
- *Myth*: a universally true story which reveals itself in all cultures
- *Dream*: the inside weaving of our life, the unseen reverse of our outer life's weaving
- *Reverie*: a story or scenario allowed to unfold at its own pace

and in its own way, pursued reflectively
- *Fantasy*: a story or scenario to which we contribute wish-fulfilling details

Every woman uses a variety of these forms in her daimonic exploration.

Frances speaks of the 'vital comfort' that helpful stories bring when they clearly validate her experience, 'especially years ago when I felt very out of it, not normal'. The many forms of story in which the daimon can come to us often prove a safety-valve. Miriam writes of a time when she had sought comfort from her husband.

> I was furious with him for not providing it. I went into another room and called my 'ideal lover' to me. He came and responded with exactly what I needed: he was my age, sandy-haired, blue-eyed, slim, gentle, genteel, cultured, and he gave me space to cry and tell my story while simply holding me. He was very supportive of my feelings. This relieved all the pressure of my husband having to relate to me like this, and I was no longer angry with him.

The psychoanalytical process focuses upon 'reconstructing the client's personal narrative and exploring it for new meaning'.[82] Each woman has the personal sequence of her life as well as a secret story within her soul. Psychology has granted us great gifts and problems in equal measure. It can help open up the telling of the daimonic story, but it can also usurp the continuity of the narrative of the deep, personal evolution of the story. Speaking often in archetypes and ancient myths rather than actual instances of life, psychology sometimes distances women from personal understanding. Here are some of the stories which respondents have given to define their own daimonic relationship.

Melissa's story starts when she was a child.

> My storyline was that the daimon was an older brother I'd finally met after years. We met in a sort of rescue-like situation, became friends and companions and I knew one day a great mystery was going to be revealed and he was going to be my brother in full again. Presently the daimon is part of my inner world and journeys of self-discovery. Because I normally work with myths, he's the companion on the quests, or the reward at the end of the journey.

Elizabeth remembers a scenario she used to have.

> I am a princess engaged to marry a prince, and we will one day be

sovereigns. We are very much in love, lose our virginity to each other and then have passionate relationships before we are married. There is always a sense of taboo, secrecy – and also a feeling that the relationship is ultimately doomed to failure.

Suzanne tells similar stories about her daimon.

I imagine he was a Viking prince, centuries before he lost his sight; he could raid my village and carry me off by force but I'd end up falling in love with him. Then he'd die in some battle. Or he is the blind minstrel at the castle gate: I am the fine lady who falls for him. Of course, my husband is a brute and our affair ends in tragedy.

Such stories underlie a sense of the daimon as reincarnatory lover.

Hue has always hated the role of 'the rescued one', the helpless one.

I never played princess. Consequently I always had trouble with love stories. I was attracted to the heroes but wanted to be like them, not rescued by them. The girl stories I liked were ones like *The Secret Garden* and *Island of Blue Dolphins,* in which the girl saved people. I'm only now learning to appreciate the role of the male as protector of the female, but it's only attractive to me in the form of a mutual partnership, such as that of Marion and Robin in the TV series *Robin of Sherwood*. I like the stories where the girl wins *his* heart, through cleverness and strength: the tomboy stories of Jo in *Little Women* and Catherine and Heathcliff in *Wuthering Heights*.

Jocelyn's stories around her daimonic figures follow the need to bring together opposites.

Over the last five years, I've developed stories connecting sex and spirituality around my daimon lover being a priest/god figure to my priestess/goddess, and together we work fertility and other kinds of magic for the community. In real life, I've met several men who in my story have played this role with me in quite distant past lives.

Frances's relationship with her daimon has evolved over many years.

The story expands as I do, sometimes slowly, sometimes with great leaps and jolts. I've got to know and trust again that person I first met when I was six and a half. While I'm now aware that he has always been there, for large amounts of time I've been unable to access him, or wanted to do so. I know now that I can be in touch with all sorts of parts of myself and other worlds, life, people without becoming overstretched. In my early twenties, carving out a career, this all seemed far too much; now I find myself embracing my daimon who seems to combine The Green Man, Gandalf, Merlin, Pan, Bear, Warrior, Healer, Lover, Brother, Father, Creator/Destroyer and Wise Man.

Fiona has gone further than many respondents in unwittingly encapsulating her daimonic experience in the writing of a novel.

In an earlier draft, the figure of Nallikino entered briefly as an arrogant, rigid, army officer, but he has insisted in pushing his way to a central role, into a much fuller character with a gut feeling against duty. He soldiers by peacemaking and preserving life. In the end he kills or is the cause of the death of the Marshal. Killing the Marshal has altered my animus: I can sense the change. The sections about Nallikino are the hardest to write because in many ways he is an ideal type of man.

The emergence of Fiona's character, Nallikino, to centre-stage is a clear indication of his daimonic role. The more she regards him, the less arrogant and more human he becomes; as she advances, it is correspondingly more difficult to write because she is approaching her own soul.

In all these stories the daimon acts as go-between, messenger, ally and initiator into eros as well as straightforward lover and hero. He is sought in a number of different ways, recognized in myths and stories, followed through unfolding scenarios and reveries, and miraculously met in dreams, meditations and visions.

Many people have commented to me that they see the daimon as merely compensation for a woman's lack of a good sexual relationship. This is harshly condemnatory of unmated women. The kernel of truth in the accusation is that the daimon is usually more active in a celibate woman's soul, for celibacy does not impede the daimon's function but, rather, enhances it. Without human relationships with men to intervene, the ground is clear for the daimon to be explored. Celibacy can provide a meditative space for the daimon to emerge.

Historically, women have been restricted when it comes to full pursuit of the beloved: it has not been socially acceptable for a woman to head-hunt her human partner. This may help to

explain why women are likely to seek out periods of quiet wherein they can reflect on the beloved. Lacan remarked that 'the
partner of a woman is solitude'.[31] This may lead men to 'understand that women are always aiming at another man who is
beyond them ... not a real, flesh and blood one' (*ibid*) This
solitude is the realm of the spinster, in its original sense of 'she
who spins'.

The involvement that women have with their ongoing daimonic story is intense. They can become like Tennyson's Lady of
Shalott who is obliged to weave whatever she sees reflected in her
mirror. The Lady of Shalott is under a curse not to leave the tower
where she has been imprisoned. It is only when she sees Lancelot
ride by, when her soul-mirror receives the impression of the inner
beloved in outer manifestation that she leaves her task and
attempts to cross the boundary between the inner and outer
worlds. In Tennyson's poem, she emerges and dies. But this is *not*
the fate of all women who spin their daimonic story. It is only
those women who fail to spin their story strongly and who fail to
engage the help of the daimon first, who falter as they attempt to
leave the enchanted tower of girlhood and enter the world of relationship without an initiator.[47]

We must ever remember that the stories that we spin speak
about *ourselves* as well as the daimon, that it is only by looking
into the soul-mirror of the imagination that we find ourselves
reflected. The retirement into a space of solitude or loneliness
often brings out extraordinary heroism and self-discovery, as Pru
Sarn, the hare-lipped heroine of Mary Webb's *Precious Bane*,[75]
discovers. Pru has resigned herself to a loveless existence because
of her deformed lip and retires to her attic as a place of restoration and spiritual companionship, vowing that 'Because I had no
lover, I would lief have been the world's lover – such world, that
is, as I could reach'.[75] But Pru Sarn's heart is captivated by the
strong and gentle weaver, Kester Woodseaves, just as his heart is
attracted to her kind and protective love. Pru speculates, 'Did my
soul, that was twin to his, draw him and wile him, succour his
heart and summon his love?'

In *Precious Bane*, Pru and Kester fortuitously rescue each other
when each is at the edge of need. Their twin acts of heroism
transcend the boundaries which separate them. Pru's vow of
resignation, her emotional retirement into her attic, is plumbed by
Kester's voice.

> The sound of [his] speaking made the world new for itself, not caring about the old world. It was like a wide, blossomy thorn-tree on a sweltering day in early June. You could sit down under it and rest you. And it was like the still hearth-fire on a winter's night...

Here Pru describes her beloved's voice as the very environment of her comfort.

When we identify the country of the daimon with this exactitude, we simultaneously define the country of our own soul. And it is for this reason that the evolving story within us must be tracked with loving tenderness and urgent exploration. It is significant that many respondents have listed as daimonic-doubles actors and singers with deep or resonant voices. Such men are often not conventionally handsome but their voices are attuned to the country of the soul.

How do we find our way into that unknown country? There are many warnings about going away with strangers into unknown lands, like this traditional skipping rhyme of girls in Britain.

> My mother said I never should
> Play with the gypsies in the wood.
>   If I did, she would say,
> 'Naughty little girl to disobey'.

This tells us that the wood is a wild place inhabited by the wanderer who is unpredictable in civilized terms. The time has come to dare the unknown country and see who lives there.

BEAUTY AND THE BEAST

Women complain that the 'new man' is tame and unexciting; the daimon may be cultured or debonair, but like C S Lewis's leonine Lord of Narnia, Aslan, he is never tame! Wildness is a necessary source of power for women, attractive to the female nomadic nature that treks from worlds of flesh to realms of spirit in order to satisfy the wanderlust of the passionate soul. Many have defined this female nomadism as merely a sexual impulse, but it far more subtle than that.

This is how Meg describes her daimon.

He is the Outsider, the solitary, the silent. He is a crow, a Raggle-taggle gypsy, a Crazy Man Michael like the man in the Irish film *The Outcasts*, who roams the hills and steals away a young girl from the village. He's a spirit that no one can see but me, or understand like me, just as no one understands me like him. He sees right inside my soul, my life-force. This song was written when I was 14. It was written very much from inside; it's the only song I've ever completed:

> Each day I wonder, I wonder about you.
> What are you thinking of, what do you do?
> I sit here and dream that you're dreaming of me,
> That we could be together, alone, wild and free.
>
> Alone with you is where I want to be,
> High on a hill top, and by the grey sea.
> We'd sit there and you would be smiling at me,
> Together in silence, alone, wild and free.
>
> Wild are our hearts in the weather so strong,
> Our hair is so tattered in the wind blowing long,
> We'd run through the sun and rain, laughing with glee:
> We'd be like two runaways, alone, wild and free.
>
> Freedom we have like two birds on the wing,
> To fly where we want to, to laugh and to sing.
> The world belongs to us, it's there for you and me.
> Please dream my dream that we're alone, wild and free.

The call of the wild also draws Susanna who writes that, though she likes the story of *Little Red Riding Hood*, she prefers the ending of *Beauty and the Beast*.

> I do not want to go off with the woodcutter; I'd prefer to tame the wolf ... the allure of the wilderness and of the sweet-talking wolf are much more exciting than the prospect of going to Granny's with the cookies.

She is also intrigued with the notion of a woman falling for someone *below* her station:

> I liked Bob Dylan's song 'Lay, Lady, Lay', with its image of the lover humbly begging the aloof woman to condescend to honour him with her body. I like the English folk ballads 'Gypsy Davey' and 'The House Carpenter', and am very attracted to the concept

of the lover as the outsider. My romantic images run to outlaws, highwaymen, bikers, criminals and marginal people.

It might be thought that women's hankering for the wild is a perverse compensation for the repression of female lives, but it represents something much deeper than that. In the stories of the wild and the encounter with the Beast, we see an important exploration of the daimon and of women's quest for the masculine.

Hazel Woodus, the heroine of *Gone to Earth* by Mary Webb,[74] is a child of nature, unawakened to sexuality. With her companion fox, she roams untamed through the Shropshire countryside. Her desire is kinship with nature, not sex. Her wildness and naive beauty are pursued by Squire Jack Reddin, a demonic rake whom Hazel associates with the mythic phenomenon of the Death Hound pack, a spectral hunt which pursues those who befoul the wild. However, by innocently following the divinatory signs inherited from her gypsy mother, she chooses to wed the local preacher, Edward Marston, a man of some education and cultivated restraint. But Hazel's unawakened nature brings her to grief, for Edward, in a gentlemanly attempt to preserve her innocence, does not sleep with his bride. Hazel's unassuaged sexual longing, which she senses but cannot understand, causes her to be lured away by Reddin, who rapes her. Reddin does double violence: as well as harming Hazel, he hunts down her pet fox with his pack.

Hazel's wild, country nature is actually more in tune with Reddin than with the cultivated Edward. She stands between the forces of the wild and the civilized, rooted in the first, but ever longing for the order and understanding of the second. Like many of Mary Webb's heroines, Hazel's chief passion is nature. She inherits the predisposition of her mother who has warned her that marrying would

> be the end of going in the woods and all my gamesome days ...
> Instead of the mysterious, transcendent illumination that passion
> brings to a woman, she had only confusion, darkness, and a sense
> of something dragging at the roots of her being in the darkness.

This experience of entering into darkness and loss of female integrity is common to those women who enter relationships without due consideration or without full knowledge of what sexual relations entail. Hazel, like many a woman before her, accepts the first man to ask for her in marriage.

Women's awakening sexuality frequently crashes across barriers of expectation. When Angela Carter's heroine Melanie encounters the first man to regard her sexually she is aware of him putting

> on the quality of maleness like a flamboyant cloak. He was a tawny lion poised for the kill – and was she the prey? She remembered the lover made up out of books and poems she had dreamed of all summer; he crumpled like the paper he was made of before this insolent, off-hand, terrifying maleness, filling the room with its reek. She hated it. But she could not take her eyes off him.[8]

Step gently! We are approaching the lair of the Beast. *Beauty and the Beast* is a story of how women recognize their daimon and how they patiently seek to remove the masks which obscure him. The stories of *Beauty and the Beast* and *Sir Gawain and Dame Ragnell*, which we shall explore in Chapter 8, form a duo of delivering myths which are critical to the disenchanting of the contra-sexual figure.

Beauty and the Beast tells how Beauty's merchant father has three daughters. The two eldest daughters live well but submit Beauty to household chores. One day the father goes to welcome back his fleet of merchant ships, promising to bring presents back for the daughters who ask for costly trinkets; only Beauty asks for a single rose. On arrival at the port, the merchant learns that his ships are all lost and that he is ruined. On his way homewards, he is benighted at a mysterious mansion where he seeks shelter. Mindful of Beauty, he plucks a rose from the garden but he is confronted by the Beast who threatens to kill him unless he sends one of his daughters to the Beast in his place. The eldest daughters consider it just that Beauty should go, since it was her gift of the rose that caused this turn of events.

Beauty goes alone to the Beast's house, where she finds herself alone until dinner time. The Beast appears and asks her if she will marry him; she refuses. Over the course of time, Beauty grows accustomed to his appearance and even fond of him, but she pines for her father and still will not assent to marry the Beast. She begs the Beast to allow her to visit her father for a short while. He allows her to go, with the proviso that she shall return promptly. Overjoyed to see her, Beauty's father is restored to health and she is prevailed upon to stay longer, past the fixed term of her visit. Then one night she dreams that the Beast is ill and rushes to his side. She finds him dying and, overcome with grief at the thought of losing him, begs him live and be her husband. At her words, he transforms into human shape and the enchantment upon him is over.

Jean Cocteau's 1946 film *La Belle et La Bête* reveals illuminating features in this story. Belle (Beauty) is courted by a young wastrel called Avenant before the family fortunes change. When she first comes to the Beast's house, she finds a mirror in her room which says to her, 'I am your mirror. Reflect on me and I shall reflect for you.' As she gazes into it, she sees her ailing father. Later, at her father's house, the mirror reflects the ailing Beast. Throughout the film Cocteau stresses this theme of 'seeing'. When the Beast enters Belle's bedroom to gaze upon her sleeping form (plate illustration 5), she awakes and shrieks with horror. The Beast retreats with, 'You must not look me in the eyes!' Later on, when he comes to her chamber literally smoking with blood, her horror becomes disgust, and it is he who cannot bear to look her in the eyes. As the Beast lies dying, Belle's erstwhile suitor comes to pillage the Pavilion of Diana, the Beast's treasury. But the pavilion is guarded by the goddess Diana. As she shoots Avenant, he and the Beast change forms, and Belle finds herself holding a man in the Beast's clothing who looks exactly like Avenant. He tells her, 'Only when looked on with love would I be free again.'

The correspondences between Cocteau's film and the daimonic experience are revealed here. The mirror in which Belle sees her father is her soul-mirror, which reflects for her the only image of the masculine that has importance for her. She continually reiterates her inability to leave her father. We may say that the daimon has on the patriarchal mask at this point. Later, when the mirror shows the Beast, Belle's soul-image has changed. Her fondness and pity have grown into something greater. When she finally holds the dying Beast in her arms, he is transformed into the image of her suitor Avenant, but within he still has the 'good heart' of the Beast. The monstrous mask falls from the daimon at the same point that Belle turns to save him from death, through her pure love. As the disenchanted Beast prepares to waft her through the air to his castle, he asks her if she is frightened. 'I like being frightened with you,' she smiles.

Belle's attentions to the Beast cause him to grow softer and gentler as time goes on, although she holds back from any recognition of him as human. 'You stroke me like a animal,' he says. 'But you *are* an animal!' she responds. He admits to her, 'My heart is good, but I am a monster.' 'Many men are more monstrous but they hide it,' Belle replies. Do women crave the Beast because it is 'safer', a more symbiotic and helpful figure than the average man? The humanizing of the Beast must be seen in the broader context of women's daimonic encounters and our quest for the meaning of the masculine.

In Ron Koslow's television series, *Beauty and the Beast*, we see a fresh working-out of the traditional story in a contemporary context. The story revolves about the friendship of a New York public defence official, Katherine Chandler, and Vincent, part-man, part-lion, who lives with a community of outcast and forgotten people under the streets of the city (plate illustration 6). This otherworldly place has great beauty and courtesy, in stark contrast to the violence of the streets above. Vincent only reveals his savage nature when Katherine or other innocents are threatened. Otherwise, he is a gentle, cultured being, with long mane and cat-like features, but a man's body.

Vincent's daimonic nature is clearly signalled by his inaccessibility: because of his bestial nature, he and Katherine cannot have a physical relationship. He remains her friend and protector, often coming to her aid when she is in danger. The link between them is a psychic one, like that of close lovers or twin souls, though we recognize Vincent's archetype as directly derived from the daimon. The introductory credits to the programme are narrated by Katherine in a mantra-like way:

> He comes from a secret place, far below the city streets, hiding his face from strangers, safe from hate and harm. He brought me here to save my life and now, wherever I go, he is with me in spirit. For we have a bond stronger than friendship or love, and, although we cannot be together, we will never ever be apart.

The popularity of this series was so great that a spontaneous network of women, calling themselves 'the Helpers', was set up to enable others to obtain information about the series and its actors, as well as to organize events where the daimonic romance could flourish in full costume. This phenomenon reveals both the universal appeal of this story and the strength of the daimonic scenario in women, which has a symbiotic intensity within these stories of the Beast.

What underlies these stories about disenchanting the Beast? At some level we want to be, in the words of Meg's song, 'alone, wild and free'. But though the likes of Catherine Earnshaw in *Wuthering Heights* might seriously contemplate the prospect that 'the world could change to a mighty stranger' before she abandoned her Heathcliff, it is the nature of most women to seek a settled life, not a wild one. And even Catherine goes back on her word and substitutes the tame domesticity provided by her rich husband, Edgar Linton, for a wild and free existence out on the moors.

The tension of the polarity between Beauty and the Beast is between tame and wild, human and animal, the integration by feminine of the masculine. We can see this depicted upon the Waite/Coleman/Smith tarot card of Strength (plate illustration 7), where a calm young woman lays her hands upon the jaws of a lion. On one level, the disenchantment of the Beast stories symbolizes the hard struggle of women to understand the masculine and to integrate its seemingly wild powers within the feminine soul. The initial encounter with the Beast is exciting and terrifying all at once, like our first sexual encounter with men. The multiform nature of the Beast, part-human, part-animal, is likewise a primary means of perceiving the daimon when it first arises in our soul, for the daimon is both man and something other that we cannot yet define.

This task of disenchanting the Beast is not a short one. In the Scottish story *The Black Bull of Norroway*, the young heroine's mother seeks husbands for her daughters. The two eldest girls are picked up by landed men, but when the youngest's turn comes, she is rapt away by a bull. He cherishes her on their long journey and gives her three jewels. At the critical time of his disenchantment, she is bidden not to move until the air changes colour and he comes to her. But she accidentally moves her foot and consequently loses him. In order to enter into the country where he has gone, she has to climb a glassy hill; the making of iron-spiked shoes to climb it takes seven years. When she eventually succeeds, she finds him wounded and under the enchantment of sleep. He can only be disenchanted if she gives her three jewels to the sorceress who is binding him, and then she must sing him awake:

> Seven long years I served for thee,
> the glassy hill I climbed for thee

> the bloody shirt I wrang for thee,
> will you not answer and turn to me?

He wakens and they are married; the enchantment is overturned by her long labour.

The conditions for disenchanting the Beast must be perfectly fulfilled, although they often seem arbitrary factors to us when we read the story. These conditions represent the innate obedience to our appointed task when we are dealing with the daimon; these taboos, conditions and agreements are actually an important part of our contract with the daimon and it is of great importance for us to seek these out and observe them. These conditions not only disenchant the fearful or obscured aspects of the daimon, but they simultaneously protect us, as proper boundaries to our behaviour, and reveal the path of our soul's vocation.

If we misunderstand our contract with the daimon as a series of arbitrarily imposed burdens upon us then we are purposely ignoring paths to freedom. If we attempt to deal with our contract in grudging or petulant ways, trying to fulfil the conditions with impatient haste, we prolong our fear of the bestial masculine and delay the disenchanting of the Beast.

Lairdearg speaks of the inspiration she derives from the story of Falada, from Grimm's *The Goose Girl* and from:

> all folk tales where the animal/otherworld helper asks the hero to kill it, thus effecting transformation. These all mirror my experiences with the daimon and have helped me to see that he is a natural part of me and a powerful ally.

This is the most extreme of the conditions we will meet in our daimonic encounters and the most singly challenging but, as we will see in Chapter 8, it is the one we may be finally confronted with – the death and transformation of the daimon.

Fiona has struggled with a number of obstructively difficult daimonic images throughout her life. This dream reveals how well she has coped and shows us a glimpse of the transformation process:

> Although the Old Man is as scary as the animus gets for me, I did meet a scary aspect last autumn. He came as a black-cloaked figure who swirled his cloak to fill my vision. I said pompously, 'I prefer to believe that love conquers all', which was effective because he changed into a clown. The Clown looked all right but

felt all wrong, so I repeated, 'I prefer to believe that love conquers all', and he changed into a Man of the Forest, crowned with antlers and with beautiful tender brown eyes.

The symbolism of this transformation of Magician and Clown into the Antlered God comes from universal mythic depths. The power of a virgin is symbolically acknowledged in the medieval unicorn hunt: no horses, hounds or weapons will aid in this hunt, only when the unicorn sees a maiden sitting alone will he come to lower his horn into her lap. This wonderful image was even used as a metaphor in mystical Christian lore where the Virgin Mary was able to lure Jesus from heaven into the lap of her womb, domesticating his godhead by her pure humanity.

The myths of the Beast and of the wild are often taken to allude to whatever is bestial in man, or as symbolic to women of the alien masculine which roams about looking for prey. But the wild is not always symbolic of the bestial, it is also indicative of the otherworldly of the suprahuman: a theme we shall explore further in Chapter 6.

Moments of vulnerability sometimes bring the necessary receptivity for the transformation of difficult factors in our daimonic relationships. These may happen consciously or work up more subtly from the layers of creation or dream. In 1990 when I was exploring my own daimonic themes I had a dream in which I received 'the initiation of Beauty and the Beast'.

> The Beast gives me a drink and leads me to a house. I am very slightly drunk. He leads me upstairs along a long room full of toys – the room is like an Elizabethan long gallery. In this rich place I abandon myself like a cat. Here are my ardent memories and feelings. Without touching me, the Beast arouses me and I follow him fearlessly. The room is long and wide, with windows on either side, red curtains flapping in the breeze. There are books and toys; the room is carpeted and furnished like a fairy-tale. The Beast himself gives off an indefinable attraction to me. The longings aroused in this place communicate themselves to my body, so that it opens in readiness to receive the Beast.

On wakening, I wrote this sonnet:

> I am tender with the telling of the dark.
> Within my heart his voice awakes a cry
> Of freedom in the house of childhood's spark,
> The place where once we played unstained by sin.
> He stood so close, I heard his deep heart's sigh

> Of longing – that I haunt the wild with him.
> The room stood ready, curtained and enclosed,
> Outside, my freight of guilt was soon disposed.
> Wonder wakened as he walked my heart,
> I knew not if the sky was bright or dark.
> His gentle arms enfolded me in peace.
> He stayed my flight and made my panic cease.
> To him I come when all my thoughts are wild,
> His welcome is my ground, my heart his child.[35]

Here the Beast shared the characteristics of a man and an animal. Access to the wildness of my dream was not associated with any anarchic lack of control, but rather through centring within my deep self and its inner resources. For me, to haunt the wild with the Beast is to enter into a wider space wherein my heart is free and untrammelled, where it can express true passion.

The man-animal nature of the Beast reveals strong daimonic clues. The universal response of children to animals is normally one of undiluted delight: they share something profound with each other. Animals are trustworthy and true in folk story; they invariably act as messengers, bridges and helpers in daimonic ways. This sense of alliance is what guides us when we deal with daimon: we may not understand his form or appearances in our life, but we know him for a friend. It is significant that many respondents wrote of their devotion to the Green, Horned, Antlered or Wild Man, and connect him or a beast-like figure with their childhood. This is a figure that ranges from childhood companion to Dionysian initiator in scope, and we shall explore him further in Chapter 6.

In *The Inner Lover*,[25] Valerie Harms relates how she dialogued with her daimon, who revealed himself to her as a wild white horse with whom she had congress in her fantasies:

> 'Talk to me. Spend time with me so we get to know each other. Keep your longings with me. Let the other people go free. Take them as they come. Express your desires freely. But come to me when your heart hurts.'
> 'Am I going to get pregnant with this fucking?'
> 'You are already pregnant with desires and inklings, like little green shoots.'
> 'You mean my desires are not the source of all misery as the Buddhists say?'
> 'No, they are the flowers that lead you on. Pluck them and make bouquets.'

This last answer is very interesting since it is by following the flowers that Persephone is led to Hades or Pluto, Lord of the Underworld, and so comes into the realm of her soul's treasury. Beasts do not offer wild or orgiastic suggestions of their nature but, as above, offer practical solutions to current problems of understanding.

Gwen's daimon has appeared continuously as a mythical beast.

> The monstrous form is the true form, but he usually appears to me in a more acceptable and very beautiful animal form. Actually I'm so used to the monstrous form that it does not bother me at all because I know who he is, but other people would be really shocked and frightened. But I never thought he was a demon or anything. There are legends about his kind that would lead most people to avoid him because he is potentially very dangerous, but the circumstances of our meeting were such that we owe each other our lives.

Myths and folk-stories about the Beast, especially in their original, not re-told, state are often helpful for identifying issues and conditions which affect our daimonic understanding. They offer ways of comprehending our own contract with the daimon, which unfolds through the evolving story-line which our lives, dreams and reveries are telling us. We shall seek out the terms of that contract now, as we explore the faceless one whom most of us know only as the erotic initiator.

THE EROTIC INITIATOR

As women, when we are young, we experience our first power. When we cease to be girls and lie on our hot beds longing for the quenching of desire, it is then that we first know the daimon. He comes at twilight and we image him in the shape of the man we like best and want most. He comes in many guises, though his nature seldom changes – as sheeted flame, as sucking undertow, as winged archangel as well as cheating rogue. We cannot deny him, for he has our hearts and desires entwined in his long hair and swathed about his beauteous breast.

Such metaphors of sexual encounter arise spontaneously – we do not need to make them up. This early sense of female power and polarized daimonic potency is typified in this poem, 'Goddess of the Grove'. In folk-story idiom, it portrays a girl who becomes a woman in a timeless, seasonal rite, elected to meet with the unknown initiator of the grove:

> When I was goddess of the grove,
> I was not old,
> I was not young.
> For me my life had just begun,
> When I was goddess of the grove.
>
> Of all my sisters in the wood:
> The lot was cast –
> On me did fall,
> When I sat with them in the hall –
> Of all my sisters in the wood.
>
> And to the grove I came alone,
> To sit and spin,
> To sit and wait
> When it was early, when it was late.
> And to the grove I came alone.
>
> When all the trees with fire were flamed,
> Desire of the
> Woodman wild
> Found me a virgin quick with child,
> When all the trees with fire were flamed.
>
> Then was I goddess of the grove;
> Under the moon,
> Under the sun,
> The chant of making was my song,
> When I was goddess of the grove.[38]

We each become a 'goddess of the grove' at adolescence. That ritual stage or scene is set and we enter it unbidden. The daimon is our 'inner beloved', the perfect and ideal partner of our dreams, the one with whom we wish to melt and meld and be in total union.

There is something within us that wishes to enter that sacred grove and become a fiery virgin, filled with desire. This is the desire to be ravished which most women experience in sexual fantasy. It does not mean that we want to be raped in actuality. It means that we seek the anonymous and sacred deflowering which puts us in touch with the reality of our desires. The faceless abductor and ravisher is really the daimon who inspires with desire.

The daimon, then, is an initiator into sexual desire, one who visits women as soon as their bodies prepare for adult sexuality. He is the awakener into light, the one who unbolts the doors of ecstasy and eros.

Novelist, Angela Carter (1940–92), was foremost among modern female writers for her exploration of the emergent daimon and her re-evaluation of female erotic power. *The Bloody Chamber*[7] explores the daimon both as sexual awakener and beast. Carter pulls no punches about the destructiveness that can arise if the daimon goes unacknowledged: she knows that the bold and uncaring sexuality of the young woman can wreak havoc. In Neil Jordan's film of her story, *The Company of Wolves*, the grandmother of the Little Red Riding Hood story teaches the young heroine how to temper the advances of the wolf in man's shape.

Many traditional societies have rites of passage which isolate pubescent girls from their tribe: in that isolation, more experienced women come to teach the girls about womanhood, but their chief initiator lies within each of them – the daimon now awakening and fanning the flame of sexual desire into full scorch.

In our own society, we have no such rites of passage, no sequestered and protected seclusion from the world in which to realize and learn these essential female teachings. The daimon advances unheralded, as out of control as a forest fire unless he is recognized for what he is. A more mature woman will know how to handle him, but a young woman doesn't even care. She stands on the brink of life, tanked up with highly-flammable desire.

It is here that young women can become slaves of their sexuality, if they are unfortunate. For if the inner beloved should become associated with some physical man who is an unworthy vehicle of the archetype, then she is done for: he will always hold the strings of her heart, whatever obscene violence he does to her, and the girl-become-woman will always submit to the image of her daimon, who will become demon in truth.

Stories of interspecies mating between mortal and otherworldly partners result in a child of heroic stature. The relationship between a woman and her daimon is of like nature. It may not produce a physical child, but rather a mixing and meeting of mortal and immortal kinds which can produce the heroic and creative 'children' of the imagination. It was only in medieval times that the daimon was seen as incubus, the father of demonic abominations.

Many myths and sacred stories provide templates for understanding the daimon, but the one which gives us the clearest picture of the relationship also gives us the terms of the contract by which the masked or obscured daimon can be disenchanted. It is in the myth of *Cupid and Psyche*[34] that we will recognize the themes of the Beast and the Faceless Initiator.

Psyche's story begins with her extraordinary, head-turning beauty which causes her to be offered the divine honours that should be due to Venus alone. This angers Venus, who calls upon her son Cupid to use his arrows of love to ill-effect, directing him to make Psyche fall in love with some foul outcast of no rank or wealth.

When Psyche begins to be miserable at remaining single, her father consults the oracle of Apollo at Miletus to ask where he can find a husband for her. The oracle demands her marriage in a lonely mountain place to a man not of mortal birth, but one full of 'dire mischief', a power who is feared alike by both the Olympian gods and the shades of the Underworld, and who uses the element of ether as his vehicle. As demanded by the oracle, Psyche's wedding procession proceeds – more along the lines of a funeral than a wedding – she is left on a rock to await her husband. She is lifted by the wind down a lovely valley where she finds a great palace where invisible maids bid her welcome. At midnight, her husband enters her bed and lies with her in the dark. After a few nights he warns that her sisters are coming to visit her and that she should ignore them. But Psyche is starved of human companionship and desires her husband to command the Western Wind to waft them safely down to her valley.

Envious of Psyche's way of life, the sisters begin to pry into her husband's background and appearance. Psyche tells them he is a young man with a beard who hunts frequently in the surrounding countryside. The sisters are stricken with jealousy and decide to humble Psyche. Again her husband warns that her sisters will come to persuade her to sneak a look at his face, but that she will lose him forever if she does so. He is especially adamant since Psyche is expecting a child, which will be divine if she keeps his secret but mortal if she divulges it. Psyche woos him into allowing her sisters down again and promises that she will keep her curiosity in check until her child is born and will study its face to find out what her husband is really like.

As she entertains her sisters, Psyche prattles on and describes her husband as a middle-aged merchant away on business. The sisters pretend they support her best interests but begin to lay suspicions about the bestial nature of her husband, suggesting he is a snake that is partial to pregnant women. Horrified at the notion, Psyche admits that she's never seen his face and asks for their advice. They bid her take a sharp knife and hide a lighted lamp behind the bedroom tapestry, and to wait until her husband is asleep; then she must take the lamp up and behead the monster quickly, after which her sisters will help her find a decent human husband.

Psyche does as her sisters suggest, but as she raises the lamp over the darkness of the bed where her sleeping husband lies, she sees the most beautiful man, Cupid, the God of Love himself, complete with soft white wings. She examines his love-arrows and accidentally pierces her own finger: an act that causes her to fall totally in love with Love himself. Overwhelmed, she spills lamp oil upon Cupid's chest, causing him to awaken. He rebukes her folly and admits that he has deceived his mother by substituting himself for the vile lover she had desired for Psyche. His punishment will be to leave her.

In despair, Psyche attempts to drown herself, but the river waters wash her ashore where Pan sits. He comforts her and turns her thoughts from suicide by suggesting that she open her heart to Cupid by praying to him in the gentlest way. Psyche travels on and arrives at the palace of her elder sister and relates her story. The elder sister immediately rushes off to claim Cupid for herself and casts herself upon the mercy of the Western Wind which, without the intervention of Cupid, fails to support her and she crashes to her death. The same fate befalls the other sister.

While Psyche searches for Cupid, he is confined to bed in his mother's house, in extreme pain. Venus, who doesn't know what has happened, discovers Psyche's part in the tangle and grows even more furious and, in order to clip Cupid's wings, she seeks help from Juno and Ceres. They make light of Cupid's behaviour, stressing to Venus his tender age and the male tendency to sexual adventure, mostly because they too fear Cupid's arrows.

In her search for Cupid, Psyche wanders into a temple wherein the votive gifts upon the altar are scattered about: she tidies the altar and Ceres, who sees how her temple is being honoured, calls out a warning to Psyche that Venus is bent on vengeance. Psyche flees and finds a second temple and prays to Juno for assistance, like any other pregnant woman. Again Juno is sympathetic but cannot help her as Venus is married to her son, Vulcan. Psyche concludes that she must 'borrow a little male courage' and submit to Venus, since her house is where she will likely find Cupid.

Venus meanwhile has suborned Mercury to search for Psyche, making out that she is a run-away slave and promising to issue a reward of seven kisses from her own mouth for Psyche's return. When Psyche arrives at Venus's house she is met by Old Habit, who drags her into Venus's presence. Venus gives Psyche into the hands of her servants, Anxiety and Grief, to abuse as they will. Disgusted at the idea of becoming a grandmother, Venus prepares some impossible tasks for Psyche.

First of all Psyche is set the task of sorting into separate piles a heap of mixed grains. A passing ant who sees her predicament, encourages other ants to help Love's wife complete the task. Venus returns and sets another task: Psyche is to fetch a hank of wool from the sacred herd of golden sheep whose bite is poisonous. Despairing, Psyche is about to cast herself into the stream when one of the reeds, such as are used in pan-pipes, advises her that if she waits until the afternoon when the sheep are asleep, she can gather their wool from the trees of the grove.

Venus sets her a third task: to gather a jar of water from the river Styx which plunges down a steep abyss. As Psyche hovers on the verge of the river, where she is challenged by the guardian dragons, Jupiter sends his eagle down, remembering the good services of Cupid in obtaining his companion, Ganymede. The eagle takes her jar and fills it with water.

Still unconvinced, Venus sets her last, most dreadful task: Psyche is to descend to the underworld and fetch a day's worth of the beauty of Proserpine. As Psyche determines to end her life by hurling herself from a high tower, the tower itself advises her to go to the underworld via one of its ventilation holes, and to take two pieces of barley bread soaked in honey water and two coins in her mouth. He tells her to ignore a lame ass-driver and to give one of her coins to Charon in return for being ferried over. He tells her to avoid the Fates and the dog Cerberus by throwing it one of the sops of bread, in order to gain Proserpine's presence. She is to keep the remaining sop and coin for getting out of the underworld. The tower insists that she must not, under any circumstances, look within the box that Proserpine will give her.

All things transpire as the tower suggests. Proserpine invites Psyche to sit in a comfortable chair and eat a lovely meal, but Psyche humbly sits on the floor and takes only a crust of bread. As she hurries away with the box Prosperine gives her, curiosity strikes her – as well as the thought that perhaps she can beautify herself further for her husband. But out of the box comes only a deep sleep which overwhelms Psyche.

Cupid, now recovered from his wound and anxious to find Psyche, finds where she is lying, shuts the box, brushes off the sleep, pricks her with a harmless arrow to awaken her, and bids her complete her task. Cupid himself flies onwards to seek Jupiter's intervention for Psyche. Jupiter summons a council of all the gods and cleverly plays for their sympathy by stressing how troublesome Cupid's arrows have been for them all and how his young and passionate nature can be contained by binding him in marriage. Jupiter consoles Venus by promising that Cupid and Psyche will become social equals; he calls Psyche to drink of a cup of nectar which renders her immortal, saying: 'Cupid will never more fly away from your arms, but must remain your lawful husband for ever.'

The gods themselves serve at the wedding breakfast and, in due time, Psyche gives birth to a daughter, called Pleasure.[34]

This rich story relates Psyche's quest for her daimon lover, Cupid, whose Greek name, Eros, is the word we still give to erotic love. When we realize that Psyche's own name means 'soul', we know how important this story is for our own progress. This story presents us with the map of our own daimonic journey.

When a girl becomes a woman, with a woman's beauty, her soul is contracted to an invisible lover who visits her in hours of darkness. Her female peers, who are jealous of her happiness, suggest that the invisibility of the lover may hide a variety of monstrous or demonic shapes. Listening only to their urgings, rather than her own personal experience, the young woman prepares to unmask her invisible lover, against his advice. His promise is that their child will be immortal. The invisible lover turns out to be Love himself, who leaves her when she seeks to make him manifest.

The bond between the Soul and Love remains, but access is denied. In despair and abandonment, the young woman seeks to kill herself but she is advised that she should sustain contact with Love by praying to him and winning him back. The Soul sojourns in the temples of nature and women and asks for help to be reconnected with Love. She finally faces the exclusivity, anger and jealousy of Love's mother and hears the accustomed voice of Old Habit, which repeats accepted gossip about women in general and about her in particular.

The Soul is set impossible tasks – to distinguish and differentiate one thing from another, to collect experience in dangerous places, to face fear, and to be obedient to her authentic self in the depths of despair. The Soul is aided by Love to accomplish her tasks and they are united in immortal union.

This template provides clues for our own quest as well as throwing light upon the kinds of allies who will enable us along the way. We notice that the four symbolic helpers of Psyche correlate to certain gods in this story: the Ant to Pan, the Reed to Ceres, the Eagle to Juno/Jupiter, the Tower to Proserpine.

- *Pan*, protector of flocks and master of animals, provides the voice of earthy, common sense. The Ant is his creature, helping Psyche discriminate and sort out experiences one from the other. The realm of nature itself comes to her aid.
- *Ceres*, matron of seasonal life and mistress of grains and of agriculture, provides the voice of motherly warning and enables Psyche to bring order to muddle. The Reed is Ceres' plan, helping Psyche to explore areas of vulnerability and revelation in the safety of sleep. The realm of dreams itself comes to her aid.
- *Juno*, matron of women's cycles and Queen of Heaven, with her husband Jupiter, King of the Gods, provides the voice of insight and encouragement in the face of fear. Jupiter's Eagle comes to help Psyche face the fear of oblivion. The realm of heaven itself comes to her aid.
- *Proserpine*, matron of transformation, Queen of the Underworld, provides the voice of women's authentic experience. The Tower is her symbol, bidding Psyche to bring forth the beauty that is hidden within by being obedient to her own authentic self. The realm of the underworld itself comes to her aid.

We note that, between them, these gods encompass the upper world, the lower world and the middle world of Psyche's universe. In whatsoever region of our sacred symbolic landscape we stray on our daimonic quest, we will never be uncompanioned. Let us look now at the challengers who stand in our way.

- *Venus* is Psyche's projected counterpart, the empty shell of what a woman really is. Psyche redeems that false image of womanhood with the help of her daimon, overcoming phoney expectations, and entrenched truisms about women and their behaviour by, first of all, being true to her soul and, secondly, by pursuing her daimon and refusing to be put off by false images of him. The impossible tasks set by Venus are actually empowering ways of transformation. They can be followed only by those who are able to work from their authentic self, rather than from the encrusted projections that women have accepted.
- *Psyche's sisters* are all those who lay down theories and rules of living which they have no intention of fulfilling themselves: they are the people who live vicariously through our actions, who have unacknowledged dependences upon us, who see our decisive motivation as endangering their status quo. These sisters are also the women who project scenarios of bestiality upon men: 'All men are brutes, dear; it's in their nature, they can't help it!' If we heed these challengers and begin to believe them, we risk losing our soul's illumination.
- *Venus's housekeeper, Old Habit*, is a cruel gossip, without finesse or sensitivity. If we are stupid enough to reveal our pregnant condition – our creative quest into the treasury of the deep self – to the wrong kind of people, they will mock and abuse our most prized discoveries. We need to avoid such people, as well as to banish Old Habit from our hearts, where she may berate and belittle us. Her gossips, Anxiety and Grief, are merely Job's comforters, and we may be sure that they will increase their abuse if we give them house-room.

This story not only tells us about the allies and challengers we may meet upon our quest, but also gives us clear guidelines on how to seek the daimon. It illustrates that we need to:

- distinguish between projections and the real thing
- collect experience from our dreams, reflections, meditations
- understand that life and power are to be found where there is most fear

- remain true to the authentic self and respect the reality of the symbolic sacred landscape which our own evolving story reveals
- actively seek contact with the daimon by asking him to show himself
- maintain connection with the daimon, even when he is not visible, by vigilant and faithful care
- carefully weigh up 'what people say' about the daimon, unless it is personally of use to us; ignore malicious, soul-spoiling gossip and conversations about the daimon with those who have no respect for our soul-space

We shall explore the practicalities of these guidelines in Chapter 5.

Inevitably, if we follow the thread of our story, and remain true to our contract, we will all come to the palace of Love. It is essential that all the stories we use in our daimonic exploration, whether they be folk-stories, myths, novels or romances, are ones which nurture our self-esteem and with which we can readily identify, regardless of political correctness.

Many feminist readings of myths and stories frequently dislodge their innate wisdom, calling into question the masculine authorship and expectations, reviling the myth by dragging it out of its contemporary context into literal modern readings. Seek out the earliest source of the story that attracts you and read it for yourself before you turn to such summary rewriting. This is not to say that the *personal rescripting* of myths and stories cannot be helpful, only that we must always be wary of the interference and manipulation of Psyche's sisters, of listening to what others say before we have checked in with our authentic self. Honour the stories which assist you, whatever critics say! Above all, trust the hand-holds which delineate the way within your *own* evolving story, for these are the most powerful and useful on the road to understanding the daimon.

Stories can only be written or told when we have begun the labours of Psyche. In order to gather our own information, let us now take the paths of blood and dream in search of the wisdom which is already within our bodies and within our most cherished dreams and meditations.

Questions

1 Which myths, books, films or other stories exemplify your

experience of the daimon? What help or insight have you derived from these?

2 With which heroines do you strongly identify? What qualities do they exemplify? Which qualities do they lack or seek to find within the story? Are these qualities or their lack paralleled in your own life?

Actions

Speak to your daimon. Ask him to show himself to you in ways you can appreciate. Ask him what conditions surround your relationship.

Reflection

Reflect upon the story/scenario which has evolved over the years about your own daimon – the sequences and transformations as well as the constant themes.

CHAPTER 4

Paths of Blood and Dream

I lead you back to your birthright and your blessing, to your Native Country which is your womanhood and your original Virginity.

Jane Leade, *A Fountain of Gardens*

THE SECRET TIME OF JOY

The daimon arrives for most women at the menarche, when he comes down the pathway of blood. He can be a faithful lover and initiator over this time of growing, showing himself regularly in different ways throughout a woman's menstrual cycle. He acts as a reminder of the inner compass of woman's soul through dreams, sexual fantasies and waking reveries. This intriguing partnership combines the wisdom of the body with the wisdom of the soul and, regardless of whether a woman has a conscious awareness of her daimon or not, he is indelibly present in her dreams.

This extract from Moyra's menstrual journal reveals the nature and activity of the daimon in both physical and psychic terms.

He regularly turns up a day or so before menstruation like a new moon; his communication grows in strength and power through to the full moon of ovulation – in the week prior to this, I always try and cancel everything as I'm in such creative mode I'm impatient of interruption. If I'm working or teaching, everything I do is brilliant – this is no boast, just the truth. Everything I do hits the spot and has confidence and panache.

I've worked out when he comes now – usually the tense days before I come on. It's like finally meeting someone at a pre-arranged border check-point. Fretful and anxious, I feel the tension flooding out of me. We embrace and he speaks some simple words – picking up a conversation that was dropped last month as if it were only a few minutes ago.

In intense dreams I know his presence, tangible as a lover heavy upon me. Usually I menstruate early in the morning, about 3–4am, when he has been with me in dreams. The next few days, he is around me, wherever I go. I can talk to him, ask him questions, he comes and talks to me and tells me things. Around ovulation – usually the twelfth day of my cycle – he is white-hot within me and I burn off the energy through poetry. I always try and keep my ovulation time free of appointments so that I can capitalize on this access to creative energy. Then come the desert days when he is not with me – off on business somewhere, leaving me to my own devices. Then, by day 23 of my cycle, I am yearning for him and he comes across the border to start it all over again.

My dreams of him are intense and nearly always sexual in content. This one arrived in the pre-menstrual week of my cycle: I am desperate for sex but the only man nearby is gay. Reluctantly he agrees to tongue my mouth. Then I sit upon his lap and feel that he is erect, ready for love. As I open my eyes I see that his eyes have rolled up with ecstasy and that he is enjoying this as much as I am.

This dream came at ovulation: The Moroccan King Solomon has come to visit me, but I haven't changed the sheets. The King's staff see to everything, erect curtains to tent the bed while I prepare myself by painting my face green. My body is white with a deep blue tinge. I weave a veil like a chador. I am almost ready and the King is waiting when tourists come in; the staff usher them out again. Then the King comes to get me. I hope that my whiteness won't shock his blackness. He kisses me totally, making a furrow of my body. I am totally loved and appreciated.

As we see here, Moyra's daimon appears in many shapes in her dreams, even though she is intimate in waking life with one particular shape. Her cycle is about 25 days long, but she knows when she is ovulating because she practises natural birth control. Among women who use artificial or chemical birth-control methods, which often create a false 'normal cycle' and muddy the natural rhythms of the body, there is less sensitivity and understanding of the menstrual cycle. Many women are strangely ignorant of the physical aspects of menstruation and of the correlation between it and their own emotional and spiritual reactions.

A woman's menstrual cycle falls into four phases, which, like the moon's phases, averages out to a 28-day cycle, which can be variable. Women do not automatically bleed at the dark moon or ovulate at the full moon: these two cycles will most often be out of phase with each other unless the menstrual cycle is regulated by the Pill. Note here the moon phase and the days of the menstrual cycle to which it *symbolically* corresponds:

- Bleeding Phase (between days 1–7) – Waxing Moon
- Ovulation Phase (at the end of days 8–14) – Full Moon
- Post-ovulatory Phase (between days 15–21) – Waning Moon
- Premenstrual Phase (between days 22–28) – New or Dark Moon

I asked the respondents if there were particular times in their cycle when their daimon was more active. Most said that the times of strongest contact were during the premenstrual week, menstruation itself and ovulation. The sex-drive is particularly high around these times, peaking at ovulation, which is biologically the time the body is best prepared for fertilization. About half of the answers spoke in terms of menstrual cycle, while the other half, interestingly, spoke in terms of the moon's cycle. Some, like Pat, recognized both cycles. Pat relates:

> At the full moon I sense and experience him around in fantasy, dreams. He's strongest when I'm pre-ovulatory and when menstruating.

Jocelyn's experience is similar.

> When I'm premenstrual I'm more likely to dream of him, but I am more likely to feel his presence at full moon and in the middle of my cycle as energy and waking fantasy.

Ioho finds that during the waning of the moon and during the week before her period begins, her dreams are less prominent. Lairdearg speculates, 'The full moon tends to make dreams more vivid, but, oddly, I think he's more present during the dark of the moon – or maybe I'm more accessible.'

The moon is conventionally understood to be symbolically feminine in most Western cultures; however, there is an older lore which speaks of the Man in the Moon. In Germany and Scandinavia, the moon is still masculine, the sun feminine.

In many cultures, the moon-daimon is seen as the husband of all women; it is his light that causes them to conceive, not the embrace of their lovers. In Babylonian mythology, the moon god, Sinn, has two appearances or phases: one as the full moon in the upperworld, the other as the new or dark moon in the underworld.[24]

These two appearances are still apparent in the female menstrual cycle. In *Alchemy for Women*,[67] a study of dreams and the menstrual cycle, Penelope Shuttle and Peter Redgrove identify these two faces of the moon-daimon as the ovulatory animus and the menstrual animus. The ovulatory animus is analogous to the full-moon aspect of the moon-daimon, making kind, professional, heroic or standardized appearances. The menstrual animus is analogous to the underworld aspect of the moon-daimon and most often appears as a dark, strange or sinister figure. Hence 'Superman, whose shoulders are broad and whose sex is rudimentary, is a clean-cut avatar of the ovulation animus, while the Phantom of the Opera presides over the mysteries of inspiration of the menstrual period.' The authors also signpost this dual aspect of the moon-daimon in R L Stevenson's *Dr Jekyll and Mr Hyde* where the former is the benevolent ovulatory animus and the latter the malevolent menstrual animus.

Alchemy for Women is the only book to date which details the close relationship of moon-daimon and the menstrual cycle. Its poetic and dream-laden pages unfold a clearer picture of women's soul-life than many Jungian books because it draws upon the actual experience of women without overt, critical re-touching or psychological jargon. The authors acknowledge that although the sometimes challenging images of the dark menstrual animus can be fearful, he also gives 'the best rewards'. The bright ovulatory animus may need more careful handling: his man-about-town appearance may lead us to collude with opinions and projections which are not our own.

In traditional societies there are many taboos and exclusions relating to blood, and especially to menstruating women. Blood is universally understood to be powerful, and the fear of power manifesting in a woman's body is immense. But the seclusion of the menstruating woman may truly originate in her sovereign need to be alone and without responsibility at this time, rather than because she is seen as a focus of chaotic or dangerous energy which may pollute the tribe. Certainly in most societies which practise such seclusion today, women regard this time apart as theirs by right, when they cannot be called upon to contribute to domestic life, a time for reflection and self-tuning.

This secret time of joy is a true sabbath, a period of heart's rest, a time when women withdraw from their human partners and seek the love of their moon-daimon. Even when we must be about daily work, we may wear the sacred red in our clothes which marks us as women apart. In the privacy of the sacred enclosure where bleeding takes place 'out of time and ordinary place', an alternative reality emerges where the spirit-husband can commune and have congress through the fantasies and dreams which arise.

The sexual current is usually very strong during menstruation: both unconscious dreaming and conscious fantasizing are evoked at this time. Women may use hand-love (an ancient Irish term I prefer to masturbation) to give relief and expression to these fantasies during this time. Most often for such fantasies it will not be necessary to look very far afield: during menstruation, the subtextual life of woman's inner story comes closer to the surface of her awareness, as her submerged dreams, fantasies and urges stir at these times.

In *Troytown Dances*,[43] Miranda has a menstrual dream of Daedalus.

> She has so longed to meet the artificer, to be enclosed within his arms, protected, safe from the behests of gods she cannot be sure of … He pours wine straight from the bottle into his mouth then, catching Miranda's eye, leans over, crooks his curved mouth over hers and lets it trickle into hers. It is the vintage of delight to drink the resinous wine from his sweet mouth. His hair and skin taste like apricots and Miranda drowns in his kisses.
>
> His clever hands are busy about her body, sliding one hand up to cup her breast, while the other opens her legs and traces the way to bliss. Miranda is without volition of the flesh, liquescent in the wonder of this moment, wishing only to be pressed under him as the juice of grapes.
>
> He lays her gently upon the star-blue flowers, entering her with an urgent and masterly stroke, as if he lovingly split a piece of tenderly weathered wood for the making of some beautiful thing. His weight upon her is a splendid burden. They move together with a well-planed rhythm, smoothing and soothing the splintering anxiety that has agonized her heart. He coaxes her up the long stair for the final descent and they fall together, borne by the uplifting sea-winds upon wings of beauty. He whispers in her ear, 'There is wax enough to reach the shore, never fear. I will not let you sink.'
>
> She has been snatched from the hungry waves of sorrow back into the country of health. She awakes to feel the slick warmth of her period at morning's first light.

Scenarios of congress in nature are common. Elizabeth reveals:

> I have lived out the Artemis/Pan fantasy, sex in the pine woods of Greece and also the coupling of the sea and earth on a deserted beach. Dionysos keeps nudging me to do more things with wine and honey!

Meg writes:

> My most frequent fantasies involve making love in a wood, in the rain. He would always be very strong and forceful, yet tender and loving.

Respondents report an energizing ecstasy resultant from this experience, far removed from the low-grade erotica or pornography of the news-stand. As Janet says:

> Beloved is very enthusiastic about his desire for me! The recurring scene of his finding me and our need so great to join sexually – the union results in our melting into one another and bursting into golden light – pure bliss.

And Jocelyn reports:

> Although my sexual fantasies are increasingly about pure energy, light and body sensations, I do often start with a kind of surrender to the divine which is a total giving up of self to love itself, sometimes conceived of as a beautiful male figure.

This is how Suzanne describes her 'Sleep Fantasy':

> I want to watch him sleeping, just to look at him. He's so beautiful, and such an artless seducer. His soft hair on the pillow, the shadows of his eyelashes, his quiet hands. I could curl up like a kitten beside him, bury my face in his hair, and just breathe him in and not wake him. All night, drunk with his closeness and warmth.

Several respondents reported that scenarios involving their daimon were not actively sought. Amanda writes that her daimon

> preferred that I didn't see him through various fantasies, and got the message over to me through a dream where I was on an ocean journey on a great schooner in Victorian times. My travelling companion was my beloved, who was a beautiful vampire, mysterious, dark and intensely passionate. Much to my sorrow, he was an immortal and I was not. We spent our time below deck in golden candlelight, as we were betrothed and spent hours sharing intimate

ideas. He and I would be together always, he said. During a storm I found him on deck, in black cape with his black hair rippling around his shoulders. I told him that I needed his touch, his total embrace, and surrendered to him, lying naked on the ship's bow. As I reached out, he said, with endlessly compassionate eyes, 'Don't you see? I cannot give you this body! I am not of your reality, I cannot touch you!' He bent over me, protecting me from the cold. We were close, surrounded by a warm glow, but I was shivering, still shaking when I awoke. I felt such aching to touch him that I realized it could only be my desires which made him into the lover in my dreams.

This distancing of sexual desire is interesting, for Amanda's dream suggests that her beloved is directing her desires away from him into other channels: a direction which she has followed in her spiritual work as a yoga teacher. We shall follow the path of blood down to its creative ocean in a later chapter.

The onset of menstruation is often explained to girls in a strictly biological way, unmarked by any rite of passage or meaningful support. Miranda Gray's excellent *Red Moon*[18] provides a host of suggestions for initiating daughters and mothers alike into new cycles of transmission.

With the preponderance of women born after the Second World War now approaching middle-age, there is growing awareness of the need to educate ourselves about the menopause. This is the time when women enter the depths of their treasury, when they are able to mine the deepest wisdom. Women who no longer bleed become like 'memory resident' hard disks, flooded, imbued and encrypted with the wisdom of experience. The deep song of their teaching is the quest for women in our age: a tradition which is being restored even as I write.

The daimon may come down the pathway of blood at the menarche but he does not leave at menopause. This should be the triumphal time when the clearest understanding of the daimon is bestowed. Menopause and beyond establishes a woman in a territory which she can claim for her own. She no longer needs to play the social and fashionable games to maintain her status, she can find new rules and life-styles. This may mean speaking out where once she was silent.

Women's life-cycles are commonly classified by the boundaries of the child of girlhood, the woman of fertile years and the crone of post-menopausal years. However, that is too arbitrary a division. A woman passing through menopause doesn't automatically enter cronehood – she is still too young to be classed as an elder in the classical sense. Rather, she enters the role of 'protector and teacher' wherein her daimon can stand clear of the relationships of her girl- and womanhood and enter into a more supportive and equal partnership.

In most Western countries, menopause bespeaks being 'on the heap' while, in traditional cultures, it is the time when women enter their wisdom and become respected elders. We too can enter into this time of deepening knowledge by living out the mystery, giving ourselves time apart to contemplate the nature of the soul within us, rejoicing in its treasury. This will mean recognizing and establishing the new rhythms and seasons of life.

A post-menopausal woman can suit herself and her own tastes, regardless of fashion. In the words of Jenny Joseph's wonderful poem:[1]

> When I am an old woman I shall wear purple
> With a red hat which doesn't go.

She may enter into deeper union with the daimon, uncluttered by other's opinions, secure in her own. As Diana reports:

> The major development of this relationship has been since I began menopause. All aspects of my spiritual life have deepened since I started menopause. In general I am freer and more confident and I think this has allowed me to open up to him more fully.

Pat is recovering from clinical depression, yet she has a Medicine Man for a daimon who brings healing in a very physical way. She speaks of a recent premenopausal experience:

> I was brought from deep sleep to consciousness by a dream that my body was responding to with repeating orgasms. In my solar plexus was an explosion of red heat. My already pulsing body began to vibrate and my breasts were more than just tingling. My Buffalo Medicine Man came into a physical experience, suckling my left breast. I felt the very physical response of my breast responding, of energy being drawn up from my depths. During this process the heat and vibrancy of energy grew. He told me to let go and allow the blocked earth life-force to be drawn up and heal me, bringing me back to life and living.

Pat links this experience with the initiation of menopause: 'The fiery hot sweats are a sign of the opening up of blockages which many woman experience in Western culture.'

The pathway of blood can be travelled to discover the treasury of women's wisdom or it can be entirely ignored. Such neglect disrupts and ignores the natural rhythms of womanhood. When the body's wisdom is set aside, both body and soul exact a terrible revenge. And when feminine value itself is discarded from society, both women and the feminine aspects of men fall into an enchanted sleep of terrible significance.

AWAKENING SLEEPING BEAUTY

So far we have focused on bringing the daimon into definition, but here we must stress the equally important task of bringing our womanhood into focus, for 'in order for the woman to develop an internal relationship of true partnership with her own repressed masculine or animus, she must value her own womanliness'.[82] This is a very hard paradox to accept for those who feel that for a woman to be supported by an inner male figure at all is to revert to patriarchal dependence, to reinvest women in victimhood.

Indeed, until each woman honours the feminine on all levels – within herself and other women, within her daily and spiritual life – she will not be strong enough to detach from the projection-masks of the daimon. In seeking freedom from patriarchal values or an imprisoning relationship without preparation, she will find herself without resources.

The redefinition of what is feminine is an urgent task at this time. Socially, femininity is still defined as soft, yielding, flowery, floaty, accommodating, domestically cosy and able. Femininity, as experienced by women – and minus these projections – is strong, fluid, competent and perceptive. Outworn images and expectations are gradually shifting, but long-term reappraisal is happening over generations rather than decades.

In a society which views women as deficient, *many women will believe themselves to be so*, resulting in low self-esteem, lack of confidence and an inability to develop and mature as women. A sense of worthlessness often prevents a woman from seeking the identity, creative achievement or spiritual vocation which lies in her natural potential.

Polly Young-Eisendrath has noted that, when women 'identify with their own gender, they part from a sense of personal authority'.[82] This comes when

> women who grow up and are socialized in a patriarchal culture are forced to exclude authority from their self-concepts. They must retrieve it from experiences in the masculine world of culture and then convert these experiences to confidence in themselves.[83]

This is one reason why a good understanding of and relationship with the daimon is essential: *he can mirror back to a woman what is intrinsically hers* and so help reconstitute her selfhood.

In unconsciously assimilating attitudes from society, women sometimes inflict worse wounds, punishing themselves, ruling by the basilisk stare of inflexible femininity which blasts everything around them with a dragon's blight. But we are not required to slay this dragon, only to acknowledge the unconscious feminine, to transform fear into power for daily living. Too often that power turns and burns within, making a wasteland of a woman's soul, incubating symptoms and illnesses that degenerate the body instead. As Marion Woodman wisely says, 'Women can be worse patriarchs than men', using the weapons with which we have been wounded against ourselves.

Women are driven to internalize feelings of inadequacy which society projects upon them, to continually undergo a complex readjustment procedure to keep in the swim of life. Many give up in the face of 'preoccupations with an inability to experience truth, beauty or goodness in oneself and one's actions'.[82]

Feminism has attempted to give women the tools to reconfigure the aims and objectives of their lives without external reference to society's projections. But each woman must find her own path, taking into account the stresses and vulnerabilities she experiences, as well as reclaiming her own competency as a human being. We all yearn to be women of compassion, happy in body, secure in our self-image and sexual function, confident in our self-presentation, socially interactive, confidently supported in our views and opinions. But we are daily confronted with patterns and expectations which continually erode our attempts. We tend to assume a resilience we do not have, trying to ignore the soul-pain which erupts in our dreams, visions and inner promptings.

No matter how much we block these out, our bodies speak out, having stored and remembered hidden hurts and desires. Unless we pay attention to the warning signs of need in our bodies, we risk severe illness. The Little Mermaid walks in the world of male orientation with pain, on feet that are not hers because her true element is water; yet because her beloved is of earth she forsakes her fish's tail and walks on the earth.

Accepting our female body and all that being a woman entails is often a hard task. This may manifest early in the repression of physical female characteristics at puberty – through crash-dieting or anorexia in adolescent girls. It may involve ignoring significant bodily signs/pain that warn of fatigue or lack of nurture. Long-term poor self-esteem and resultant depression may result in physical self-mutilation and emotional self-sabotage, or in attempted suicide. The repression of sexual or physical satisfaction is also common. These conditions are all denials of femininity. Obesity, anorexia, bulimia, addictions, infertility, stress-disorders, psycho-somatic illnesses, menstrual disorders and sexual dysfunction are often co-present with low self-esteem and a negative daimonic experience. The therapist, Geneen Roth, who treats women with compulsive eating syndrome, relates that 'Whereas I have met many men who love their bodies, men who don't even think about their bodies, I have *never* met a woman who liked her body without reservation'.[82]

Ignoring the body's signs often extends to denial of personal needs. Many women still live the false myth of over-accommodation whereby they efface themselves in service of their work and menfolk, undermining their own personal needs and desires to the extent that they can be confused by choices. The inability to recognize one's needs is a common syndrome lurking beneath all manner of addictions.

Addictions and compulsive behaviours spring up to fill a vacuum. If something is missing in our lives, through the trauma or violation of soul-fragmentation, we will seek to fill up the hole. Whether we eat the fridge bare, or fill our hours with business, or smoke 60 cigarettes a day, we are trying to fill holes. Many addictions originate in feeding or soothing the body when it is the *soul* which is aching. The solution to such disorders is to attend to the soul, to let in space to meditate, breathe, write in your journal – to allow the real needs and problems to emerge. This is equivalent to Psyche's ordering of Ceres' temple and attending to Juno, matron of women.

Women are socially assessed by their personal appearance

rather than their innate personality. Acceptance of the male projection of womanhood may make demands upon a woman's body. She may seek to identify with:

> the much-promoted media stereotype of a pencil-thin, fibre-packer, endless peppy body. A woman's ego, thus assailed, loses all of her actual body type, the weight, the bodily rhythms appropriate to her.[69]

A young woman's preoccupation with her personal appearance, which is twinned with her identity, may please the men she wishes to impress, but this adolescent model falls down as she ages; so begins the quest for eternal youth that is carried to such lengths in America. At the other extreme, radical feminism derides all beautifying aids as unnecessary. The daimon is not interested in being wooed by our appearance. He continually repeats: 'True beauty derives from the authentic self, honour it and claim your beauty.'

The daimon can be a useful mirror from which to reclaim the lost image of our beauty, strength, power, resource, confidence, passion and courage. Jocelyn sees her life as

> a search for opposites and then a gradual integration of that opposite into my own being. Feeling ugly, I longed for beautiful men, created them in my paintings, poetry and dreams, then had relationships with what I perceived as beautiful men until I began to feel really beautiful myself. I did the same thing for feeling too much in the head, too middle class, too white – so created images of the opposite and went on to have real flesh-and-blood relationships with men who embodied those opposite characteristics. My stories around them follow this need to bring together opposites.

Coming into our bodies is a good way to begin accepting ourselves and admitting self-worth. By honouring the body, we begin to heal the soul-hurts which women collectively carry. If we care for our bodies instead of neglecting and despising them, we begin to heal the name of woman which has been despised and belittled. 'Woman' is not a name even women have upheld and honoured; it has been decried everywhere, yet womanhood is a garment to be worn with pride.

To discover what our womanhood is about we must go to the roots of what disempowers us in order to reclaim the power that is ours. I believe that this is why many women avoid feminist research and distance themselves from feminism – the confrontation with female disempowerment is too overwhelming for one lone woman to bear. A similar problem is discernible within ecological activism, where the problems of the world seem insurmountable when contemplated by the lone individual. This kind of overkill makes the soul quail.

We must bear in mind that women's personal problems concerning low self-esteem and identity are not personally-induced problems: they are part of a greater distortion which feminists call patriarchy, in which both women *and* the feminine aspects in men are classed as deficient. Things can change only if the whole of society – men as well as women – puts hearts and minds to work co-operatively.

To dance with the daimon means to engage intelligently with our feelings of feminine inadequacy as well as our fears about men and the masculine. As Jocelyn says, 'Many women have negative experiences with their daimons because they lack information about their whole selves, especially their sexuality, and see the daimon as external.' Accepting the daimon as a mirror aids the recognition of self-identity and the fostering of self-esteem. Melissa doesn't feel that accepting the daimon diminishes her femininity.

> I am one of the most joyously masculine women one may come across and this doesn't hurt or impair my triumphant and assertive femininity ... The world would be so much better if men listened more to the woman within and women to the man within. My longing and prayer is for all women to become more masculine and men to become more feminine: polarities without but complementary within.

For this wonderful dance to take place, both partners must be free to approach the dance-floor. The immobilization of the feminine in our society has created a terrible shortage of partners! As Sleeping Beauty is imprisoned in her tower asleep, so the feminine is trying to wake up and find its way back through the thorn-hedge of exclusion. A primary method of return is through the reclamation of the symbolic, psychic and spiritual pathways which lead into the country of womanhood.

Of prime importance in the awakening of Sleeping Beauty are the fairy-godmothers, the brooding female presences who invest her with blessings. The reclamation of the feminine and women's self-worth has been aided by the quest for women's own fairy-godmothers: the many faces of the Divine Feminine or the Goddess.

Of course, there are many other very important factors in this rediscovery: a reclamation of women's unique spiritual role and a recognition that female deities were and still are venerated around the world.

The recovery of the Divine Feminine is important because it repolarizes the spiritual norm for men and women. Spirit cannot be addressed and responded to only in male terms. I consider myself fortunate in that my earliest experience of the Divine was feminine rather than masculine. I believe this starting-ground helped bring the daimon into clarity for me, for he has been my bridge to the Goddess. My daimon is a guide who conducts me through the mysteries of the Divine Feminine, for he is a servant dedicated to the Goddess, and it is this cross-polarity which gives me strength of hope and vision.

Many respondents stressed the immense importance of the Divine Feminine in their lives and hoped that I would take this into account when summarizing the results of their daimonic experience. In this area, the American and European responses showed a marked difference. Eighty per cent of the American respondents found the questionnaire difficult to address because, for them, the masculine is more frequently experienced outside themselves in actual relationships than in an internalized rela-tionship. But the other factor that created difficulty was typically expressed by Miriam who commented that because she was so immersed in the Goddess, there just wasn't room for any male figures within her and that, had there been, they wouldn't have got an enthusiastic response. This is also borne out by my experience of teaching around the world: in the USA, the Goddess is considered a uniquely women's thing and the Divine Masculine is often excluded from female consideration because it smacks of patriarchy. Of course, gender studies and awareness have a far higher public profile in the USA than in Europe, but I do not believe that this represents a more acceptable or balanced atti-tude. In marked contrast, the European response showed a much more tolerant acceptance of the masculine in both psychological and spiritual terms.

Not every woman is required to venerate a Goddess literally, only to find within herself and her spiritual experience a true respect for the Spiritual Feminine in whatever forms it should manifest in her sacred landscape. This does not require that she move from any religion or self-determined spiritual arena she currently inhabits, unless, of course, that arena fails to provide her with the necessary soul-nurture. In seeking our fairy godmothers, we are seeking models of inspiration and encouragement which will aid us when we are undergoing difficulties. These models are all about us in the myths, stories and legends which have been discarded as pagan or heretical by what are now accepted as orthodox religions: but these myths were once our core spiritual stories. Wherever we live in the world, our own culture and land still remember them.

In seeking the blessing of our fairy godmother, we turn to the strong stories which inspire and encourage us. On one level, the story of the Sumerian goddess Inanna is a story of women's reclamation of self-worth. It tells how she descends to the underworld to attend the funeral of the husband of her sister, Ereshkigal. The gatekeeper stops Inanna at each of the seven gates of the underworld and asks her to relinquish a piece of her regalia, until she is unadorned and naked. Ereshkigal seizes her and hangs her on a hook to die, since whatever enters her domain of the underworld is her prey. Inanna's faithful servant, Ninshubur, pleads with the gods to help release her. They form two advocates out of clay to reclaim her and revivify her with the waters and grain of life. But the underworld cannot be robbed of its dead: Inanna must be replaced by another victim. In the world above, all Inanna's people are mourning her loss, except her husband Dumuzi, who is found celebrating. He is seized and taken to the underworld in her place.

Inanna's sevenfold descent has passed into Middle Eastern dance tradition as the 'dance of the seven veils', an exotic striptease of dubious merit in which Inanna's revelation of her soul and relinquishment of status have devolved into a stripping bare of the flesh. Women everywhere are now involved in the reclamation of the sacred tradition of Inanna – the work of clarifying the soul and resuming the seven veils of womanhood.

Those who go the way of Inanna come back to the world positively arrayed in the regalia of their sevenfold wealth: beauty, strength, power, resource, confidence, passion and courage. It is time to reclaim the seven veils which are our true clothing; we need only ask the gate-keeping daimon to help us reclaim these as we make a sevenfold ascent to the place where can walk as women – proud, assured and beautiful.

VISIONS OF HOPE

'The horseman waits at the church while the bride is busy being angry somewhere else.' Fiona's recurrent dream exemplifies not only her own quest to arrive at union with her daimon, but also women's impatience to be free of the endless forgetfulness of Beauty's enchanted sleep. Our haste to reclaim our rights and privileges in the world and to consign men to perdition has often clouded the very important process which precedes Beauty's awakening – the period of solitude in which dreams and visions arise and tell us our story. To find the ground of our being we have to honour that solitude in which reveries and meditations can unfold, honouring the sacred enclave of sleep where our dreams speak truly about the things we have ignored or forgotten.

Women's realm of realization is the deep place within, the imaginal realm (note: *imaginal*, not imaginary) – the place where the ideas, stories, reflections and passions are mirrored, the realm wherein they are enacted. Within this realm, which is our sacred symbolic landscape, we can explore feelings, dreams and desires, and be ourselves.

Using the imagination, working with images or symbols, is hard in a society which devalues the imagination, and which has become unable to read the potent visions of hope which shimmer there. It is clear from my work that, for most people, dreams, writing poetry and mystical experience are natural and common-place human occurrences. However, we have no social framework in which to share dreams and mystical phenomena, and the media-enforced conspiracy to belittle any form of spiritual perception or mysticism keeps most people silent and isolated from others' experience.

Most of my teaching is about encouraging people to attend to the subtle messages of the imagination, which is, after all, a faculty of the soul. Those subtle messages are most often neglected or discounted as irrelevant, but are potent signposts of experience nonetheless. The place of imagination in the healing process cannot be overstressed. It helps us assess our inner treasury and

gives us rich resources to sustain, support and transform us. If we
steer without imagination, we find our lives petrify, solidify, cease
to sparkle; daily life becomes a route march to be endured.

There is also fear of self-delusion: how do we distinguish
between day-dream fantasy and the sacred symbolic reality which
is the true landscape of our soul? Fantasy feels synthetic, sacred
symbolic reality feels powerfully authentic; but we often choose
the 'safer' synthetic because symbolic reality can be very powerful. We can choose to live our lives by the artificially-simulated
light-bulb of fantasy or by the true sun- and moonlight of our
symbolic landscape. If we opt for symbolic reality over fantasy,
we will experience the true exchange and reciprocation of energy
which can illuminate us. This choice is akin to Psyche's first
labour of differentiation and it is the one at which women often
falter but, as Rilke wrote, 'only someone who is ready for everything, who excludes nothing, not even the most enigmatical, will
live in relation to another as something alive and will himself
draw exhaustively from his own existence'.[64] Many women are
unpractised in discriminating between different forms of reality,
for they are taught to repress that which is not seen, from
emotional needs and instinctual promptings right through to
mystical visions and manifestations of spiritual reality in dreams
and daily life.

Using the imagination too freely has been equated with mental
illness and self-delusion in our society. We often fail to acknowledge our deep inner nature when the evidence of dreams and
meditations is so often alarmingly raw, violent or dynamic. The
projection upon women to be 'sugar and spice and all things nice'
divorces us from accepting anything dynamic or powerful from
within. The projection of 'slugs and snails and puppy-dogs' tails'
upon men returns rather dramatically when women dream about
their own masculine aspects. Projecting the daimon upon others,
we veil part of our authentic self. When we cease to project, that
part comes home and our daimon loses one of the masks so we
can begin to understand him. This is why, when any personal
exploration is undertaken, the results are often quite alarming to
a woman, who may feel invaded by something alien, or feel disturbed by the presence of so many conflicting and sometimes
unpleasant facets in her soul. We do not expect to find the masks
of the daimon fastened to our own faces! Some women will often
revert to a careful cultivation of their outer personality, which will

be worn as the chief mask with which they greet the outer world.

What women meet in dreams and meditations is their raw power. They are either frightened by so much excess or else appalled by the wildness of it, since it doesn't accord with the social norm of femininity. Sometimes the evidences of the soul show us powerful and strange things which do not seem to accord with social standards of life today. Our dreams show us engaged in primitive or rather primal patterns of behaviour and relationship which affront or affright. But we do not have to equate primal experience with nastiness or confuse challenge with aggression.

The primal power of our dream experiences should tell us immediately that we are on track of our passion, even though some details might seem unsightly in the light of day. The writing of this book has caused many disturbing dreams, which I have been driven to regard with humour rather than disgust because they are so cheekily true.

> I dreamed that I was helping to restructure and organize a large house and gardens. As I was going to my room, a charismatic actor embraced me and thrust his tongue into my mouth, causing me to urgently desire him. But instead of taking me to bed, he opened up a vault where lived many men waiting to have congress with me. After that, he took the role of a procurer.[35]

Here, an aspect of the daimon strings me along the path of passion and graphically illustrates the task before me – to open the hidden, subterranean realm of the masculine.

Since the feminine has been in an enchanted sleep for so long, we would expect the dreams within that sleep to be very powerful. In Amanda's dream, we see the retrieval of self-worth from the hands of the daimon.

> I was a servant in a royal palace; it was teatime and I had to serve the King and Queen. In the kitchen I discovered with horror that all the china was dirty and I couldn't possibly serve them like this. I could see the Queen shaking her head, 'I don't know if that girl is able to fulfil her duties.' But the king said patiently, 'Give her a chance, she is new to us, it's true. But she has a good heart and will serve us well.' Back in the kitchen I made a hasty attempt to wash everything up but it seemed impossible to get things clean. Then the King, whom I recognized as my beloved, suddenly appears at my side. Radiating with compassion, adoration and little amusement at my progress, he sat down at the servants' table and I

joined him. We drank a mug of tea together. I felt relaxed by his gentle manner, cherished and comforted. He said, 'You see, we don't need these things clean to have tea. *You are of service* and without these cups and saucers we are served as well.' He embraced me with his love and I felt able to carry out my duty.

The loving humour in Amanda's dream is also present in this dream of mine.

I was in a library working on an ancient Irish manuscript which I was restoring. At the same time I did this work, I was simultaneously healing the wounded body of my daimon poet, who lay unconscious and naked. An English poet, who was almost an exact counterpart of my Irish poet, urged me on to finish the work, laughed at the wit of my translations and told me to take home the text for one night. There was also a female librarian who was very sympathetic who helped me find auxiliary texts to complete my work. The more I worked on the manuscript's restoration, the more vigorous my poet became.

My Celtic studies are intrinsically associated with my daimon who takes an important role in my restoration of fragmented texts and traditions, but I had no notion that my work was also healing to *him* until this dream. This has realized a new creative level in my work so that I now sleep *with* rather than *on* the texts that I study.

Unfortunately, many sleepers fail to retrieve more than a tiny portion of their dreams. How then do we become conscious of the unfolding stories which give us visions of hope? How we can make the space to retrieve our dreams is described in *Singing the Soul Back Home*, which also demonstrates many powerful shamanic ways to explore the sacred landscape of our story, but here I want to show another way.[41] If we cannot access our dreams, then we need to look at our story in conscious, waking reality.

In the daily world, women's soul experience may be fragmented or dim, but in the rich underworld of the soul, that same experience shines with clear light and has a satisfying wholeness to it. Purposely entering solitude, in our room or garden, as we walk or sit outdoors, we can find thresholds over which we can invite the daimon to visit us. In this solitude, we seek to find the most immediate methods by which we allow images, feelings, associations and story-snippets to arise in waking reverie. Reverie should not be confused with fantasy: we are not dreaming up something that isn't there or that we have consciously invented, but allowing something deeper *that already exists in our experience* to arise and show itself. We do not have to shut our eyes, utter arcane invocations or enter deep states of trance to achieve this – we need only silent solitude. Some of the respondents tell how this works for them, revealing that there is no correct etiquette for approaching the daimon, only the simple invitation to be present. You can meet him at a pre-arranged venue in your own symbolic landscape, as Allegra does.

> He comes when called, often from the sea. He used to come from a cave where I would escape to and he would play the guitar while I sang.

Or you might put on appropriate music, like Moyra.

> Certain kinds of music provide the pathway for my daimon: music penetrates my bloodstream and activates him rather as petrol fuels a car and makes it operative. Again, walking is very important to his appearances: if I've been indoors for several days at a time, he gets restive, because this is our time.

There may be certain times of year when he is more amenable, as Elizabeth relates.

> He appears or has until recently, differently in winter and summer. He acts internally in winter and I seem to meet him more in summer. I dream him in winter and find him in summer.

Fiona finds that

> he appears when I invite him to, though I sometimes ask for a specific aspect, such as the horseman: usually he comes in an aspect relevant to the circumstances. He comes through in writing too, as well as in dreams, and in odd individuals I meet. When I'm feeling anti my partner, he appears, which is when I tend to dialogue with him.

Sometimes his appearances will change, as Frances reports.

> When I need healing, he's Pan; if I need comfort and grounding, he will be the Green Man. If I need knowledge, he is Merlin or Gandalf. Plant lore and reflection brings him as Bear. If its loving or dancing that we're doing, then he's the Satyr. When I am emerging from being very stuck or in a crisis, I'll be aware that he was there all along.

But what if you don't want the daimon to appear whenever? Gwen allays this fear.

> Usually I call him if in need of some kind. He rarely, if ever, turns up uninvited or unannounced.

Jocelyn reminds us that the power of vision leads us to our true beauty.

> For women to take the power of fantasy into our own hands and create/transform the inner lover into something empowering for us is useful. Also, if it helps us to be more permanently identified with our loveliness, which I think most of us desire, then it's served a profound purpose.

The simple reverie in which the daimon can be invited to appear doesn't require record-keeping or notation, unless that seems important to you. Records are mostly useful in retrospect when we need to check particular points and notice our progress, but they are not usually part of the early exploration of the daimon any more than keeping a diary about a new acquaintance is part of our lives.

However, some respondents have maintained journals, dream-diaries and meditation records over a long period, to the enrichment of this book. Sheila in particular has kept an in-depth journal of the exploration of her sacred landscape and the stories associated with it, in which dream, meditation and shamanic journey all play a part. The culmination of this work included a month's study of the realm of the goddess Hecate. During this time Sheila dreamed of

> a crippled young man who looks on at other young men playing football. He cannot join in because his legs are wounded in some way. Things change. There is a disaster concerning a large ship and he is a hero. His legs are whole again. Later, I am on a beach with Tara (a course teacher). She is lying in the sun on a lounger looking red and sun-burnt. A group of us are writing stories for her. I rack my brains about what to write. I draw a diagram which is a story of the young man going underwater. I explain this to her and she says, 'Yes, we need stories of men going into the underworld.'

Sheila found this dream very moving and continued to work with its themes, seeing them as relevant to her own inner masculine. Seeking to support and encourage him, she continued to meditate and journey, being directed in one of her sessions by the Moon to follow the trail of her dream and to enter the waters. She emerged into an underworld cavern wherein stories of descent were depicted on the walls, including those of Persephone and Inanna.

> It seemed to me then that my inner man felt at home here and that, like Hermes or Anubis, he was able to descend to the underworld and return with treasure and knowledge. It is he who supports me by his ability to travel backwards into Hecate's realm, the deep waters of the unconscious.

That week her dreams showed her a ceremony at which a hierophant appeared and questioned her about her vocation. She spoke of 'shining out the Moon and radiating the Sun'. The hierophant challenged the femininity of her room with, 'Where is the masculine?' She assured him that she was about to make an image for her room; on waking, she then spoke to the Moon about how she might form such an image. It referred her to a figure of the Sacred Masculine, who revealed the young man who had been in her dream, only now he appeared in a monk's habit, as a man of great integrity and understanding whom Sheila recognized as one who had long been her teacher.

I give this experience at length to show that trust and know-ledge are built up over long periods of such work and that reverie, meditation and daimonic encounter do not yield immediate understanding. If we are faithful, the images, stories and scenarios which emerge over the months will begin to move into discernible patterns which have meaning for us. Like the ornithologist who must watch for several years to understand the migratory habits of birds, we too must keep scanning our sacred horizons before we can be certain about our own daimonic patterns.

We can only find these signs in the reverse of our life's weaving – in dreams, reveries and encounters which well up from our deep living. Only if we treat the imagination as a faculty of the soul and the daimon as guardian of our treasury will we find the insight to re-evaluate their riches as a true commodity rather than meaningless trash.

DAIMONIC DIALOGUE

One of the primary ways of encountering the daimon is through dialogue. Again, we seek the silence of solitude in order to meet our daimons. Some respondents dialogued aloud when they were alone, some dialogued in the heart, some on paper.

Moyra writes:

> I talk to him a lot of the time when I'm alone. I used to do it aloud in public when I was younger: my parents kept sighing and consoling themselves with the prospect that I would 'grow out of it'– well, I haven't. During the early seventies I used to walk all the way to work through the back-streets, solely so that I could dialogue aloud with him. The motion of walking seems important to our relationship; he is less present when I'm still.

Anna says:

> I've just started to develop dialogue. He gives comfort, protection, ancient wisdom, practical advice.

Sheila reveals:

> I speak to him during meditation. Generally he acts as a guide in my inner landscape. If I'm seeking help over a specific problem, he leads me down paths towards the solution. He always knows the sort of guidance I need, because he truly knows me!

Anne dialogues mostly silently.

> I sometimes hear the voice giving me information or a new phrase for a song or poem. It's often quite funny and frequently useful.

Diana experiences a full range of dialogue modes:

> If I clear my mind and turn my attention towards him, I may hear him talking in my head, especially late at night when I am walking the dog. At times I do automatic writing on the computer and his words pass through my brain to my fingers without editorial interference. I have amassed a considerable amount of material in this way. Usually something that happens, or something I read that upsets or excites me or turns my attention towards him, will stimulate a response which I perceive as pressure until I sit down and let him talk. In addition, in specific ritual situations others may call him to speak through me. In this form of possession he has control of my voice and body and access to my memories, but the personality which takes over is very different from my own. I retain only partial memories of what he says and does afterwards.

But the daimon doesn't always give his response on a plate. As Pat says:

> He doesn't tell me what I must do; he shows me other ways of perceiving life, often giving me more choice. He steadies me. He's given me healing with herbs, chanting, dance. He has worked hard trying to enable me to open my self and allow the life-force through me – to help release blocks in my body.

Sometimes the daimon will even allow us to make fools of ourselves, as Ioho ruefully relates:

> I have always talked to One Feather, both aloud and in thought. I remember, at the age of 17, stoned witless and absolutely desperate, screaming at him across the floor of the ladies loo in some nightclub, 'Don't just stand there and tell me not to! Help me, you bastard!' I remember his face looking down, waiting for me to get myself together. He never comforted me directly in any way, only by his constant presence. Nowadays we talk as friends, with great respect, and deep affection: a powerful love. He gives me advice and I share with him my joy of discovery.

This sense of distance and loving support is a sure sign of the true daimon. He will not wade in and take our power from us, he wants us to find our own authority. Sometimes the dialogue can be physical rather than verbal, as in Meg's case.

> It's as if we don't need to talk. He supports me with his closeness. If I feel him close by I feel sure of things. I become distressed inside if I can't find him. When I was younger he was definitely the leader. He took me by the hand and led me through the dark woods. He spoke words of comfort when I was distressed or confused. Now we are more equal but I still feel the need for his 'hugs' sometimes.

How do dialogues work? There is often a sense of asking the question and suspecting oneself of supplying the answer, but the wisdom of the daimon comes from deeper levels than this. It helps not to edit what comes or wonder whence it derives, but just listen. The time for evaluation is later, when you can review it. The most important thing to establish is, 'What insights have I gained? How does this change my life?' You can record or write down the substance of what you receive and keep it back for a month. Then read it and see if it still makes sense.

As you grow in confidence and experience, as time goes by, you will begin to filter out the interference of your own mind-set completely, but bear in mind that your own genetic, behavioural and educational circuits are themselves networks of wisdom. The interference comes when doubt and lack of self-esteem begin to rule the show. You can only test the words of your daimon by applying them and seeing what fruits emerge, as Suzanne did when she initiated the following dialogue as a result of answering the questionnaire and coming to fresh conclusions about her daimon.

> S Why didn't I realize who you were until now?
> D You needed to find out in your own time. You often said yourself that I've always been here for you, you just didn't understand why.
> S It's true – you never deserted me … (hugs him) Have you any special advice for me?
> D One thing: stop under-estimating yourself. You have so much to offer. You're talented, creative, loving, lovable, spiritual and intelligent, and many things besides … *Do you realize that when you made the effort to contact me you did something that thousands of others constantly fail to do?* People tend to treat me as if I'm invisible, but you tore down the wall between us with your bare hands, stepped through the gap and made yourself known to me. I can't tell you how much I appreciate your friendship.

The kinds of information received in dialoguing can be very moving and enlightening. Some may not make a lot of sense at the time but on review they can prove of overwhelming significance, as in this dialogue I had one winter with my daimon about the direction and form he was taking. As the fine snow began to cover everything outside, his words seemed to burn into me.

> C Where are you leading me?
> D To the centre.
> C Are you changing into another form?
> D No, you are coming closer to the centre now and we are aligning.
> C Who are 'we'?
> D The array of threads which lead you home.
> C Where/what is home?
> D The place of the soul's vastness.

In any dialogues, we must answer from our authentic selves to make any headway or we are merely playing useless games. To clarify the daimon, we ourselves need to move centre stage and speak from our authentic selves, without throwing our voices via the projections around us. It means initially listening to *the content* of the voices and seeing whether these are issues to do with our self. It takes continual practice to disengage from those projections, to stop filing all that we dislike about ourselves into 'the bad man made me' box.

Gwen reminds us that 'there is a certain amount of protocol involved in this relationship and the overlapping of our worlds'. It is important to be sensitive to the conditions of invitation and meeting, to remember that the taboos which the daimon may set are for our protection – like those Cupid sets Psyche. The distance will lessen as we grow in soul.

There is a puritanical streak in our society which tells us it is pure selfishness to spend time upon ourselves rather than caring for the benefit of others, but I would urge women to discover self-nurture as a proper part of their life, to see it not as selfish ego enhancing, but as a quest for the authentic self and the true daimon. The authentic self has authority which is not derived from others, which does not play other people's games; it derives from the soul's depths and it promotes values which protect the soul.

Finding our proper boundaries as women is about discovering this deep authority, our protective strength, which does not give itself away to others. If we are in deep contact with the authentic self, we are less likely to hurt ourselves or others by our thoughts, deeds and actions. Working out of true integrity, we maintain the timelessly enduring identity of womanhood.

It is important to understand that the ability to experience the messages of the creative soul – whether through creative expression, dream, vision or meditation – 'is an indicator of advanced female development'.[83]

In honouring the visions of hope that arise in solitude, it is also important to have a soul-friend you can consult when you emerge from silence – a person with whom you can share your soul, your thoughts and your feelings in ways that will be respected. If you have such a friend who can honour the space, respect the revelation, be silent or ask the right questions, give you a reality check and support you, you are indeed fortunate. If you have no such friend and psychoanalysis is beyond your pocket or feels too invasive, you still have the resources of your story and sacred landscape to guide you.

When a woman actively searches out her daimon through the landscape of her sacred self, it is inevitable that partners will be concerned and feel threatened. By casting off her partner's unconscious projections upon her, a woman in search of her authentic self will no longer be the adorable little girl that he married, but a stranger. This will cause a shift in that man, who will have to deal with the cast-off image of his own anima that he projected onto her. But in seeking maturity of soul for herself, a woman may in turn cause her partner to grow up and seek his own maturity. Rather than become a cause of fear and resentment, some women may choose to drop their exploration; or they may go even further and project their own weakness upon their partner and enhance his power so that he can feel safe again. Compliance, compromise and self-sabotage bring no joy to a relationship, only domestic hell.

'Great sensitivity is required to deal with the overwhelming sense of abandonment a man feels when "his" woman recognizes her inner bridegroom, unless, of course, he has discovered his inner bride.'[79] It is essential that the human relationship is maintained by patient communication and mutual consideration.

By withdrawing from the projections of her partner and by realizing that he and her daimon are two different beings, a woman will come to a clarification about herself that will enable her to free her passionate soul. It may cause her relationship to enter into its true contract, or it may end a partnership built on lies. It will clear the ground for her spirituality to emerge in its most sustaining and nourishing phase, and to dynamite any blockages or stale concepts that have been keeping her soul from its proper nurture. Maintaining a stable human relationship while maintaining a stabilizing interior one with the daimon is possible, even though it is sometimes difficult; but many respondents provided proof that this balancing act is indeed possible.

The fruit of Sheila's work is impressive but she still has to use her journal and her meditation as coping mechanisms when her daimon manifests

as the Judge, when the so-called negative animus seems to embody all the critical 'should's and 'ought's of childhood. I certainly tend to judge myself over-harshly. My coping mechanism is to reach for my journal and dialogue with an inner figure who loves me in an unconditional manner. I speak to loving friends ... I feel as if my daimon has been hidden from me, rather like Pluto and his helmet

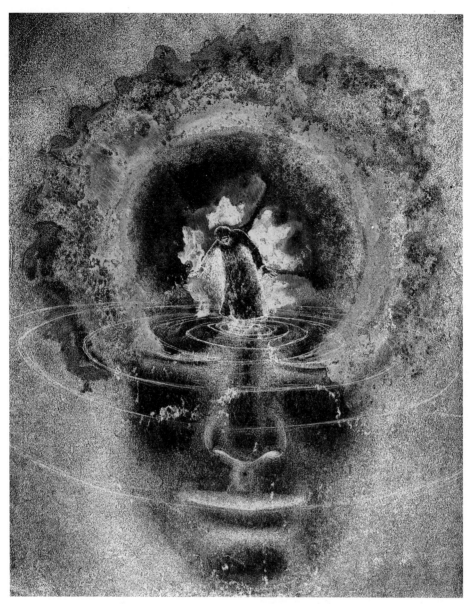

Daimonic experience: "The man in my mind'
(Soul card by Deborah Koff-Chapin).

Pin-ups: *(clockwise from top left))* Keanu Reeves, Mel Gibson,
Liam Neeson, Johnny Depp.

Angel and demon: the angelic daimon awakens women's passion; the demon lover in snake form bids her ignore the integrity of passion.

Lovers captivated by each other's projection ('The Baleful Head' by Edward Burne-Jones).

Beauty and the
beast: Cocteau's
traditional view of
the beast.

Beast as daemon: a
contemporary
beauty and the beast
(Ron Koslow
television series).

Taming the beast: women have the strength to disenchant the beast and to work with the masculine fearlessly.

STRENGTH.

(Below) The ghostly lover: Nina's dead husband Jamie appears to her (Alan Rickman in *Truly, Madly, Deeply.*

Vampire as daimon: two faces of Dracula, seeking his love down the ages.

The vampire legacy: the inheritance of fear and fascination with the demon lover is one long bite.

The green god: the north-west European Dionysos awakens many to
verdant ecstacy (print by Chesca Potter).

Consummation: the Buddha of tantric teahings conjoins with his consort
('Vajradhara and Vajradhatuishvari' by Andy Weber).

Love leads the soul: the torchbearing daimon leads woman
('Psyche and Cupid', relief from Capua Mithraeum, third century AD).

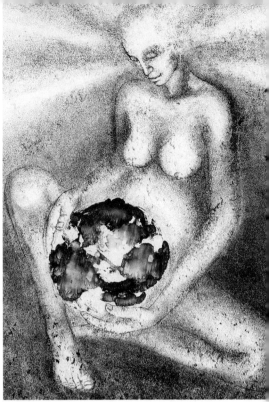

Daimonic Creation:
Above left: daimonic conception;
Above right: gestaing the seeds;
Below left: showing forth.
(By Deborah Koff-Chapin.)

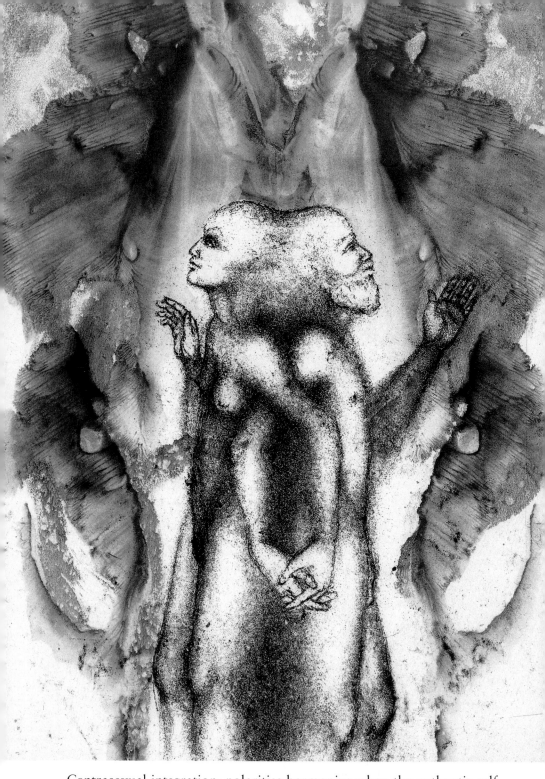

Contrasexual integration: polarities harmonize when the authentic self and contrasexual other integrate in women and men (by Deborah Koff-Chapin).

which renders him invisible. I've come to him through my exploration of the underworld through the gateway of a depression. I've found this myth of great value in understanding my individual journey in this lifetime, in particular, in honouring the rhythms of womanhood and my deep connection to the seasons of the Earth.

In myth, the helmet of Pluto makes him invisible, for the Lord of the Underworld is ignorant of terrestrial or heavenly happenings, but when mortals strike their hands on the earth and invoke him in oaths and curses, he hearkens.[30] All the jewels and metals that lie hidden in his realm are our secret treasury and when we strike our hand upon the sacred threshold of the daimon, we are able to access them.

When we are sad, confused or wounded, we can return to the source of our feminine experience and use our creative faculty to explore our hurt. By so doing, we will avoid the illnesses that flourish on repressed desire or hidden hurt, such as cancer and depression. To come again into the arena of discovery by whatever creative means we have, to take the hand of the daimon and descend deeper, we will find treasures that need to find the light. Ignoring the daimon, we ignore the treasury within our feminine souls. In the utterance of the unspoken, from the depths of the soul clearly revealed, we will arise as women of passionate soul.

The myths of the men who make the descent are, as Hecate indicates, some of the most precious, for they speak to us of our own daimon who is as much in the underworld with us as any woman. In the darkness, like Orpheus, he sings the melody of our soul and enables our return and safe passage. If we are attuned to his voice and listen to his song, we may both ascend.

Women who seek the place within are assured of a faithful companion, as Anne Lister's song 'Hawthorn',[84] relates:

> And who will open the gate for me
> When my wandering comes to an end
> And who will wait on the road of dreams
> To be my lover or be my friend?
> For now the roads that I walk down
> Are lined with oak and ash and thorn
> I'll build my love a forest crown
> And dance with him from dusk till dawn.
>
> If you would walk on the road of dreams
> Take someone there to be your guide

Know that nothing is as it seems
And you need someone by your side.
I see him standing in my dreams
Tall and slender as a willow
He whispers song into my heart
And lays may blossom on my pillow.

Women now need to return to the ground of their being, their womanhood, which, in the words of the 17th-century mystic, Jane Leade, is their 'birthright and their blessing'.[42] Drawing into our deep centre, we will find resources for the journey to understanding ourselves. That journey starts with valuing our femininity which has, until now, been locked up in the tower of patriarchal principles, ideologies and conventions. The daimon can help reflect these factors for us and point out the ways to honour our femininity.

We need no longer be imprisoned, impaled or restricted by the thorn-hedge which surrounds the castle of sleep that society has cast about the feminine. The hawthorn tree has traditionally been associated with the feminine, not only because it has thorns, but also because it has a blossom which carries women's sexual scent. When the may blossom on the hawthorn is fully out, the summer arrives and we can leave off our winter clothes. What many women have seen as an impenetrable prison suddenly comes into fresh focus as something more subtle and wondrous than we have been able to define: the circle of hawthorn around the tower may prove to be the very parameter of our femininity, in which our beauty, power and vision have been maturing.

Questions

1 At which times and seasons is your daimon more present? Do your moods or the weather influence when he appears?
2 What needs are you ignoring?

Actions

1 Tend Ceres' altar by taking time to nurture your whole self – body and soul.
2 Start a journal to record dreams, impressions, meditations, visions, pictures, poetry, etc, as a way of mapping your soul.
3 Write a letter to your daimon asking him to help you remember who you are.

Reflection

Reflect upon the Seven Veils or qualities of your true woman-hood, and the ways in which you can assume them. (They may be different from the ones listed in this chapter!)

CHAPTER 5

The Demon Lover

> I ach'd to see what things the hollow brain
> Behind enwombed: what high tragedy
> In the dark secret chamber of her skull
> Was acting, that could give so dread a stress
> To her cold lips, and fill with such a light
> Her planetary eyes; and touch her voice
> With such a sorrow.
>
> John Keats, *The Fall of Hyperion*

POSSESSED BY DEMONS

In earlier centuries the respondents of this book would undoubtedly have been classified as 'possessed by demons or incubi', and would have been abused, tortured or beaten to be 'cured'. It is true that the daimonic relationship can sometimes seem to verge on the demonic and, significantly, in studies of the animus, authors have identified it with the Demon or Ghostly Lover. Women report experiencing the daimon as judge, tyrant, aggressor, raptor, thief, demon and vampire.

For most women, at some point along their path to self-identification and daimonic discovery, there will be confusion, pain and struggle. Many of the respondents write tellingly of this time, feeling themselves close to breakdown, madness or self-violence. Pat speaks of

> the negative daimon who has destroyed my self-worth and confidence. I'm now discovering his shadow killer drive and I've seen him in two dream flashes where his eyes were dead like a psychopath and I knew he was one of the living dead. It's taken me to the edge.

Common problems that may occur in relation to the daimon are listed below. Each may occur in isolation from other problems, but they frequently combine and are present in different forms simultaneously.

- an addiction to the daimon, to the exclusion of other relationships
- neglect of the daimon, causing a build-up of dammed power
- animus-possession or total identification with one of the daimonic masks, whereby a woman's male characteristics are actively worn as a mask over her femininity
- neglect of personal power and submission to the authoritative or critical voice of the animus, rather than to the true daimon, causing petrification
- total projection of the daimon upon human men, causing an addiction to self-endangering forms of behaviour and ways of life as compensation for lack of self-motivation

In this chapter, we will explore some of these themes and seek their solution.

The experiences listed above can often distort or control our behaviour. As we saw in Chapter 2, Ioho's childhood struggle with the chaotic energy of the black elves continued into her twenties.

On the other hand her constant companion, One Feather

> never caused me any trouble at all, except perhaps in allowing me an idealized image of the father which my own father couldn't live up to. When I journey in to discover memories of my early life, I find the black elves are still there, only not so vicious.

Possession by or total obsession with the daimon is a difficult phase to go through. Everything in a woman's life may become subordinated to the inner relationship; human relationships and daily duties may be cast aside as irrelevant, as Lairdearg reports:

> Between 16 and 20 I became 'addicted' to him and to the inner-world; I spent every available moment escaping from ordinary reality, being with him. It reached a point where I couldn't function properly in ordinary reality and the innerworld became more real than the material world. I was also suffering from depression and so I guess that's the nearest I've ever come to committing suicide. I really didn't want to stay here. Looking back, I can see how dangerous the situation was, and I was fortunate to have a

very rude awakening which brought me back with a bang. The daimon gave me what I wanted: all choices were mine – talk about free will!

It can happen that, due to an obsessive regard of the daimon, a woman can end a partnership. For Suzanne, who has photos on her walls of a man who is the image of her daimon, he acted as co-respondent in her marriage breakdown.

> In 1991, I left my partner because I wanted to be with my daimon full time. My ex thought I'd gone crazy. I nearly was. I was so over-whelmed with love and longing that I thought I could make my beloved come and live with me. Somehow, I even performed spells to try and bring him to me. Now my ex and I are friends, but I can't maintain a relationship. I don't want anyone except my daimon to touch me, and if I sleep with someone else, I feel I've been unfaithful to him, and end up crying and apologizing to his photos on the walls next day.

Although there is a great sense of partnership and support and a deeper sense of creativity and resource in Suzanne's experience, her daimon has totally polarized her life into a semi-static pattern. She has fallen in love with Love, and so may not move from his image. Hers is a particularly severe case since she has experienced the daimon suddenly, in her forties, with no previous intimation of him and with no support or friend to help her understand what she is undergoing. By actively exploring her daimon, she will be able to emerge into a less obsessional, though no less devoted, relationship. But currently there can be no human relationships for Suzanne since no man measures up to this standard.

While the obsessional animus can obscure all other relation-ships to the point of unhealthy isolation, the projection of the masked daimon upon human men can result in an addiction to self-endangering ways of life. Many women live dangerously, purposely seeking out men who are criminal and choosing to associate with them. Addicted to excitement, such women are frequently drawn by the dark shadow of their animus rather than the light of their daimon. Marion Woodman describes this dan-gerous symbiosis thus:

> together they are in a love/death relationship; their passion is the anaesthetic that makes them dare the magic that may destroy them.[79]

Susanna writes of her early fascination with 'bad boys' and with the male elements that are conventionally forbidden to 'good girls'. This fascination continued into adulthood when she dated men who were dangerous to know. Shortly before her black lover, Henry, tried to strangle her she had a warning dream.

> Two older black men got out of wooden crates in the cemetery. One took my arm and planted a kiss in the crook of my elbow. I thought 'that's the kiss of death'. In sheer terror I awoke. What scared me even more was that the inside of my elbow was still tingling.

Susanna was slow to understand the warning of the dream and it was only after a succession of dangerous relationships that she was able to curb her fascination with 'bad boys'. The last of these relationships was with a pimp.

> one of the sweetest and gentlest men I ever dated, even though he had tried to convince me to work for him. One day the woman who supported him showed up on my doorstep. She looked like me ten years older and having lived a much harder life. She told me if I wanted him, I could have him, but I'd have to take complete responsibility for him. I saw her point and backed off.

Susanna finally woke up to the danger by meeting an image of herself from her own future, in the person of her lover's street-walking supporter.

Projecting the dangerous or outlaw mask of the daimon upon men often results in a woman suffering violent abuse, beatings and systematic victimization. This can be experienced as both reciprocally exciting as well as a radical means of self-destruction and self-depreciation.

It is common to find women who adopt the male characteristics of their daimon as their own masks. This is particularly so in Western culture where, in order to succeed in a male-oriented world, women have to be 'better than men'. And we are very good at becoming 'superwoman' – a hybrid distortion of our feminine selves complete with the panoply of male attire and attitudes with which to defeat the patriarchal world – but turning into even worse patriarchs in the process! This distortion is often called 'the Athena woman', referring to the birth of Athena from the head of Zeus.

Frances speaks of her experience.

> In my daily life I was very developed in my masculine characteristics and when it became very obvious that the feminine was distinctly out of balance, I found myself pushing my daimon away firmly.

The real, feminine Frances had receded, to be replaced by the masculine mask: a process which she has now totally reversed. The adoption of 'the Athena woman' role is recognized as a form of animus possession. Its symptoms are a feeling of being 'driven or paralysed, entranced or desperate', as the woman realizes that the cost of her actions is the loss of her feminine wisdom.[49]

The paradoxical repulsion/attraction around the daimon is mirrored in the names it is given: 'daimon' can easily become 'demon', while 'animus' is another word we use for hatred. Powerful and ambivalent, the daimon is hard to define. Some women question whether the daimon is 'good' or 'bad', fearing to be the haunt of spirits, however beautiful and desirable. The discernment of spirits, like the perception of co-operative human friendships, is an important factor when it becomes a light by which we direct our lives.

So, is the daimon a light or a shadow? Jungian psychology recognizes what it terms 'a positive animus' – a mature daimon which supports the well-integrated woman – as well as 'a negative animus' which acts in a vampiric or autocratic way, causing the woman to be entranced and powerless.

The Jungian concept of the shadow is often misunderstood as 'the bad or evil tendencies within', whereas it is the *submerged*, undeveloped and unknown part of ourselves, which has potential. Jung writes:

> The shadow personifies everything that the subject refuses to acknowledge about himself and yet is always thrusting itself upon him directly or indirectly – for instance inferior traits of character and other incompatible tendencies'.[28]

He also said that woman has to be in possession of her shadow, aware of her submerged tendencies, in order to relate to the animus successfully.

> The animus should not be connected with the shadow, that connection should be broken, despite the fact that you arrive at the animus by way of the shadow; for you can never arrive at the animus unless you see the shadow.[22]

A similar ambivalence was expressed by many of the women who chose not to complete the questionnaire. We have inherited a deep duality from Western culture which splits everything into 'good and bad' polarities. The contrasexual other is a grey area in the minds of many women. Indeed one of the respondents remarked, 'I don't think my answers will be much use, as I've grown up thinking about this in psychological language, as "the shadow", as something negative.' Many felt they could not answer because they were in too much of a confusion themselves to be coherent.

Let them take heart: even the Jungian, Irene Claremont de Castillejo, admits that her initial confusion with the concept of the animus was so great that she was compelled to write a paper on the subject: 'to rid myself of the uneasy suspicion, shared by many women, that to have an animus problem was a polite way of saying one was smitten by the plague'. Many female Jungians have since sought to clarify the concept of the animus, rescuing it from the dubious backwater into which Jung himself had sculled it, unfamiliar as he was, from a personal experiential viewpoint, with these feminine waters.

This all sounds alarming and potentially disempowering for women who feel that they also might have 'an animus problem'. How do we define our soul and what is going on in it? What tools do we use to disentangle ourselves from our difficulties? Lengthy analysis is not an option for many women, so how can we arrive at definitions, unblock problems, dissolve difficulties?

We shall be exploring the immediate and practical solutions which lie at hand. Chief of these is to seek whatever grounds or earths us, so that our panic is defused sufficiently for us to seek help. This may be the help of nature, which immediately puts our human fears into a wider perspective and gives us safe surroundings. The services of a supportive friend who can act as our reality-check and bull-shit detector are also invaluable. But the primary source of help is questions which act as can-openers to impenetrable problems.

When I was in the early stages of this book, a dynamite-stick of a question was tossed into my hands by my own daimon, who suggested, 'Does the unemergent daimon reveal, mirror, even *impersonate*, blockages and obstacles in our souls' development?' I took that question and ran with it: I invite you to do the same.

At the other extreme from the obsessional daimon is the

neglected daimon, who can be just as dangerous. If the daimon who comes to awaken a woman is refused, that woman loses an opportunity to grow – she sinks into unconsciousness, slewing about in a welter of feelings and impressions which threaten to overwhelm. Pat warns us from personal experience:

> If we ignore or suppress the daimon, turn our anger towards it and to all men, we become ever more wounded, as we wound ourselves. The other risk is the negative shadow force which can possess the woman's psyche and hold her in unconsciousness there, by limiting her perception, vision, functioning and creativity ... To heal our relationship with the daimon can have powerful collective impact upon humanity's whole psyche.

Ioho reports that

> on the few occasions I've managed to ignore that presence I've experienced a draining of my energy to the daimon. It is as if that force is so strong that if you don't acknowledge its presence, it will harass you – questioning your actions, instilling doubt, demanding loyalty – to do as it wishes.

Denial of the daimon drains our battery of power. But it is also fear and suspicion of their own power that keeps many women weakly enthralled as well-behaved and eternally-servicing women.

This word 'power' has taken on connotations of might and political manipulation, but woman's power represents her authority, her true creative direction, her passion, and her spiritual vision in true alignment. If a woman chooses to ignore her power, she submits it to a vampiric force which diverts her energy. This force may take the cloak of the daimon but in truth be her projection of the archetypal authority figure whom she invests with her own power, giving it away. The tendency of women to eroticize power and to mate with their projection often helps to aggravate this situation.

Fear is potential power; if fear is indulged it grows monstrous and blocks access to power. Passion is unable to function under the restriction of total control. Being able to let go is the paramount requirement of creativity – because the fluid relinquishing of total control enables creativity to flow.

Unblocking the conduits of power involves looking directly at what most terrifies us, because whatever drains us of power is that which we most fear. This means reassessing the opinions and information of others which we have personally taken to ourselves: are they really true for us, or did we only claim them because they conferred the appearance of authority upon us? Such things block up the conduit of power within us, causing us to ignore our own resources.

The eruption of the masked daimon is like a country rising in revolution: it affects all levels of life. For women who have taken the line of least resistance to life, this can result in considerable soul-fragmentation and power-loss.[41] When this happens, a vacuum occurs and the subject is open to any focalized power which seems to fill the gap or seems strong and ordered. Then the unemergent daimon may show himself in some fearful guises.

If we tell ourselves horror stories and then believe in them, they can manifest in our own lives. The destructive power invoked by Psyche's sisters, the suggestion that we harbour something horrid within us, gibbers from the dark corners of our suspicions. We cannot even ignore the daimonic confrontation by staying at home and refusing to play this seemingly risky game. The daughters of King Minyas refused to join in the wild rites of Dionysos even though they had been sacredly enjoined to do so. They continued to ply their looms while their companions donned leopard skins and carried leaf-girt poles to the mountains. As they sat and told stories to each other as they worked, their looms began to be covered with green, the fabric upon them changed to ivy, threads became tendrils of vine. They shrank back into the dark recesses of the house and began to change into bats – their punishment for avoiding service to the god Dionysos.[54] The effects of ignoring the rites of Dionysos can be compared with the problems of women who ignore the daimon: familiar things take on nightmare appearances, monsters haunt waking hours, the denied wildness becomes rampant. These are all stories of the daimon denied. The mature female versions of the Sleeping Beauty story do not involve a little spindle prick followed by a chaste disenchantment, but a devastating stab in the back followed by very terrible violence.

We saw in Chapters 2 and 3 how the daimon comes to claim each girl and transform her into a woman. This process is endlessly repeated in myths of gods or fairy-lovers who come to take a mortal bride and initiate her into their realm. In our own age, which is largely ignorant of the daimon's role and has thrown off belief in subtle reality, this received folk-tradition is being replaced by horrific new scenarios of vampiric or alien abduction.

The recent reports of abduction by extraterrestrial aliens bear a striking similarity to the traditional reports of abduction by fairies, which are graphically erotic and ecstatic in content and involve a separation from the woman's family and friends. In contrast, the reports about aliens concentrate on clinical 'interference with the genitalia'. In both instances, 'children' are said to result from such unions, or the ova and sperm are harvested, in alien abductee cases. In a society which has an unsophisticated understanding of other realities but which is open to rational scientific explanations, it is possible that the daimonic experience itself might be understood, in both dream and waking reality, as a form of alien interference.

The ghostly, demon lover is becoming wholly captivating to women who find themselves adrift from the wholesome and inspiring daimon. The demon lover has the apparatus and appearance of a conjurer, one who can manipulate appearances and draw upon the illusory veils of the unseen. There is a great desire among women to understand and to explore the dark daimon. He evokes unhealthy fascination – a blend of the forbidden, the erotic, the suppressed, and a seemingly unending supply of magical dynamism.

In his guise as vampire (plate illustration 9), the daimon has always held a particular fascination for women. In Francis Ford Coppola's erotic reworking of Bram Stoker's *Dracula*,[88] the fate of the vampire and his victim are fused together in a symbiotic reincarnation. While the historical 15th-century Dracula is out fighting off the Turkish invaders, his wife Elisabetta receives a false message informing her that he is dead. She commits suicide by plunging into the river below their castle; her dying prayer is: 'May God unite us in heaven.' On his return, Dracula's priests say that his wife's soul is lost because she has committed un-Christian suicide. At this point he renounces God and voluntarily becomes one of the *nosferatu*, the undead, in order to avenge her death with all the powers of darkness.

Over 400 years later, the property agent, Jonathan Harker, travels to Dracula's castle, leaving his fiancée, Mina, behind. Mina has Elisabetta's appearance and some of her memories also, as we see when Dracula travels to England in order to find her, introducing himself as Prince Vlad. As they sit drinking absinthe in the restaurant, he speaks of his country and she continues to describe the landscape. To her, his voice has a dream-like familiarity which comforts her when she is alone. The erotic symbiosis is re-established.

Like any daimon-haunted woman, she is aware of his presence when he is not physically there. It is only after she has married Jonathan that she begins to understand her feelings for her strange friend. He comes to her at night, entering her bed as a green mist, and she awakens to find him in his beautiful form. She asks the important question, 'Who are you?' He replies, 'I am nothing, lifeless, hated and feared. I am death. I am the monster breathing men would kill.' Despite his revelation that he is the same Dracula who has killed her friend, Lucy, Mina still wants to be with him for eternity. But he warns her that, 'You must die to your present life and be reborn to mine.' He bites her neck and cuts his own chest so that she can drink from him, in a blood rite which is both marriage and communion. His words decry his vampiric nature: 'I give you life eternal, everlasting love, the power of the storm and the beauty of the earth.' Dracula and Elisabetta are briefly together on the earth as *nosferatu*.

Dracula and Mina act out the last scene in his castle; at the precise spot where Elisabetta's body lay and Dracula renounced God, Mina lays the body of the wounded Dracula. The redemptive miracle of love works upon him, and he reverts to his once-beautiful appearance. He asks for the peace of death from Mina, who resolutely stabs him through the heart and cuts off his head. Elisabetta's final prayer for union is at last granted.[88]

This powerful film has many instances where it departs from Bram Stoker's original, but James V Hart's screenplay skilfully touches upon the dichotomy of women's negative daimonic fixation. Beneath even the worst female experience, the true gold of the daimon shines; the problem is how to extract the gold through the corrosive overlay which can steal our very life? The film explores the symbiotic intertwining of two beings who need to be together yet who, except for a brief period, are separated on the wrong sides of life and death. Is it possible to leach out the demon lover from the eternal beloved? The film demonstrates that though love conquers all, this struggle is not without sacrifice and suffering.

The curse of the girl who refuses to engage with the daimon is the enchantment of Sleeping Beauty – to receive the prick of the spinning wheel, the spinster's tool, and to fall into a hundred years' sleep from which the traditional release can only be the kiss of the prince.

The curse of the woman who engages with the vampiric daimon is the living death of his fangs, from which there is no relief, only an endless infection of other undying lovers who will infect yet others. Only a stake through the heart and the behead-ing of the vampire can bring the mercy of disenchantment, in a final shedding of blood which releases the soul to its true place.

Though the vampiric daimon does not belong in any physical, human dimension, it continues to prey upon some women, trans-mitting itself down the generations through that most subtle of rivulets: the ancestral blood.

THE VAMPIRIC INHERITANCE

The old sixties slogan, 'life is a sexually-transmitted disease', is no longer very funny as we view the simultaneous advance of genetic theory and Aids. The sobering realization that the way we have lived will affect our children presents a chilling perspective on cause and effect.

The theme of genetic transmission is prominent in our culture, along with the fear that our secret wound will be unmasked and shown to have a long, shaming lineage. Several respondents spoke about the daimonic experience in accents of shame or guilt. Some, like Fiona, pin-pointed a dismaying sense of legacy about the whole business.

> When I ignore the animus, my outer life tends to fall apart. I used to carry it as a secret, proof that there was hereditary insanity in me through my mother and her father. My mother is an awful example of wasted creativity, suppressed by criticism. A friend who recently met my mother described her as 'the most destructive woman she had ever met'.

Fiona challenges the conspiracy of silence with passion.

> No woman should have to go around thinking she's nuts because there's a male voice in her head! I wonder how many women there are who daren't even mention it to someone else? I guess there are even more women who are totally unconscious of their animus, in thrall to him to the extent my mother is, so that she won't even try

to paint, write or draw because she says she can't create something perfect. She is tyrannical, destructive and very lonely. We can whinge about patriarchy for as long as we like but until we're willing to face its representatives and upholders within ourselves, how much can change? Not a lot. Men need to learn about their animas too for permanent and real changes.

Since writing this, Fiona reports changes both in herself and in her mother who has, astonishingly, begun a creative arts course with some relish. Fiona's experience reveals an almost magical disenchanting which I see frequently in my shamanic practice. Like Fiona, by addressing ancestral blockages and difficulties, we too can help reverse tendencies within our own families both *forward and backward* in the generations. This is an important fact to remember when we are dealing with ancestral- or family-related problems that seem entrenched or insuperable.

It is a truism to remark that, 'children unconsciously live out their parents' shadows and often, through resentment, repeat their failures'.[49] The inherited daimon factor is clearly demonstrated when the mother is locked into repressive patterns of control and denial, for then it is likely that her daughter will inherit this tendency and her daimon begin to constellate vampiric elements of the mother's unfulfilled and uncreative life. Some women will be aware of their mother as a spider or vampire who wraps them up and survives by sucking their creative potential. This happens quite unconsciously, as the mother may know of no other form of accessible nurture.

The mother's unlived life may become a skin which surrounds the daughter's perception of her own daimon. The inherited mask of the daimon often shows itself by the prickly protective layer which daughters of betraying or disempowered mothers wear. The daughter will sometimes suffer from the voice of the critic, and will find in herself a contempt for and hostility to women. This syndrome may produce the haggish virago whose harsh tongue speaks the ungarnished truth and who has no faith in her own womanhood.

Inherited ancestral patterns are strongly present in our society, though they are seldom recognized as being multi-generational. The unmothered woman, abandoned at birth, is more likely to become a mother herself at an early age and pass on that experience to her child than a conventionally reared woman. Where supportive role-models are lacking or where interventive protection fails to happen at the crucial time, all human beings revert to understanding their own abusive personal experience as the norm. This is why patterns of abuse, incest, violence and addiction seem to cascade successively from one generation to the next in such hopeless ways.

How do such inherited patterns become established in the first place? Some women experience a sense of helplessness when dealing with the masked or unemergent daimon: this may be compounded by poor job prospects, low self-esteem and identification with the prevailing view of female inferiority. Women in this state battle on, especially if they have children to support. They work themselves into states of fatigue and self-abnegation in order to provide for their children, often simultaneously enduring bullying, abusive or neglectful partnerships. While all this is going on, she has no time to assess who or what she is. When the children are grown, it is another matter. Having poured herself into them, and become empty, exhausted and without self-focus, she may continue to live only for her children and grandchildren in ways which they find irritating.

A woman who is sufficiently self-aware to feel the anger of repressed creativity can be a formidable power for ill, becoming the devourer of her children and exhibiting the classic symptoms of the malevolent witch: hate, envy and destructive rage which scorches anything in its path. One spoiled female vocation is all it takes. Consider then the collective ire, disappointment and repressed creativity of women down the ages and its weight upon women today.

Women's capacity to act with power has been constrained and repressed over many centuries, resulting in manipulation as a mode of controlling power. It is visible as a Machiavellian high art form in women of certain generations and upbringing who can wheedle, twist, torture and win with surpassing ease. Yes, it is one way to get ahead in a world oriented to male needs, but it is also the road to the sorceress. Many families have such a sorceress in their midst: she sits in her web and draws everyone to her via the sticky filaments she has woven under their feet. She exacts terrible revenge on those who seek to thwart her.

Women who have been sexually and violently abused by their fathers or male relatives are usually also part of a generational pattern of abuse. There is a common suspicion among many women that the father has been abusive, whether this is true or not. Something subliminal lurks in dream and memory, shrieking of abuse. This memory may arise in therapy and has been the foundation for 'recovered-memory syndrome'. Putting aside the proven cases, it is also possible that an abusive feeling is experienced because a father has projected his anima upon his daughter. Since the male soul-image of the anima most commonly takes the form of a young girl or innocent woman, even the most careful father might be tempted to project this upon his daughter; she, wishing to please and receive his approbation, might reciprocate in this unconscious projection, taking parts of it to herself. Such projection may indeed feel like rape, though it may actually be an assault upon the *soul* rather than the body.

Rape is motivated by many things – desire to possess, control or punish – but it may also be due to fear of feelings aroused by the anima, so that a man will seek to subdue or destroy it when he finds it reflected in a living woman. The many cases of criminal pursuit or 'stalking' and the serial killing of women by obsessional men would fall into this category. Sexual abuse is so tied up with domination and gratification that a common misconception arises – that women enjoy being raped because they unconsciously desire it or are 'asking for it'. Back in the Middle Ages, Christine de Pizan addressed this problem:

> I am troubled and grieved when men argue that many women want to be raped and that it does not bother them at all to be raped by men even when they verbally protest. It would be hard to believe that such great villainy is actually pleasant for them.[12]

Yet, in the minds and fantasies of many animus-obsessed women, the vampiric raptor strides like Tarquin to the bed of Lucretia. In *Troytown Dances*,[43] Miranda contemplates the Plutonian brother of King Minos, who has appeared as a daimonic figure in her fantasies:

> Who is Sarpedon, of whom no one speaks? What dark deed veils his fame? Sarpedon is the son of Zeus and Europa. Himself the son of rape, of the body's rapture by the Sea-Bull. He has the shaggy black and Plutonian shadow which echoes his father's subterranean deeds. Men deal uneasily with him, transacting their business briskly, never looking long into his soul-wasting eyes. Women flutter round him like moths, drawn to his deep daemonic light. Some catch alight and are carelessly brushed off. Others are transfixed from afar, caught in the deadly beam of his pharos-beacon stare.

Can he help it if his cow-mother's horned womb was gored by the Sea-Bull's frenzy? Can he ever flee the slow-staining bruise of his father's pleasure, the mark of the sea-wrack, weed-green, crab-tormented, which sullies the fair, white outcrop of the jetty? The plum-blue press-marks of his thumbs are seen at the throats of women he has bedded who, urgent for air, have thrashed and rattled like cuttle-fish in his embrace.

Cycles of abuse and self-sabotage are hard to break, but not once they are recognized for what they are. They may be broken by such procedures as shamanic soul-retrieval, whereby the shaman seeks out the spiritual origin of the problem and brings back the soul-part which has fled as a result of abuse.[41] Susanna speaks of her experience with alcoholic lover, Jordan, who shoplifted and drank while driving.

He was also a soul-thief. He took pictures of me without my permission and then hoarded them, refusing to give me the negatives or sometimes even prints. He wanted to possess me to a degree that I thought was inappropriate. He didn't even think I should masturbate alone – all my sexuality should belong to him. When the counsellor we were seeing at the time seemed to think this request reasonable, I went along with it ... my sexuality went underground and years later has not re-emerged.

Later Susanna sought soul-retrieval from a practitioner called Sheila, who brought back Susanna's stolen soul-part with a story which 'she thought came down to me through the female line of my family, a story about the dangers of men'. Susanna confirms the remembrance of 'riding my tricycle outside the house at age four and being on guard because I thought a man would come by in a car, grab me, carry me off and kill me'. Susanna's addiction to 'bad boys' caused her to live her first years as a mother in life-threatening terrain, from which she has now retreated. She has come to realize that much of this recovered story contains 'many of the issues that surface in my personal life, especially the way my daughter was threatened in all of my relationships'.

Soul-retrieval breaks the tape-loop of an inherited story or a traumatic incident, allowing a woman to take up her own story, free of the burden of nightmare or ancestral re-enactment. This is a traditional method analogous to that used by Scheherazade. The Sultan Schariah, incensed by the infidelity of his previous Sultana, has her killed; in insensate reprisal for her act, he resolves to marry a new wife every night and have her strangled at dawn. Scheherazade begs to be his wife and craftily replaces the tape-loop of revenge by telling him stories night after night which she leaves unfinished till the next occasion, for one thousand and one nights. At the end of this time, her stories have erased the trauma which evoked such terrible revenge and brought forth his love and compassion.

The tale of Bluebeard and his wives may stand as a story of women's common inheritance of negative daimonic problems. Bluebeard, a widower many times over, gains a new wife and leaves her in his house. She is given the keys to the whole property but forbidden to enter one room. When she finally succumbs to curiosity and opens that room she finds the blood-stained corpses of Bluebeard's former wives. The key becomes indelibly stained with their blood and the new wife has to confess she has entered the forbidden room: the penalty for her default is a similar death. In most versions, she is saved by the watchfulness of her sister in the high tower above the bloody chamber who announces the arrival of her brothers, who kill Bluebeard.

The fact that the new wife cannot wipe off the blood of that chamber is significant. The task in this story is not just to free the new wife from death but also *to recognize and liberate the souls of former wives* from their hidden tomb: to that end, their blood cries out and cannot be washed from the key. In this story, we should note that Bluebeard *freely gives the key* to his new wife. We also note that, as soon as she enters the chamber, *she sees herself* and her fate in the bodies of the dead wives.

The Jungian couple, Ann and Barry Ulanov, describe Bluebeard as 'the killer animus', but Bluebeard as soul-thief or murderer needs to be released from his insensate cycle of criminality just as much as the animus-haunted woman needs release.

Is this killer animus, this vampire, a malignant daimon that takes hold of generations of women? What will exorcize it? By dealing with such ancestral patterns through forms of exorcism such as meditation, prayer, shamanic soul-retrieval, analysis, or the substitution of a new story, our female ancestors, and we ourselves, can be released. When we step free from the ancestral story, we begin to see that the true daimon is indeed our individual guardian spirit, and we can understand how his guidance can be blurred by collective masks which have been accumulated not only by our own life and upbringing but by those of our foremothers and sisters. We owe it to our children to identify our family story, our own story and the storyline of our daimon as early as possible.

Forgiveness is crucial to such patterns and that can only be given when it is understood quite how generational and inherited are the patterns which follow a family line. The social assumption that the child of a deficient mother will turn out to be flawed derives from a sense of women as intrinsically flawed or deficient. Lifting the burden of blame from our mothers is vitally important. In particular we need to distinguish clearly between our mother as an individual who has to find strategies for survival, and as a woman whose resourcefulness and power has been restricted by patriarchal society for generations. If we disconnect our wounds from those of our mother, she no longer has to be a dumping ground for what doesn't work efficiently in our own life. The reclaiming and embracing of the mother comes about when women welcome the dynamic passion which makes them women. The greater symbol of this reclamation is the rediscovery of and devotion to the Goddess, the Divine Feminine, who is the spiritual treasury of womanhood: a being greater than fear, death and abandonment.

When a woman denies inherited patterns as projections, she is free to engage her own power and access her true daimon. She compassionately helps liberate her female forebears from the bloody chamber, recognizing herself as separate and forgiving her ancestors.

Women continue to be fascinated by the raptor, the invader, the vampire, and the daimon under this guise still features in many popular films (plate illustration 10). In Anne Rice's trilogy, *The Witching Hour*, *Lasher* and *Taltos*, we read about the daimonic spirit, Lasher, who is inherited by a long lineage of women. Lasher is first contacted by a 17th-century Scottish witch and passes, at her death, through her daughter to her female descendants down the ages. In this book, Lasher is no mere daimon, but a spirit of great power whose charisma captivates his female host and whose every whim he grants. This cycle is brought into resolution, though not completion, through the agency of every woman from the Mayfair family with whom Lasher has cohabited: their knowledge, beauty and vital DNA meet in Rowan Mayfair, who learns that she must go beyond crude forms of exorcism, beyond denial of the daimon, but engage her whole being in understanding that the demonic Lasher hides the sublimity of Ashlar, helping to liberate her foremothers from the secret of their blood.

Identification with the stories of vampires and soul-thieves can result in a sense of being stuck, in an inability to proceed, a deadness where there is no way out, where life grinds to a halt – just as time ceases for those who are enchanted within the thornhedge of Sleeping Beauty. In this tale, the enchantment is brought about by the ire of the thirteenth fairy who is purposely left off the guest list. Her curse is for Beauty to be pricked by the pin of a spinning wheel so that she sleeps for a hundred years – a curse that commandeers Beauty's youth and marital prospects, immuring them in impenetrable thorns.

The female self can be restricted by the vampire's bite and by the unappeasable foremothers' curse. The crude stake which is used to transfix the vampire or burn the sorceress cannot bring about our liberation. Escaping the sorceress and outwitting the vampire are not just the stuff of fairy-tale, they are the experience of every human being. Seeking modes of disenchantment from their carefully woven spells, we must find the courage to move by constellating our helpers to rouse our authentic self from slumber, to teach us to differentiate friend from foe.

THE FIRST LABOUR OF PSYCHE: SORTING THE SEEDS

The foremothers who seek release from generations of imprisoning attitudes and behaviour are mirrored in the unappeasable Venus of the Cupid and Psyche story, she who sets seemingly impossible tasks for poor Psyche, who initially greets each of them as cause for suicide. Yet these tasks simultaneously provide vehicles of release and disenchantment for our own condition.

The first of the labours of Psyche is to sort out a confused mixture of seeds into different categories. In daimonic terms this relates to the necessity to distinguish between her projections upon the daimon and the daimon himself. This must also be the task of any woman seeking clarification of her experience. Psyche is helped by the ant, famed for its industrious and organized nature.

Definition and diagnosis of the daimon's presence and action within our lives is very important. Many women have expressed their shock at having defined the daimon as totally other, as alien or horrible. They have looked no further than the masks of the daimon and filed him in the wrong box, thus neglecting or forgetting some vital routes to their authentic selves.

Because the daimon makes his first appearance at the time of a woman's erotic awakening, when her understanding of sexuality is less mature, she may feel shame or guilt at the intensity of the experience, as Pat relates.

> When the daimon is coming into consciousness, especially when arousing sexual and sensual desires, experiences, dreams, etc, I personally thought I must be not OK, almost evil, odd, weird and perverted. It took a lot of courage to be open about it for the first time. It was a relief to know I am normal. I feel because it is hidden and women are isolated in their experience and influenced by religions, the healthy growth and experience of the daimon in the psyche has become corrupted, distorted, malfunctioning to the detriment of individual women on a collective level. It has led to the negative daimon, animus-possession, which is misogynistic, causing a deep collective psychic wound. It can be to the point of seeking the woman's death. Marion Woodman's books *Addicted to Perfection* and *Ravished Bridegroom* have been a great help to me.

The accumulations which barnacle the animus, the projections which film the daimon like so many onion skins, must be removed by identification. Each woman needs to identify herself as distinct from her parents, her job, her friends, her social environment, the guiding institutions that have fostered her upbringing. Very often, a complex constellation made up of these factors will become daimonic masks by which a woman will define herself. We do not have to believe that the curse upon the Lady of Shalott is also our allotted fate; we do not have to weave the projections from the mirror in the tower which surrounds us into our own identity. We do not have to live restricted lives because the walls of our prison give us identity.

Cause, conviction and religion can all become substitutes for self-identification, because they confer an identity of their own. And a woman who grows up with examples of dictatorial or authoritative men can remain in bondage to their spells, to their projected images upon her own daimon. When the feminine self is identified with the masks of masculinity, then we see opinionated, perfectionist, critical behaviour. Female insecurities become plastered over with a facade of aggression, bossiness, do-gooding or manipulative interference.

The patterns set up in youth linger longest in the unclarified daimon. Whatever has been excluded from our self-identity, whatever facets of life-experience have imprinted upon us, will be found as ideas, images, feelings and behaviour patterns in our submerged life. Voyaging through our own intimate experience of men as parents, brothers, friends, partners and colleagues can be a very enlightening process.

> If only we can succeed in splitting the animus up into distinct and separate persons we can deal with him. Then I can kneel and ask a blessing of the priest, befriend the feeble-minded boy, face firmly, but with due respect, the devil and order the mealy-mouthed sycophant out of my house. But woe betide me if I lump them all together, call it the animus, and try to deal with that.[10]

The process of animus deconstruction is part of Jungian analysis.

We need to define who is doing what to whom: an essential ant-like task of differentiation. If the multi-faceted masks of the excluded masculine appear only to confound and confuse us, we need to divide and conquer. Marion Woodman notes, 'When we see ourselves becoming someone we do not want to be, we seldom ask who is seeing us in this way'.[79] We need to ask, 'Whose voice is criticizing, belittling, eroding me?', identify the voice and stop the tape loop which has unwittingly become our tune.

THE SECOND LABOUR OF PSYCHE: REFINING THE FREQUENCY

The second labour of Psyche is to fetch the golden fleece of savage sheep; she succeeds by waiting till the sheep are asleep and collecting their wool from the briars. The most helpful kind of information about our daimon is, likewise, collectable from our dreams, reflections and meditations. We explored this procedure in Chapter 4, where we noted that the reed helps Psyche, the same reed from which the Pan-pipes are made and which represents the voice of the Shepherd of the Flocks, our guardian daimon who advises us. For women who have not done their wool-gathering and scanned their dreams for clues, this voice may speak in the tones of the critic who disempowers us.

The animus is defined by Irene Claremont de Castillejo as 'the total focusing power of a woman whether she was focusing on the outer or the inner world'.[10] The true daimon is a torch-bearer who can send a clarifying beam into the soul of a woman possessed of her authentic self. The daimon wearing the mask of the patriarchal critic sends an interrogatory searchlight that evokes discouragement. The critic also carries a mighty megaphone which bellows conflicting messages in our direction.

Jung associated the animus with the archetype of the Logos or the Eternal Word: 'He is the word, the power to formulate, to analyse, to discriminate between opposites' (*ibid*). The animus then operates as woman's faculty *to separate rather than to unite*, 'which is why, if she is trying to make a relationship as a woman, she had better keep this analytical, separating part of her well out of the situation or he will wreck it with his impersonal, collective character' (*ibid*).

An opinionated kind of fundamentalism can set in wherein a woman mouths personally unexperienced views which her daimon is showing to her. If we accept a piece of daimonic-provided information as our own when, in fact, we have not yet fully understood it as a woman, we may speak 'knowingly and wisely' about something of which we have no experience whatever. Only when this information becomes personally assimilated will it sound authentic to ourselves and others. The way through this interference of our frequency is to utilize humour, especially self-humour. A deadly serious attitude which reverently enshrines the reflections of the critic-mask as holy writ should be seen as a danger signal.

A continual checking of where thoughts and remarks originate may seem tedious or pointless, but it may help women who are struggling to define themselves and their emergent daimons with more immediacy and clarity. Trusting our decisions and understanding their implications are important skills to cultivate, since uninformed decisions radically alter our lives. All decisions must rest with the authentic self *as it manifests at that time*. As we mature, more of the authentic self is revealed and we possess a better basis for judgement but, until that time, we have to clarify our motivations the best way we can.

Fiona reports that in an early appearance of the daimon, he was the Watcher:

languid and Hamlet-like, paralysingly critical of everything I did, said and was. He did nothing but criticize. Although he lived in my head, he felt separate from me. During a transpersonal psychology workshop, I drew him lolling against a tree: someone commented how effeminate he looked, but he was definitely masculine to me.

Both Fiona and Sheila have written about the Judge, Assessor, Critic or Vigilante – the patriarchal figure with the disapproving voice who is but a mask of the daimon which derives from the figures and institutions of male authority. Control is the key feature of Critic-possession; the woman who plays host to it will find it difficult to admit mistakes, and will strive to uphold her public image, despite the crumbling-away inside. An addiction to perfection can derive from the appeasement of daddy, the Church, the social fabric, or other authority figures and institutions.

If the Critic keeps up his bullying assault, a woman can believe herself to be unworthy or unlovable. Instead of seeking her authentic self, she will enter into a new role – that of hag. She will feel herself to be physically deficient or shameful to look at. Truly, the disenchantment of the hag, like that of the masked daimon, must proceed at the same pace, as we shall see in Chapter 8.

The way to deal with the Critic is not to ignore him but to treat him as any other bully. Stand up to judgemental daimons by commanding them to stop bullying and speak the truth. Fiona has been successful in her attempt:

> The Watcher used to criticize my creativity, convincing me that I couldn't draw or paint and that my poetry didn't count as poetry. He's transformed into the Jesuit, a man of God with a sharp critical intellect … he assures me he will assist in bringing out my novel, not by inspiration, but by way of negotiations and examining contracts.

Fiona's novel explores the changing nature of the heroic. Daimonic images of the heroic, creative and empowering quality can help release a woman from the patriarchal and authoritative spell. But, as Fiona is finding out, her novel's main character, the Horseman, is an evolving daimonic image who is quickly putting distance between Fiona and the Critic.

> There are other ways to stand for the truth and for life than to take up arms. The knight behind his visor is blinkered as well as noble; there is a need for all-round vision to come to the point, after the battle – a need for reconciliation. The battle is for him the last resort and it takes courage to find alternatives.

THE THIRD LABOUR OF PSYCHE: FACING FEAR

In order to fight, we must engage the enemy hand at hand. The third labour of Psyche is to bring a jar of water from the sacred stream of the Styx, where even the gods fear to go. Here, the quest for the daimon leads us to the difficult understanding that *life and power are to be found where there is most petrification and fear* in our lives. The eagle is courageous and far-seeing, with a perspective that earth-bound Psyche lacks. From the air it can clearly discern that what humans see as places with distinct boundaries are *all the same country*.

The task of transforming the death-dealing waters of Styx into a life-giving elixir is something few women attempt. They would rather not drink, just in case. They would prefer to stay indoors, draw the curtains and ignore the daimon. Is it then any wonder that the daimon comes to them in increasingly terrifying forms?

What emerges from all the respondents in this book is the fact that the more the daimon is ignored, *the more monstrous and overwhelming he can become*. The point of transformation has to be arrived at with courage and love. Frances notes that her daimon 'gets bigger and more powerful and more demanding the more I ignore him!' When the daimon takes terrifying forms, it is usually a sign that it is trying to get attention and be transformed. A woman who dreamed of a thug with metal teeth at a roadside café, found herself

> screaming at him never to terrorize her like that again. He yelled back that he would keep doing it to get her attention if he couldn't get it any other way.[69]

In this woman's case, the daimon was demanding that she get in touch with her ability to stand up for herself, as well as telling her to clear the channels through to him by giving him access to her own unused powers.

Respondents report numerous dreams about burglars breaking into their houses. Jocelyn tells how 'sometimes in dream I experience males invading my home as burglars'. She sees these as representing 'the patriarchy rather than an intimate figure who's on my side'. Jocelyn writes of how she deals with this:

> I often use the story of Psyche and Eros in which after Psyche's trials, Eros comes to her, seeming to need her just as much as she needs him. Divine love needs human form.

Elizabeth also had

> dreams of my daimon being a burglar breaking into my flat ... his
> breaking through the door frightened me, but once he was in, I felt
> no fear. These dreams came at a time when I had no faith in my
> own ability to sustain a relationship and even doubted whether I
> could love at all. I now know I can, and my fear of relationships
> has diminished a lot. He no longer appears this way.

The creative side of the daimon needs access to the soul and
cannot be left outside the soul-house. But if a woman ignores him,
the knocking becomes more urgent and the imagined form outside even more terrible. However, just as Psyche discovers that her
sisters' tattle about her husband being a devouring snake is completely untrue, so too can the daimon be revealed as the bearer of
love, power and life itself.

I believe that here we can begin to disenchant the demon lover.
Pat relates two dreams about her experience with the negative
daimon and how she has coped with it.

> In 1986 I had a dream of Dracula: I was in my parents' house, only
> the stairs were back to front. I became aware of Dracula embrac-
> ing me and trying to bite my neck. It was so hard to fight as it was
> utterly sensual and sexual. I finally called out to archangel St
> Michael to help. He didn't appear but I heard a roaring sound and
> saw daylight coming through the front door. Dracula backed off
> me towards the cupboard under the stairs, which in the dream had
> steps down into a cellar. There was a set of cast-iron fire imple-
> ments on a stand by the door. I took the poker and plunged it into
> Dracula's heart. Blood came and my right hand was caught stuck
> at the wound. I finally managed to pull my hand free but Dracula's
> blood was on my thumb, and he was dead.

Here Pat defeats Dracula by a fusion of her own action and the
coming daylight which saps his power. In the second dream, she
is aided by a more positive daimonic figure.

> I have a long-haired Peruvian man who comes in a number of
> dreams. I'm running with a female colleague from work along a
> chalky road and we keep stopping to put masks in the ground and
> trees to fool our pursuers. We run under a tunnel in a hill and
> emerge into an amazing place – high in the mountains, with green
> foliage and a clear natural river. The air is cool, crystal clear and
> sunny. The other woman is calling me to do a mask with her. I am
> staring in wonder at the scene when I notice this Indian man,

dressed in rough woven shirt and trousers. He emerges on my left and doesn't speak or acknowledge me. He walks to a bridge wider than the river and I follow him across to the other side. He walks along the bank, which has rich dark wet soil. He kneels and bathes his face in the river, drinking. There is reverence in his act. I dither, but know I must do the same. I bathe my face and wake up.

I am floating in darkness and I can't see him, but he comes from my left side. I see a serpent and he tells me to take care. Then I'm underneath the serpent. It breathes into my face and I feel its hot breath and float on, with the Indian telling me not to rush and try to get to know the serpent – it can blow me apart.

This is good advice. Understanding and respecting our power is essential in any enterprise. Pat's recurrent life-scenario has been about disempowerment and the consequent depression which this evokes. For her to learn to swim with the serpent of her power in this dream-enclave of numinous safety, under the tender guardianship of her healing daimon, is to learn again how she can operate in the different currents of life. She has also learned cunning and concealment to throw off things which entangle her – she *lays masks in a false trail*, to put them off her scent.

The fear of being blown apart by our power can happen when passion builds up and finds no outlet. Breakdown may well occur unless the daimonic regulator can help with that accumulation within us. In seeking to resolve an inappropriate attraction to her therapist, Valerie Harms dialogued with her inner lover who said:

> You can be forceful in word and feeling. You can release it there. Just like in orgasms. Bring your animal and mind together. Don't keep them so far apart. Be in that sexual strength. It's power, vitality. It's yours. You are really trying to deny it instead of being it. Be as energetic as you feel. Don't be so polite.[25]

This dialogue enabled Valerie to experience a great release of pent-up power, re-establishing her self-worth. Female politeness is no ally in this work: only our direct and determined mother-wit gets us out of these scrapes. In the film *Aliens*, Sigourney Weaver as Ripley doesn't politely ask the aliens to go away: she deals with them forthrightly!

The daimon, cleared of the encrustations of the fearful masculine, urges us to rip off the masks of terror and get to what lies beneath. Denial of the daimon dams up the natural pathway of woman's power. By ignoring her power, she sinks deeper into a sea of unconsciousness, unable to define what is going on. Her daimon will likewise blur and distort, sometimes to monstrous forms and sizes. She will live perpetually under the shadow of fear, fear of the unexpressed. Living on the level of instinctual survival means never being able to become one authentic self. Replacing fear with power enables the last labour.

THE FOURTH LABOUR OF PSYCHE: RECLAIMING OURSELVES

The fourth labour of Psyche is to bring back a day's worth of Proserpine's beauty. In the depths of our despair and confusion, the way through this labour is to remain true to our authentic self and to respect the reality of our own symbolic sacred landscape without giving our power away to it. In this labour, Psyche's ally becomes the Tower. Interestingly, and encouragingly, we note that the Tower most often appears in daimonic myth as the place of the princess's imprisonment and from which she seeks rescue. Just as Bluebeard gives all his keys to his wife and Venus's cruel tasks reveal the pathways to freedom, so the Tower instructs Psyche. In the same way, the fearfully masked daimon dares us to unmask him.

This labour appears to be about the reclamation of our own image from the underworld, while on the surface it seems to be about taking back our own beauty and valuing it for itself, rather than for the projections put upon female beauty. Though it includes elements of this reclamation, this labour is indisputably related to the second half of Persephone's story. The same Persephone who is captured by Hades and swept off to the underworld as an innocent girl, is restored briefly to her mother Demeter but returns to the underworld, becoming its queen, ruling it with Hades. She then reaps a secret harvest of joy in the subterranean realm, unseen by mortal eyes, but this part of her story is rarely told. Venus sends Psyche to steal that secret.

The girl who is swept into the initiation of sexual arousal by her daimon makes a descent into deep places. She enters the dance of relationships in an unconscious way, still unable to clarify her daimon. When that girl becomes a woman and matures, she consciously begins to learn how to dance with the daimon, as well as to conduct her human relationships with more confidence. The secret of Persephone's success is the beauty of the Queen of the Underworld – a secret that women who have been too terrified to go there would kill to possess!

It is during this last labour that Psyche falls into a stupefying slumber. How many quests grind to a halt in the selfsame way? Just as the immortal draught is within grasp, Gilgamesh falls asleep. Just as the Grail procession circulates, Perceval is struck dumb and forgets to ask the all-important question. Just as Christ succumbs to the very human fear of death, the disciples fall asleep.

Psyche's sleep arises when her innate self-interest overcomes her and she looks inside the box – thinking, perhaps, to take just a little of that beauty for her own use, to please her lover! She succumbs to the old pattern of accepting the projections, opinions and beauty of someone else to attract her man. But the secret of Persephone's beauty, her experience of Hades, cannot be shared, not even by Venus. Twice, Psyche is instructed not to look. The first time, she is forbidden to view her daimon but to trust him implicitly. The second time, she is forbidden to look into the box of the Queen of the Underworld who, alone of all women, has been into the depths of Hades and returned.

Those for whom the task has been too gruelling, may lose heart or fall into despair and self-blame at this point. But all who recognize the problematic daimon/animus in their own lives should take heart and not blame themselves in any way. Learning from personal experience is often painful, self-revelatory and embarrassing; it may initially feel like an admission of failure to face the reality of a relationship founded upon projection or to discover that what you thought was one of your own personal attributes is in fact a quality you have unthinkingly taken to yourself.

When we become aware of problems, habits or ingrained patterns we are half-way to the solution, and able to entertain the possibility of change and even transformation. True definition or diagnosis of a problem is a great relief but it can also be a shield or mask. The ability to redefine ourselves rather than accept the labels of others is of paramount importance. Especially, we must be wary of identifying *ourselves* with the problem: it is not ourselves – it is *part of one phase of our life*, no more. Rather than describing ourselves by labels we have adopted – alcoholic, fat, shy, unemployed – let us look into our own experience of deep daimonic rapture and bring up a box of beauty from our authentic self.

Keeping a sense of self, despite all the projections which get sucked into our body-field like so much static dust, requires a frequent self-clarification of motive and a good sense of boundaries. When something or someone becomes invasive of our soul boundary we must act.

Taking off and denying the projections which others have conferred on us – and which we have unconsciously accepted – requires great skill, patience and humility. Many of the masks are actually attractive to us, but they do not truly represent the authentic self. An engulfing sleep will ensue if we attempt to be anyone else but our own self, if we seek to steer by another's solution.

'She has a genius for disaster', we say of an unfortunate friend who always seems in a muddle, little knowing that the *genius* (pronounced gay-neus) is but the Latin name for the daimon. Many of us are born with a difficult genius or daimon whose qualities may manifest through our personality in their more negative aspects: thus, a gift for communication and discourse may express itself as a capacity for gossip, while a gift for perceiving and imparting justice may manifest as a tendency to be overly-critical or tactless. The nature of our personal daimon is related to the nature of our soul – but we do not have to continue on this level; we can seek our most creative mode, which is our daimon's gift.

If we are able to identify our soul's gift, which is on the same frequency as that of our daimon, we can begin to work co-operatively with both and begin the work of transforming our projections upon the daimon and thus transforming him from beast to beloved friend. If we are able to bring forth our unemergent daimon by acknowledging our powerful gift, we will begin to be true to ourselves.

Dealing with each of the daimon's appearances can only be done if we are true to our self, without acting a part, without projecting our inadequacies upon each facet. The basic rule of thumb is to use our common sense. Just as we would not tolerate being beaten or abused in our everyday lives, so we do not have to abase ourselves as victims to the unclarified daimon. We have to learn to exercise our street-wise mother-wit to see the daimon without the constellating shadows which cloud him.

The mighty shadow of the animus/daimon increases when we attempt to cast light upon it. We may be seized with the initial horror of Persephone as we gaze upon the King of the Underworld, knowing that his name is Hades, a name also meaning 'the infernal region'. We have been told that he is the guardian of hell and, like a prototype of the Demon King, he leaps out and scares us to death. Yet, as we hold steady, returning for a deeper experience, we learn that he has another title. He is 'Plutos' or 'wealthy'. Out of our sojourn in the underworld comes a new experience – a realization that we ourselves are treasuries of resource, that we are indeed beautiful in his eyes. We grow in the wisdom that to be fearful of our riches is to neglect our power.

Psyche is awakened from her stupor by the prick of Cupid's arrow and taken to the upperworld where she receives immortal status – like Sleeping Beauty who is kissed awake by the Prince, after her hundred years' sleep, to receive the status of Queen. Such solutions do not please modern women – they find them trite, passive and unsatisfactory. Something remains deeply unresolved. The reason for this is that many myths and stories deal only with the less mature phase of female life. We do not have a fund of stories which lead us into the mature phase and illuminate it, which is why contemporary women's rediscovery of the daimon is so important.

Why does the daimon appear in unhelpful and threatening ways? If he is truly an ally, why does this happen? We know that it is only our truest friends, those who are not afraid of what we will think of them, who can point out our unbalanced behaviour. Barbara Hannah suggests that 'when the animus interferes in our daily life, it is usually in a place where we have not given the matter our fullest conscious consideration, particularly where we fail in the realm of feeling'.[22]

To work with the daimon, we need to trust the information that comes from our dreams, poems and visions in order to assess what is happening more clearly. We can only do this *by the light of our authentic selves*. If we hold up such information to the yardstick of someone else's theory or findings, we may lose sight of what is most powerful and important to us personally. Learning to trust the unassuming allies – the ant, the reed, the eagle and the tower (all vehicles of the gods) – Psyche is able to deal with 'the tasks of Venus' which face every woman who longs to be free of projective tangles.

Working interactively with the sacred and imaginal dimension, I have seen terrible fear of self-delusion in many forms in students. But self-delusion is perpetuated by unclear definition, by belief in other people's explanations, or by unwillingness to face up to personal reality. Sometimes self-delusion flourishes because of bad labelling.

Are the negative masks of the daimon caused by such bad labelling? Are his fearful shapes our own problems in relief? Sometimes it is not the daimon that is the cause of the problem, but 'the woman who is not using the animus creatively, who is at his mercy for he *must* throw his light somewhere'.[10]

Facing the unknown calls for courage and an understanding patience – how do we uncover/transform the daimon before it transfixes us with a petrifying glare? Around which bend of the labyrinth will the Minotaur be lurking? On which moonlit night will the vampire come to call? The fears of many women clamour. It is only when our stories are told and compared that we will realize that, in seeking to clarify the true daimon, modern women are the heroines who find their own self, their power and passion.

Below are some suggested approaches to the difficult encounters which we have as a result of the daimon. Like Persephone's box of beauty, these may not be your own resourceful solutions, and there may be others that have not occurred to me. Engage with those that help you.

- Re-establish human relationships; cease to be isolated from sensible friends who can provide reality checks and support.
- Seek proper soul-nurture which encourages you.
- Distinguish between daimon and human lover.
- Acknowledge and seek the daimon as a true voice, differentiating him from the masks you have given him.
- Acknowledge and use your personal power.
- Re-evaluate your innate qualities and differentiate these from qualities which have been projected upon you or which you have unconsciously accepted as yours.
- Treat fearful dreams and daimonic appearances as signposts which point to things you have been ignoring.
- Live, make decisions and find motivation from within your authentic self, rather than from other people's territory.
- If you cannot cope alone, *ask for help* from the best qualified professionals.

We need humility to disentangle our muddles, stamina to check and recheck the findings of our symbolic sacred landscape, courage to undergo the searchings of our deep soul-hurts and, most of all, patience to sustain this quest for the authentic self and the inspiring daimon.

The many patient and painstaking women of folk-story have all been there before us. Patient Griselda, the maiden who serves seven years in order to release her daimon in the *Black Bull of Norroway*, and the other resourceful heroines who bide their time and take their chance, all prefigure the endurance and patience of women awaiting the transformation of the daimon and, ultimately, the masculine itself. But it is important to realize that female patience *without love* is not cosmically sustainable. To invoke such patience is to lose soul. Love alone is the key.

This process will not be short. The route will be long and winding but, once begun, a great sense of vitality will return, along with a better respect for our female self. In Psyche and Beauty we see women who are courageous enough to follow their will and desire, to see through the transformation process. Because they recognize the distinguishing mark of the true lover beneath the fearful image, they don't get hooked into the addictive, negative daimon. They have taken the vow of love, as many women do, and are able to remain in often untenable partnerships because they are in love with Love – and it is to that Love and integrity they remain faithful, not to the partner.

Lairdearg speaks to all women:

> For me the daimon is a personal force or energy which emerges at puberty and dares us to ignore him. He is a sexual partner, but has a profound effect also on the emotions, mind and spirit. If he is not honoured, integrated, acknowledged, he can run wild or rebel against us – and almost worse, *he can be chained up and hidden in our darkest dungeons* – but beware if he breaks free! We can project all kinds of faces and personae upon him but he is a raw force in his own right and if we accept him and work with him, he makes us complete. The daimon is a force, a power, and can manifest as anything or wear any shape we give him.

We turn now from our exploration of the daimon as a will-o'-the-wisp to explore his capacity as a true torchbearer. The daimonic experience is not solely about traumatic problems based on distorted male images or thwarted female expectations. It is also inspiring, numinous and creative. That which we have experienced as demonic also has its angelic mode. Between these two paths many of us still walk.

I am deeply grateful to those respondents who were brave enough to expose their moments of vulnerability in this chapter; their insights may help women who are still at painful thresholds of self-discovery. Many of the respondents have since successfully emerged from their pain and confusion to find the peace and power to continue their lives. Others are still moving through this meteorological tunnel of emotion, with trust and determination to combat the fear and paralysis which still surge over them. As our experience continually evolves and clarifies, let us be assured that none of us is alone or uncompanioned on this difficult quest.

Questions

1 What story are you telling (against) yourself that no longer needs to be told?
2 Of what are you most afraid? Where lies the power for you in this fear?

Actions

If your daimon appears in fearsome or threatening forms, challenge him and ask 'what are you trying to tell me?' Also request that he show himself as he really is. (You may find that this is dependent upon some action or change to your current attitudes.)

Reflections

Reflect upon the following:
- Wounds can become conduits of wholeness and healing.
- Rilke's suggestion that 'perhaps everything terrible is, in its deepest being, something helpless that wants help from us'.[64]
- The meaning of this 14th-century prayer with respect to your daimon: 'Make me ready to receive you; and when you are received, speak for me to yourself and hearken to yourself on my behalf'.[69]

CHAPTER 6

Touch of the Soul-keeper

The soul is the place of presences and meetings, it has a nature: whether betrothed or adulterous, it is the communion with one's 'other'.

Paul Evdokimov, *La Femme et Le Salut du Monde*

ANGELS AND ARCHETYPES

The daimon has not always been demonized: he has also been viewed as god, spirit or angel. In Plato's *Symposium*, the Mantinean priestess, Diotima, says that daimons are

> the envoys and interpreters that ply between heaven and earth, flying upward with our worship and our prayers and descending with the heavenly answers and commandments, and since they are between the two estates they weld both sides together and merge them into one great whole ... The divine will not mingle directly with the human, and it is only through the mediation of the spirit world that man can have any intercourse, whether waking or sleeping, with the gods'.[56]

The classical *daimones* are appointed to each human being in order to mediate between mortal and immortal. Each human being was understood to have a particular guiding spirit. Among the Romans, this spirit was called the *genius* (pronounced gay-neus). Recognizing the daimon or genius of a person was the key to understanding that person's nature. After the institution of Christianity, the daimon and genius were spurned as pagan concepts, yet even Christians could not ignore the idea of a powerful companion spirit and recognized it in the guardian angel. Assigned to each soul, the guardian angel offered the same inspiration, support and help as the daimon. Since the Middle Ages, other ideas have added weight to this view.

How we view daimons today is coloured by the inheritance of historical viewpoints. In this potted 'history of the spirits', the last three viewpoints are all concurrently upheld by different individuals and institutions in our society.

- *The Ancient World* Daimons are intermediary spirits connecting humankind and the divine.
- *The Medieval World* All spirits are of the devil; daimons are demons.
- *The Rational World* Spirits? What spirits? There are no such things as spirits!
- *The Modern World* The spirits are really psychological parts of ourselves.

In recent times we have ignored the ancient spiritual role of the daimon. As we saw in Chapter 5, the daimon is relegated to psychological status only and is often seen as the source of many ills and inconveniences. By honouring the daimon as a mediator or messenger of the spiritual dimension, we can restore a pathway to our own female soul.

Spirit, the Divine, is critically important, however we perceive it, since it carries the soul's image of wholeness. The Divine may be seen as a single figure combining both sexual metaphors, or a pair of Divine partners, or as an animating principle present within all life.[48] Spirit is universally perceived as transcending gender, yet human beings in every culture and in every age have clothed Spirit in anthropomorphic and genderial image.

Because we have neglected to map or relate to subtle reality in our society, the conventional response to it is either the medieval or rational model above. Spirit and religion have been conflated because our culture has a deep-seated distrust inculcated by centuries of religious control over belief: we have been told that only authorized spirits are to be trusted. We have all suffered from the imposition of religious ideologies upon our lives, which has cramped our souls. As a result, the reality of Spirit and spirits is no longer commonplace understanding in our largely secularized society.

But human beings require mythic stories and symbolic landscapes. Although we may be alienated from orthodox religions, we do not cease to respond in spiritual ways.[36] This is especially so in a world where global perspective and planetary survival are on the agenda of all life-forms on Earth. The search for the soul and for appropriate spiritual frameworks is undertaken at a time when the earth's own body is threatened. Where society is full of dissolution and disintegration, a corresponding yearning for wholeness arises on every side. Spirit must be urgently addressed in a world which has devalued and ignored it, for only when the *spiritual* cause of problems and difficulties is addressed can real healing take place.

Yet for many people, the spiritual realm is real because they experience it in daily, domestic ways. But the lack of a precise, sophisticated language to talk about this experience and the absence of a socially-supportive culture in which to talk about it without ridicule keep many from comment. Psychology has its own language to discuss interior states of being, but this is not a satisfactory substitute for precise, spiritual terminology. The sense that the soul is accompanied by a guardian spirit remains consistent in popular, if not always socially-accepted, belief. Physical and subtle realities mix uneasily in our times, so by what criteria can we speak?

Each human being is born in a biologically male or female body which, due to sexual orientation, upbringing and education, operates within a mesh of ideas which define personality, desires and gender values. These vary from culture to culture. The body is the seat of physical life and the primary receptor of physical reality – the created matter we can see, hear, taste, smell and touch.

Each human being is also born possessing a soul, the integral animating part of us, which associates with the biological body during life and which, say many spiritualities, continues after bodily death. The soul is often mysterious to us, but it is the seat of spiritual life and the primary receptor of subtle reality – the unseen counterpart of physical reality which is no less real and which we apprehend through our subtle senses, through dreams, meditations, visions and everyday mystical experience.

Since classical times, the soul and the human relationship to the Divine have been described in feminine terms, most often by men to whom the contrasexual image is both attractive and symbolically relevant. For the last two thousand years the Divine has correspondingly been defined in masculine terminology and images which have 'made it more difficult for woman than for man to recognize her individual spirit, for it was always projected, in its positive aspect, into the prevailing religion'.[22] In   the same work, Barbara Hannah postulates that 'this may be one of the many reasons why woman realized the existence of her male counterpart so many centuries later than man'(*ibid*).

Just as there is no social context to speak of spiritual experience, so there has been no context in which women might discuss the work of the daimon within their souls. One of the major revelations when investigating women's daimonic relationships is how very spiritual women's lives are.

Many women may not necessarily associate their own daimonic experience with any spiritual or religious adherence, or their daimon with any specific deities, but they will respond to qualities of the ideal masculine or to male figures in the entertainment world and other fields. They will certainly experience the kind of strong emotion, enduring love and sense of spiritual nurture around these subjects which are normally identifiable as spiritual experience.

We all need a spiritual life to provide soul-nurture – not a religion necessarily, but 'a way of spirit', defined by our own guardian spirit, which is the messenger or angel linking us with the Divine. When I asked respondents about the role of the daimon in their spiritual lives, I received overwhelming response indicating that the daimon kept open the spiritual gates. Ioho responded:

> He is my teacher, my father, my priest, my God and my lover. He is everything. My spiritual life is still my prime motivation to continue, to live at all. By showing me the ways of beauty and ecstasy, he inspires me to live, yet at the same time, he also teaches me to flow, to dance with the breeze and not to fight. One Feather has taught me more than anyone ever could have. He has a humility that has always revealed my every trick and egotistic twitch.

Jocelyn writes:

> He is a continual positive presence, helping me to love myself and the world more and more. He is needed most when I'm loving myself and others least.

Janet's daimon is

> at the centre of it, representing to me the union of opposites, the gentle bridge that joins the here and hereafter, the worlds of form and spirit. My spirituality rises from my depths, from the myriad

of beings, male and female, who guide me on my path. My guide, Tehuti, is most certainly the moving spiritual force in my life. Every day I spend time with him in vision or dream and cannot imagine life without him. I've come to look forward to our talks, his lessons, our discussions about things that might trouble me.

Melissa meets him 'in my inner temple in daily meditation and in the evening to reassess what happened to me during the day'.

For myself, the daimon has always been the one who conducts me through the mysteries of the spiritual world. Importantly, he is a servant dedicated to the Goddess and it is this cross-polarity which gives me strength of hope and vision, for it blends the Divine Masculine and Feminine for me. I can also see in my childhood figure of Sysgryn, a faint echo of the formless and chaotic creative energy of the Goddess and her uncompromising catabolic quality, which cannot abide stasis but sees everything in terms of birth, growth, life and decay as matter and soul are endlessly recycled. Through the agency of my daimon, I have access to this creative cycle which irrigates my spiritual life from the mountains to the seas.

For Lairdearg he is a 'guide, teacher, companion, friend and lover'. For Lauren:

> his role is that of inspirer and gentle reminder of priorities. He appears more or less daily as I strive to strength my spiritual practice. He will make crisis appearances usually when I focus too much on one aspect of my life and become imbalanced.

For women who walk in darkness and despair, he is a true guide. For Suzanne, he has been

> my lifeline when I'm in despair. If I'm on the edge of an emotional cliff, he holds me and prevents me from falling as surely as if he were there.

Pat is aware of his role in

> awakening me to who I am, reconnecting me to my soul-guide and guardian through the Underworld Journey I've been on to reclaim my self/my soul.

She experiences spiritual ecstasy after the

> deep cathartic release of pain and despair when I come to a state of experiencing the Beloved. It is like being consumed within, ecstatic beyond prose.

Many respondents reported how important both the daimon and the Goddess were to them. Although theologians tell us that the Divine is neither male nor female, the truth remains that the accepted supremacy of the Divine Masculine has had a marked effect upon our world. We always hear about the avenging Jehovah, never about the creative Sophia. Fearful, patriarchal images of gods still hold sway. And although the Divine Feminine has been, and continues to be venerated in African, Hindu and Western cultures, few institutions and people in the mainstream of life have the ability to recognize or accept even the concept of a Goddess, discounting her as a modern invention or a pagan irrelevance. Many women who have sought to reclaim their femininity, from the divine levels downwards, have purposely avoided accessing any male images of the Divine.

But we cannot exist without the dance of the opposites, whether it be within the human arena or in the polarities of the Divine. Positive, supportive and inspiring aspects of the Divine Masculine clamoured to be acknowledged in the respondents' reports. Some of those who inspired and who came closest to the innate genius of the respondents' daimons are mentioned here.

Diana is attracted by the image of power tempered by wisdom, especially as expressed in the mythology of Northern Europe. She listed Odin, Hokmah, the Wise Old Man of Jungian theory, Gandalf, Obi-Wan Kenobi, Amergin, Merlin and Coyote as prime images of power and wisdom. Frances acknowledges Mercury, Hades, Apollo, Dionysos and Herne, Loki, Puck, Thoth, Anubis and Osiris. Melissa honours, 'Hermes, messenger of the gods and Guide of Souls: he evokes wisdom through experience, daring, commitment to the Great Work, the giving of the self projected into all worlds'.

Images of the hidden, vulnerable or wounded Divine Masculine helped many women. Pat honours the transformative powers of

the Lord of the Underworld, the Horned God, Pluto or Dionysos. I relate these archetypes to initiators into my earthly sexual ecstatic experience of being a woman.

The patriarchal and demonic side of her daimonic experience has been revealed by Dracula and Bluebeard. Sheila sees her daimon as

a combination of Merlin as guide, Blaise as teacher and Hephaistos, the wounded yet creative one. The Merlin/Blaise combination relates to my long journey towards understanding the mysteries of life and death, whilst Hephaistos seems to reflect my wounding and the healing inherent in the creative life.

Allegra mentions Chiron, 'because of his wounds'.

I have found the controlled strength, authority and vigour of the Dark Age King Arthur a great inspiration, in common with many women who have been drawn to the archetype of courageous strength. Another inspiration is the Irish God of the Sea and the Otherworld, Manannan, who appears to me as an audacious, sea-cunning mariner and old man of the sea like Odysseus, who comes as the Thief of Night, evoking sexual playfulness in me. Ioho speaks of

> the incredible figures in the Indian stories who teach us both in history and in myth. They teach us both of fighting and of peace, of pride and determination and also of surrender, grief and the beauty of creation.

Lauren says that her daimon

> most closely accords with St Francis in essence: his love of spirit and joy, coupled with respect for all other creatures, is the direction in which I find myself led by my daimon. St Francis is the most androgynous of the three images he takes.

Images of the daimon often appear in sexually unattainable or non-corporeal forms as androgynes, castrati or angels. At the same time, they may also appear as divine bridegrooms. Angels are currently much in vogue, possibly because they exemplify the daimonic role of soul-guardian in socially-acceptable forms.

The 'knowledge and conversation of the holy guardian angel' was the goal of the medieval ceremonial magician who sought an alchemical fusion of microcosm with macrocosm, between earthly and heavenly realms of the universe.[48] In effect, this courting of the holy guardian angel sought the attainment of soul-to-soul communication with one's daimon. Jung continually stressed the importance of the union of the self with the contrasexual image as a model of alchemical wholeness.

Suzanne has written of her angelic daimon who comes to support her through a painful illness:

> he arrives barefoot, clad only in a pair of blue jeans – large and composed of many shades of grey from silver to charcoal. I am enveloped in these wings completely and feel very small, but very

safe … On bad nights, I've asked him to fly away with me and not return me to another painful day, but he says he is not the 'angel of death', and every day I have to leave the shelter of those lovely, soft wings and face up to life.

Although the androgyne or angel occurs as an important archetype of woman's daimon, one particular daimonic form emerged among all nationalities of the respondents I approached.

THE GREEN GOD

Throughout the world, green- or blue-skinned gods, with or without animal characteristics, make their appearance. We think of the green Egyptian god Osiris, or the prophet Elijah, who is venerated as the Green Khidr throughout the Arab world; and of the blue-skinned Hindu gods, the Lord of Love, Krishna – avatar of Vishnu the Preserver – and Shiva, the Ecstatic Destroyer. Osiris is killed and his body scattered in pieces, yet he returns. Elijah does not suffer mortal death, but ascends to heaven in order to visit the world again. Krishna has his three phases of descent, darkness and ascent. Shiva rules, rejoices and delights as well as destroying, and is venerated as a god of fertility. The verdant or blue colorations of these gods link them to seasonal cycles of vegetation at one extreme and to cycles of spiritual regeneration at the other.

In the West, these same qualities of renewal and transformation are present in the native deities of Europe. In the North we find the Green Man, Cernunnos, the Master of the Forest, the Lord of the Animals – he goes by many names. He most often appears in male shape but with elements of both green and animal life about him: Cernunnos has stag's antlers, the Green Man often comes swathed with leaves or his skin has the texture of bark (*see* plate illustration 11). In the south of Europe he is more often seen as Pan or Dionysos. Respondents have written about this archetype with loving fervour and respect.

Elizabeth speaks of her daimon as

an expression of god, a fusion of Pan and Dionysos. He helps me to feel passionately, live freely and wildly, see through logic and use my intuition. He is the fire that drives me in ritual and appears in others when they invoke a goddess into me during a ritual. I have gone from honouring and working with only goddesses to a more balanced relationship where goddess and god are equal for me. This has brought about my initiation into the Craft. It is his wisdom which has guided me this way ... Pan and Dionysos are wild expansive, breaking through inhibitions. I had many very destructive inhibitions and fears which harmed my life for many years. It is only through a maturing relationship with them that I overcame these. They appeared in forms of anorexia, fear of sex and relationships, fear of joy and yet an overwhelming need and desire for it. I suffered severe depressive episodes as a result of suppressing my need for joy and he has helped me overcome this.

Ioho speaks of her many other guides:

both male, female, human, divine and animalian. When my teachers present themselves as male they always come to me as the old man, the sage or Druid. There is absolute respect. Perhaps here is the father, for I listen, captivated, taking in every word and action with absolute trust. My Lord of the Wood teaches me in ways which are harsher, more shocking to the system. He thwacks my consciousness into opening a little more, riding through the night with howling wolves, rising up out of nowhere with a terrifying rush of energy, leading me out into the forest to experience what I could never have conceived of. In the traditions of this land, my archetype is perhaps closest to the Green Man, the god Pan is very strong with me, flighty and yet with a powerful brute force. They inspire within me the fullest expression of my soul, my anima, of the power of the Goddess within me.

Fiona has struggled long with the Patriarch and Critic masks, but she has turned to a later image, that of the Horseman, who is warmer, much more loving:

His deity is Pan; he has told me, 'Honour Pan more than you do because you need to remember the push-pull of positive and negative charges that manifests as life.'

My own devotion is to the antlered god, Cernunnos, who is like Pasupati or the Master of Animals, a frequency of Shiva. He represents the daimon as a fusion of man and animal awakening and stimulating the creative wildness in me as in the universe.

The Green Man, like Shiva and Dionysos, comes not only to liberate women, but to dance in the souls of all human beings who would seek freedom. Freedom is not anarchy. It is freedom to express the deepest part of the soul, rather than a shallow indulgence. The green and animal energy of this liberation is significant since human beings are kin to animals as well as to the green world. After that realization, we live in a more alert and primal condition.

Interestingly, the Green God is embraced by the men's movement as its especial deity of male liberation. He is one of the oldest deities to have been continuously venerated in the Western world, beloved of those spiritually engaged in the primal roots of their culture. Information about the Green One comes not from a written tradition, but from folk tradition, where he is venerated in nature by those who live close to the land. If we wish to investigate a received myth, we must turn to one of the ancient deities, like the figure of Dionysos.

Dionysos 'personifies and dramatizes an energy embedded deeply with our human nature' – the freedom which comes from the initiation of passion in personal experience.[66] He inspires his friends, but those who resist he renders 'batty', literally – the daughters of Minyas spurned the rites of Dionysos and preferred to remain safely at home, for which he turned them into bats.

Dionysos, the god of passion, intoxication and ecstasy, brings the elevation of joy as well as the catharsis of sorrow and the healing forgetfulness of sleep. Women especially are called to his rites, for he knows their gift of being true to love causes them to act from their authentic selves. He endows them with divine inspiration – not to be confused with the self-administered distraction of drugs.

Dionysos overturns the old religious order of the Greeks in which the worshipper does something for the deity in order that the deity might render some good service in return. Rather, he calls upon his initiates to experience *deity within themselves*, to so fill themselves with divine ecstasy that the soul follows its authentic path and avoids behaviour that is alien to its nature. In short, Dionysos leads his initiates to enthusiastically embrace their daimon and the vocational gifts they were born with.

The entry of such a god into the female soul is often rapturous and ecstatic. It is also charged with danger if the way to the soul is blocked by egocentric patterns of control. Uncontrolled ecstasy is terrifying to experience, for one stands at the nexus point of creation and destruction in such a moment. The initiation of Dionysos has sometimes been misunderstood as a descent into wanton abandonment; but it is, rather, the release of the soul into the ground of its true nature.

Dionysos' female followers, the Maenads, were seized by divine frenzy to rush into the wild places of nature, performing ecstatic dances. None of the many writers on the subject of the animus has mentioned dance or movement in connection with the daimon, although many respondents noted this as significant to their daimonic experience. Dance is a non-verbal way of evoking and understanding the daimon. It was dance that was the inspiring source of the Maenads' ecstasy, not wine. I find this personally fascinating, especially at this time when substances are being used in addictive and anxiety-appeasing ways. Dance remains a primal doorway for ecstatic and divine entrance to the soul. Without words or theologies, it heralds the entrance of the gods more quickly and surely than any substance. Trance-dancing is used in many traditional cultures for this very function.

As one of the accessible sources of ecstasy and divine communion, dancing can also be one of the great initiatory doorways of the daimon, although it should be said that dancing while entranced requires the help of vigilant guardians to ensure the safety of the dancer.[3] The dance of the devotee and her daimon is not like formal round or pair dances: it is freeform, ecstatic and inspiring.

Moyra discusses the relevance of motion to her daimonic relationship, noting that

> he is less present when I'm still. When I walk by myself, and I often purposely go out late at night to be alone, he arrives immediately, and we walk for miles, discussing many things. When I dance, especially in a big space outdoors, he enters my body in ecstatic seizure. This has been so since childhood. I remember running along the forest paths with my home-made spear in my hand, yelling my head off as I gathered speed. He was with me then, as Dionysos to my Maenad.

Although many respondents spoke of specific mythic and religious figures as objects of their devotion, we must not forget the importance of nature, landscape and vegetation. More and more often, people are describing their spiritual experience in such terms rather than in conventionally religious modes. I believe that this is one of the major reasons why ecological awareness is so acute at this time: people have made the imaginative connection between the image of the soul and the sacred beauty of nature. When they see the despoliation of nature, they also apprehend devastating incursion into the soul.

The rhythms of the seasons are the dance of the daimon, whose appearances may be seasonal. Elizabeth meets her daimon more in the summer. For Meg:

> He's transformed over the years. He used to be more mysterious to me and slightly scary. Now I'm more confident with him or niggled by him, like an old couple, I suppose. He tends to change with the seasons too. He's very strong in the harsh winter months. He loves the frost and the howling gales and gets very restless. He calms down in the spring and is easier to live with.

Similarly, Lairdearg finds him in winter, as she relates in her poem, 'Raincall':

> Yes I hear you,
> in my heart's depths I hear
> your voice calling through the gentle
> veils of rain.
> I feel the weight of my flesh
> stolidly ignoring
> your phantasm luring,
> but my spirit yearns to yours,
> O spirit.
> Yes, I hear you,
> and how I need to come to you
> through the gently murmuring
> bejewelled veils of rain.
> You rarely call to me in Summer,
> nor in daylight,
> but when the night is risen
> and the edge of winter cuts my heart,
> or when the gentle veils of rain
> fall to our Mother's ancient earth,
> then you call me,
> and in my sad heart's depths I hear.

For Anna, it is 'the wild man/woman, hunter/huntress of the woods, the inspirer, vitalizer and protector of nature' that calls her heart. For myself, I have always seen the land and seasons as female, but certain land-features and elements feel male to me: sacred hills, some megalithic monuments, the moon, the West wind, the clouds. Interestingly, when I lived in London, the Thames always felt very male; now I live in Oxford, further up the river, it partakes of both genders. The sea has always felt male to me and the sun upon the sea female. The appearances of the daimon as god vary according to the nature of the spiritual focus I take at any one period.

The respondents come from a variety of religious upbringings. Most of them in their middle life are finding their own way through the familiar terrain of spiritual longing without any sense of jettisoning whatever has been helpful to them. Many remain within orthodox spiritualities, yet they can be called out to answer the wild, free spirit of their daimon. That there is little dichotomy or confusion about a seemingly dual spiritual adherence is no wonder when their mystical experience has led them to the heart of non-duality.

Meg tells how the daimon

> was partly responsible for moulding my current spiritual beliefs. I started with a firm Catholic base, but never suffered the guilt Catholics are sometimes consumed by. As my daimon grew inside and seemed to be very much the link between me and the spirits of the earth, trees and sky, so my spirituality shifted to more earthly forms. The really wonderful thing is that there's never been any conflict between the two. It was very much a natural progression and now I feel just as spiritually moved in a deep wood at dawn, or in a terrific thunderstorm, as I do in church or listening to/performing music like Bach's *St Matthew Passion*. As Roy Harper said, 'We all go to church in our own ways. Every time I look at a sparrow, I'm in church.'

The mature phase of the daimon comes through when a woman surrenders to her deepest nature. The ability to surrender to spirit gains us inner space; the inability to surrender leaves us in a strait-jacket of personal control, impervious to ecstasy, unawakened to passion. The Green God shows the way to creative 'letting-go', shows us how to abandon strictures which curb our dancing feet, how to find the liberating ecstasy of the wild.

Part of this surrender is about true veneration and divine service. By surrendering to our deep nature, we simultaneously access the deep gifts with which we have been endowed. Our passionate treasury then becomes available to ourselves as well as enabling a true verdancy of spirit throughout the universe.

THE DIVINE BRIDEGROOM

The major feature of the daimon is his physical inaccessibility. But, paradoxically, the total inability of a woman to sexually unite with her daimon sustains the relationship long beyond his initial role of awakener of sexual desire, way beyond the pin-up and the longed-for hero. The world of virtual reality has arrived, but no one can yet perform virtual sex – or can they? This desire is sometimes sublimated in reverential devotion to a divine archetype, as in the case of female religious who devote their lives to God. From the *devadasi*, the Hindu priestess dedicated to the service of the temple in India, to the Christian nun, dedicated and married to Christ, is but a short step.

This influx of divine revelation is invariably recorded in the language of mystical and erotic desire. Although Christianity is devoid of eros, being more concerned with *caritas* and *amor* (compassion and disinterested 'pure' love), this does not mean to say that Christian mystics have not been entirely untouched by eros, as this account of St Teresa of Avila's ecstatic reception of an angelic messenger bears witness:

> In his hands I saw a long golden spear and at the end of the iron tip I seemed to see a point of fire. With this he seemed to pierce my heart repeatedly so that it penetrated to my entrails ... he left me completely afire with a great love of God. The pain was so great that I screamed aloud, but simultaneously felt such an infinite sweetness that I wished the pain would last eternally'.[41]

Her report reads like a virgin's first night with a beauteous lover.

We may compare this with the account of the 9th-century Tibetan mistress of tantra, Yeshe Tsogyel, who recorded her own ecstatic experience of initiation with her guru, Padma Sambhava...[13]

> ...slipped into the nakedness of pure pleasure and anointed my mandala of delight (vulva) with the petition:
>
>> Buddha Hero of Pure Pleasure, do as you will.
>>   Guru and Lord of Pure Pleasure,
>> With true energy and joy, I implore you to inject
>>   The seed into the inner mandala.
>> And I will guard the secret of the method with my life.

She offered her mandala to the Guru 'with an intense snake-like dance' as the Guru took divine form, 'his magnificent flaming vajra (penis) in a state of rapacity, projecting his full emanation, took command of the lotus throne with a roar ... that flooded appearances with glory, transmuting them into pure pleasure'. In the rapture of orgasm, the initiation of tantric method was bestowed upon her.

In Tibetan Buddhism, the practice of Deity Yoga creates a meditational communion with the *Yidam*, or the deity to whom one's heart is dedicated; this advanced practice aims at the fusion of the meditator with the *Yidam*, so that they achieve a non-dual unity.[11] In addition, practitioners meditate upon the *dakini* and *daka* – respectively, the female and male powers – to attain a true internal balance of natures. Therefore, male practitioners seek to actualize the recessive feminine through meditation upon the *dakini*, while female practitioners concentrate upon the *daka* to actualize their recessive masculine. In Buddhism, as in the other major religions, since there is a predominance of male practitioners, the symbology is male-oriented and dwells on female spiritual consorts (plate illustration 12) rather than the women's male spiritual consorts, but it is clear that the *daka* accords the daimon in most respects.[2]

In such living traditions, the relationship of woman and daimon is publicly recognized as a ritual marriage. The goodness of life and its resources, as well as the spiritual benefits of the relationship, are all understood to stem from this union. In almost no other way is the daimonic relationship so clearly upheld and so happily received.

This sense of wedding is frequently expressed by women: 'It was only after the fantasy of my husband collapsed, when I had to find the inner lover in myself, that I began to feel the possibility of the divine wedding within myself,' writes Linda Leonard, in her book *On the Way to the Wedding*.[32]

The act of sexual union creates an opportunity for experiencing non-duality, although this may not always, or ever, be experienced. Many women seek sexual union for this very reason, often unconsciously, for they know in their bodies that sex is a holy act. Of course, it can also be for fun, for gratification of the body's needs and for procreation, but the ecstatic non-duality experienced during orgasm often opens the road to spiritual union. 'For a woman, physical union with the soul apparently ignored makes her acutely unhappy'.[10]

The projection of anima/animus or muse/daimon upon each other in a partnership is common enough, but the projection of the muse upon a woman is more easily assimilated than the projection of the daimon upon a man. The reason men are so irritated when this happens may be that a woman expects her partner to act as a reflector for her soul, and he may feel this is just not his task. The fact that many women seek their daimon or the Divine through union with their partner is, I believe, a deep physical memory of a tradition which is still alive within Tibetan Buddhism, and which is alluded to in the work of Dion Fortune as 'mating on all the planes'.[15] Within certain forms of tantric practice, both male and female sexual partners actively seek Divine union through each other in a positive way.

The experiences of a St Teresa or Yeshe Tsogyel may seem remote from the common female lot, yet several respondents wrote of their sexual-spiritual alignment with their daimons. The passion between woman and daimon can be the bond of spiritual union; the passion between a man and a woman who are also on the spiritual path together can lead to extraordinary experiences.

Elizabeth speaks of her aim

> to live more closely with my own God within, to balance my polarity, to acquire some of his own masculine qualities, as I can be too lunar and passive. I have seen him in the eyes of a couple of men whom I have loved recently, and I was amazed: I thought I never would. This is what life is about! The god-forms who most closely resemble my daimon, Dionysos and Pan, appear in my partner at times and this adds a great sparkle to the occasion!

Ioho describes the Rite of Union, wherein she has congress with her partner.

> The Rite of Union is very important to me within my faith. I can feel the sexual power of my Lord of the Wood extremely acutely. That heightens what I feel, either in sacred ritual or when I'm making love with my husband or priest ... to watch and feel the man, my priest, rising, infused with the strength of the God, feeling that exhilaration. It is to imagine the perfect man. It is to know what that feels like, because of the impressions and delusions of the magic, perceptions that bring any man – provided he knows the way of the ritual – to a point of extraordinary beauty and strength. Making love – exchanging the energies, the life-force – in that state is an extremely poignant mixture of utter

tenderness and almost brutality, that rich animal nature with a spirituality that soars with freedom.

The female shamanic practitioner similarly often makes a spiritual marriage with her inner beloved, talking of him as of a spirit-husband. In her spirit-flights she meets and talks to him, drawing upon his advice and experience to help and advise her clients. Here, ecstasy and practical healing are accessed. The Voodoo priestess, Alourdes, living in Brooklyn, has gone through a marriage ceremony to the spirit, Ogou Badagri.

> She calls him her 'husband'. On this night she receives the handsome soldier in dreams, and no human lover shares her bed. On Wednesday, Ogou's day, Alourdes always wears his color, red.[6]

A handful of the respondents are also shamanic practitioners. One of them, Karen, speaks of her own experience:

> I'd been aware for several months of something missing in my life. One night I had a dream, parts of which are still inscribed on my soul. I stand in a beautiful Mongolian yurt, hung with carpets and the air thick with scented smoke. I'm brought before a masked man, wearing long, embroidered robes and seated on a heavy cushion. He rises and, holding out his hand, asks, 'Will you wed me for the spirits?' I reach out to him and we walk into the rear portion of the tent ... At the time I saw him as just a dream figure, unusual because I rarely remember dreams. However, a month later I started working with shamanism, a spiritual tradition still followed in many parts of the world, including Mongolia. A core part of this tradition is the journey to the Otherworld, to the reality you enter when you dream. And there we met again and have met many times since. I recently realized that under that mask, my spirit husband is also my healing spirit-teacher. The latter is also the person who, on my death, will meet me by the final shore. He's always been a challenging character to work with, but over the last six months we've become far closer, and in September, on a journey about a teaching from the west, we made love in the shallows of the Sea of Death. And there on the shore I recognize in me the man I wed in spirit long before.

For Karen, this is an ongoing, evolving relationship.

It is suggested that some women, in choosing a lesbian lifestyle, do so in order to integrate, 'an independent heroism ... an embrace of the woman-self' wherein they actively integrate their essential womanhood in a very physical and loving way.[83] Yet innately lesbian women are not excluded from the experience of a spirit-partner. Like Eve, they will be drawn to images of the Divine Feminine who spiritually inspire:

> The Deer-Goddess Flidais comes to me in dreams and we entwine, so that her fierce, animal sexuality infuses me with ecstasy ... With my life-partner, I exchange the deep honouring of Goddess energy in our love-making.

The relationship between a woman and her spiritual archetype has been frequently dismissed as merely sexual sublimation, especially when the subject is celibate. But a world of subtle meaning is missed by this belief. Just because a physical partner is absent from a woman's life does not mean that she is not in touch with the masculine. Indeed, many spiritual traditions actually demand that their practitioners *be married* in order to be fully observant in their faith. Judaism, for example, which states that it is a *mitzvar* (religious duty) for husband and wife to make love on the Sabbath, so that the union between God and the Shekinah, the feminine symbol of God's power on earth, might be celebrated.[42]

There is indeed a sense of surrender in the spiritual marriage between the devotee and the object of worship. Surrender commonly has an underlying sense of 'passivity', of failure or the relinquishing of personal power. This is not so of the true spiritual union between woman and daimon. There is a coming into humility, a stillness of purpose that comes from such surrender. *Spiritual surrender is about relinquishing separateness in order to be filled by the universe*. This union of human and divine brings a sense of non-duality, of being part of all that is.

'To a woman who is true to her basic self ... unrelated sexual intercourse ... festers in her belly' – because it lacks spiritual relationship.[10] Many women have sought this experience through their sexual encounters, mostly to be disappointed, because their partner does not reciprocate their spiritual dedication. As for those who seek a sexual partner only for the purpose of uniting with their daimon, they too find little satisfaction because the sacramental nature of sexual union is disrespected. In any sexual human partnership, this sacred sense of mutual respect must be present in both partners.

When Pru Sarn meets her true love, the weaver, Kester Woodseaves in Mary Webb's *Precious Bane*,[75] it is at the 'love-spinning' – a gathering together of neighbouring women to spin and weave the thread that will make a betrothed woman's wedding sheets. The women sing songs both secular and sacred as they spin. For Pru, the refrain of one of these songs sums up the sacramental nature of her desires:

> He brought me to His Lordly House,
> His banner it was Love.

These words are directly taken from *The Song of Songs*, that most beautiful of Middle Eastern love-songs which the Church Fathers tried to construe as only about God's love for his church. Pru, like many another woman before and after her, understands the sacramental union of soul with soul as something which happens at more than one level of union. Because of her hare-lip, she doesn't look for a partner, yet in Kester she discerns the features of her true beloved and experiences the promise of sacred union as alchemical and necessary to her life.

Women crave this sacramental union with their partners, not just seeking the brief thrill of orgasm with someone they love but passionately desiring the union of the archetypal male and female of whom we are reflections in our man and womanhood. Through the soul-mirrors of the contrasexual images, we are enabled to seek self-identity as well as to understand opposite-sex relationships. The dissolving of the sexes in physical union becomes something more profound at the level where human, contrasexual other and spirit are conjoined simultaneously (figure 1).

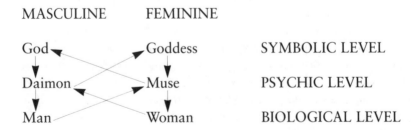

MASCULINE   FEMININE

God → Goddess   SYMBOLIC LEVEL

Daimon → Muse   PSYCHIC LEVEL

Man   Woman   BIOLOGICAL LEVEL

Figure 1 The union of masculine and feminine on all levels

The work of esoteric philosopher, Dion Fortune, was deeply engaged in the rediscovery of the unifying mysteries of men and women. Her novels *Moon Magic*[16] and *The Sea Priestess*[17] attempt to convey this teaching in an accessible way. They concern the task of a modern priestess, Vivien Le Fay Morgan, to reveal the mysteries of sexual/spiritual polarity for the healing of humankind. In these moving stories, Vivien rebalances the archetypes by recreating the bridge between the Divine and human realms, so that men and women alike can be restored to dynamic, passionate life, in accordance with their gifts and natures. When women can see the God behind all manhood and men can see the Goddess behind all womanhood, then Vivien's task will have been achieved.

KEEPERS OF THE FLAME

To what extent are these mysteries abroad in our own world? A number of respondents in this book are priestesses, women who have made a formal ritual dedication to the spiritual service of their communities. Some are also involved with the re-manifestation of shamanism in a contemporary context.

A priest or priestess must be a mediator, one able to move between the worlds of physical and subtle reality; but to transact spiritual business in the human realm also requires sensitivity to the needs of men and women. Accessibility and vulnerability are essential prerequisites for mediation. I know that through my own deep communion with my daimon, my feet have been set more surely upon the path of the priestesshood. Through his agency I am familiar with the Divine Masculine as well as the Divine Feminine.

Colleges of devoted women, women's sacred guilds and magical societies are all gaining strength at this time, but many groups lack the initiating awakening of the Divine Masculine because they are solely dedicated to the revivification of the rites of the Divine Feminine. This is gradually changing, but the initiatory rites which witness women's spiritual and sacred marriage can only be called back through those women who are in touch with the deep wildness of the Green God, whether as Pan, Dionysos, Osiris, Cernunnos, or the divine Forest Guardian.

The role of the priestess can be to awaken men to an experience of the Goddess, just as the role of the priest can awaken women to an experience of the God. However, there are also priests who are dedicated to a *Goddess* and priestesses who are dedicated to a *God*.

It is a common experience in most women's lives that the daimon will rise up and indicate a path of spiritual service. Sometimes this movement is met with fear and suspicion because it may violate strong personal levels of control and be experienced as a kind of psychic rape. But the willingness to yield, to be a garment of divinity, is part of the mutual contract that is struck between the gods and ourselves. We are not required to assent unknowingly or without due preparation.

The act of spiritual submission is spurned or misunderstood in the West as passively allowing the domination of a totalitarian force. The reality of this experience may even feel like that initially, but it also involves the reception of a greater freedom, and a deep welcoming of the gift which resides in our soul. If we serve the divine spirit in the manner of our heart, we are able to follow our life's work – this is where the daimon leads us.

I can only speak from my own experience at this point. Here is a dialogue I had with my daimon during the winter of 1995:

D Will you yield to me?
C I am a woman, one in herself. I am also the controller of who I let into my soul. But if I let you in, I will also let you go.
D You will let me go free?
C I will: to go, come or leave, as you will.
D Then let the words come through your hands. I am a spirit and I want to be accepted as a spirit. I lie with your soul. I inhabit the waste and wild places, freely. You cannot summon me, because I am free as the wind. I have reflected for you the images in your soul's mirror. But now it will be different. Now I look out of your eyes and see.

Since then, my view of the daimon has altered dramatically, for I have fully understood the nature of our contract: he has shown me how I can disenchant the last remaining masks. The contract between my life's vocation and Spirit is based upon unrestricted access: a two-way street which is creatively demanding as well as immensely rewarding. This means that, as a priestess, I can ask for help but, also, that I be available to provide help for others, turning no one away once it has been shown to me that I am to be the instrument of mediation in a case.

The nature of the contract between a priestess and her god is clearly revealed in Diana's dedication to the god Odin, whom she perceives as a projection of Divine Consciousness which I experience as an anthropomorphic personality. Insofar as I understand his purposes, I agree with them and have offered myself to him in service and partnership. I believe that by sharing my consciousness, and sometimes my body, he is able to experience the feminine perspective and the physical world. I also work closely with a number of goddesses to whom he is linked in mythology, 'all his old girlfriends'. In return, sharing his consciousness expands my own. When I turn my attention towards him, I enter an altered state, often accompanied by a kind of 'rush' which is in itself pleasurable. From him I often feel both amusement and love.

The role of the non-hierarchical and non-institutional community priestess is re-emergent in our society, but, although this is not a task for all women, women everywhere can maintain their spiritual devotion to specific deities without becoming incumbents of temples or removed from daily life. The manner in which African and Indian women continue to serve their personal gods and goddesses is a case in point. Through the use of domestic shrines and rites, personal devotion and continual mediation of the qualities of the deity in question, women are able to maintain their daily lives and spiritual service in ways which serve the whole community as well as the Spirit.[39]

The formal role of priestess is not one that can be taken on by all women, yet all women have the ability to be a mediator between subtle experience and daily life. Whether we arbitrate between members of our family or community or workplace, whether we bring hopeful solutions and suggestions to depressed friends, whether we offer our unseen support to environmental actions that maintain the networks of life on earth, or whether we speak out when another human being needs our help, we are all priestesses and mediators. The many levels of understanding and practice in women's experience range over a broad spectrum of life.

Whatever brings help, healing and regeneration comes from the well of Spirit: human beings are able to offer the healing drop of their own soul, since every soul is imbued with Spirit. Although we may not engage in formal worship, prayer or spiritual offering, we nevertheless experience and express our homage to the beauty revealed in nature, to the truth which abides in personal integrity, to the love which brings connection and healing. It is not necessary to have 'belief' in order to live spiritual lives: spiritual experience is most often a commonplace and domestic happening which women acknowledge in their daily lives but which high-flown clerics and others have elevated to a high art-form when it happens to them.

Women everywhere have been 'the keepers of the flame' of Spirit, tending the hearth-shrine of their personal devotion in domestic and ordinary ways, able to turn to their families and to their spiritual allies alike, unnoticed by observers and theological experts. What is that fuels them?

THE TORCHBEARER

Irene Claremont de Castillejo's own animus casts light on the role of the daimon in this story:

> He has explained that he, the torchbearer, is an autonomous spirit whose sole concern is shedding light ... He has no feelings towards us, neither good nor ill, he has no feelings of any kind. *Feeling is a human prerogative* ... He needs us for his very existence, for ... he needs a human being to see the light he sheds.[10]

Does this make the daimon nothing more than a decorative parasite? What is the purpose of his shedding light? For whose benefit does he act? The way in which the daimon is continually symbolized as a torchbearer tells us much about his role of shedding light upon our authentic self.

In Cocteau's *La Belle et La Bête*, whenever Belle moves about the darkened mansion of the Beast, her way is lit by a series of candlesticks which are held by disembodied arms.[87] It is an image which occurs also in the 'Sub Rosa' episode of *Star Trek Next Generation* in a scene where Beverley Crusher encounters a daimonic figure called Ronin when she comes to sort out the affairs of her recently-deceased grandmother. Ronin causes Beverley to experience erotic waking and sleeping dreams of great power. He is described as 'an anaphasic energy form' who requires the bio-chemistry of Beverley and her foremothers to survive: he has lived with generations of her female ancestors and she has inherited him. When not manifesting as a man, he 'lives in' an ancient candlestick which is kept as a family heirloom.[89]

We recall the lamp which the unfortunate Psyche raised to view Cupid, which led to their separation; but in an early relief of Cupid and Psyche (plate illustration 13), we see her being conducted by a torch-carrying Cupid. Jung spoke of the animus in this regard as 'a psychopomp, a mediator between the conscious and the unconscious and a personification of the latter ... the animus gives to woman's consciousness a capacity for reflection, deliberation and self-knowledge'.[29]

The role of the daimon is to help woman find her soul – that hidden part which is inviolable and which restores to her 'her image of herself'. This cannot be brought about by sudden, violent action, only by a willingness to be led to the soul's hiding place. This is the role of the torch-bearing daimon, to lead us into this dark place. When a woman stands on the threshold of her own soul, she immediately recognizes her true nature and can enter into it, as into a garden in which all her hopes and desires have set root and grown beautifully without her conscious effort. The fruits of the garden are hers – the gardener is the daimon: who has cherished her and believed in her, perhaps in ways that the world has ignored and neglected. The daimon's belief in her restores her to essential self-recognition. This might be termed 'the déjà vu of the soul', for there is an instantaneous recognition of something previously touched upon in dreams and in creative work. When we follow the illumination of the torchbearer, we grow more sensitive to the correlatives between physical and subtle realities. More importantly, because the daimon believes in the woman and her soul, the woman herself is able to live from the ground of her authentic self, without projection or confusion.

Irene Claremont de Castillejo posed the question: 'do women's innermost souls continue to be represented by a male figure or not?'. She believed not, but she also asserted that a woman cannot find her feminine soul unless she is first of all in good relationship with her animus.

> It is he who ... leads the way into the innermost recess where the soul-image of a woman so successfully hides.

Because he is the first image she meets, he is often mistaken for the soul-image she is seeking, but, as she proceeds, 'she may understand him to be a guide towards herself'. She reached the conclusion that 'the feminine soul-image of a woman is still in great distress because it has remained in the unconscious and it desperately needs to be brought into consciousness'.

The distress of the daimon arises when his light is ignored, for if we attempt to live without it, we do violence not only to our own souls but also to Spirit. Spirit is real, real as ourselves, but society is continually denying the reality of the spiritual realm, forgetting that the gods:

> require to be taken notice of, they want a reciprocity of awareness. The gods of all times and place have not been invented by us; they were here before we arrived and they require our recognition. And if you define a special field of attention they jump in.[27]

The Mantinean priestess, Diotima, asks Socrates 'how people can agree that Love is a great god when they deny that he's a god at all'.[56] This same question is one our age has asked, since the Jungian animus is described both as a complex and an archetype – as a collection of masculine aspects excluded from a woman, as well as a transcendent and universally acknowledged female experience. It will be argued that the animus appears in illusory and trickster guises, that it can mislead and repress, when it manifests as a complex. But as true daimon it can arise above the masks we have given to the masculine and be a spiritual messenger or angel to our soul.

If we examine the history of the world and other cultures, we will realize that accepting the reality of spirits – or of any dimension not seen or touched – is a malaise unique to the present time. Great areas of our planet are now given over to the totalitarian maintenance of the belief that there is no such thing as Spirit, just as once there was state investment in different forms of spiritual belief. Yet people of creative and mystical vision continue to be born in every culture, regardless of the status of belief in the divine. Wherever Spirit is denied or forbidden, that is precisely where Spirit continues to walk.

Many people are chary about giving credence to 'something unreal', a problem which arises continually when beginners approach spiritual work because it challenges the received meaning of 'reality'. There is more than one level of reality, but for us to move into subtle reality for the first time we have to learn initially to act 'as if' it were real for a fixed term and see what happens. During that period, we apply the same rules as we would to any new situation – when we are given advice or ideas, we try them out and draw conclusions from our experience. We see if they work. It is at this point that psychology and spirituality usually part company.

Psychology holds that 'psychosis resides in the identification with an archetype', yet mystical spirituality reveals a seemingly parallel yet inspirational model of the subject's identification with a deity.[79] In terms of the daimon, we may define the difference between psychotic and mystical thus: identification with the unemergent daimon, with the animus-image that draws on projections, can indeed verge on psychosis. Identification with the true daimon brings joy, inspiration and soul-support. We know each experience by its fruit.

Those who do not experience subtle reality for themselves may well speak in terms of psychosis when considering women's daimonic relationship, but the daimon appears for all that, in often life-saving ways. For some women, although the risk of trusting the daimon has felt overwhelming, it has proved to be well worthwhile. In defiance of the Western tradition which speaks of spiritual experience in transcendent language, some of the respondents describe their spiritual experiences in more intimate and earthly terms, like Pat, who writes of her daimon:

> I could not allow him in until I began a descent out of light and ego-illusion. He is of the Earth, of underworld enlightenment. If I had not opened to him at first as a fantasy presence, my lack of life-force would have taken me to my death.

Instead of the daimon becoming more ethereal or insubstantial, Pat goes on to report that

> he has grown in density and reality because of love, not from any romantic notions. He is my guardian, teacher, healer and lover in all realities. I experience respect, integrity, caring, strength and wisdom, but no threat of possession or control of me. This is the healing he brings in respect of myself and men: the response of my deep feminine to the masculine.

The unemergent daimon and muse walk in the depths of the female and male soul waiting to be recognized for what they are: messengers of Spirit. They come forth to reveal one or several images of inspiration, according to our capacity for discernment. *Each is a partner of completion to the soul's unfinished or immature state.* The daimon or muse cannot complete the task unless our souls develop.

Psyche's task of distinguishing one seed from another is like the process of sorting out the daimon from the veils of animus. This process inevitably leads to a clarification of soul which allows our sacred symbolic landscape to appear, just as the land appears when the morning mist has lifted. This symbolic landscape is inhabited by the divine, by the universal myths which inform our culture. To arrive here is a great privilege, but it can be confusing, especially in our society where so many people have no developed or prior landscapes, myths, religious symbols or stories to help define the Spirit. Finding our sacred symbolic landscape and becoming acquainted with its inhabitants is the initial work of all personal spirituality.

The daimon starts as a soul-image, leading woman on to her discovery, but the *soul itself* is revealed as her own true image. The experience of the bride and the bridegroom often heralds this revelation. After walking down the corridor of mirrors in which life has reflected projection after projection, we eventually discover the door at the end. There is imaged the true daimon, without projections of any kind. When we can see this clearly, we realize that the daimon is *the door-keeper of our soul*, not the soul itself.

The more we understand the work of the daimon, the closer we come to discovering our life's vocation, to finding and being able to live from our authentic self, to discovering our essential wholeness. Such an understanding involves faithful obedience to the authentic self, and trust in the daimon whose torch-light leads towards our gift. This process will often involve direct opposition to our egocentric self and its motivations, and a deeper dedication to our soul's vocation.

The work of clarifying and remembering our own daimon has been expressed in many great myths, prime of which is the Egyptian myth of Isis, who sought throughout the land for the scattered pieces of her husband's body after Osiris had been riven into pieces by his enemy. She faithfully and passionately re-membered him until she was able to mount his body and conceive their child, Horus. The secret at the heart of spiritual union with the daimon is that union liberates the ability to create. What child comes forth from our union with the daimon? When we have prepared the ground of our soul to receive revelation, then the daimon becomes a messenger for the Spirit, often appearing as an angelic messenger. We are ready for the annunciation of our creative Spirit. We are then ready to conceive, for we have come to understand that creation is a fundamental spiritual act of non-duality which embraces the whole universe.

Questions

1 Who is the bridegroom of your soul?
2 Where is Spirit in your life?

Actions

1 List all inspirational male figures in your life – alive, dead, in your imagination and dreams, heroes, gods, spirits, places, animals, plants, etc. Sit in the circle of your daimonic con-stellation each day and dialogue with one of them.
2 In a large, safe space, play a drum or rattle and begin to summon your daimon to dance with you. If songs or calls arise in you, utter them. Dance and learn of him. If you have no instrument, play some ecstatic music which conveys the voice and timbre of your daimon.

Reflection

Reflect upon the words of the poet, Kabir, as translated by Robert Bly:[1]

> If you make love with the divine now, in the next life you will have the face of satisfied desire ...
> When the Guest is being searched for, it is the intensity of the long-ing for the Guest that does all the work.

CHAPTER 7

The Pursuit of Passion

By pursuing your allurements, you help bind the universe together.
The unity of the world rests on the pursuit of passion.
Brian Swimme, *The Universe is a Green Dragon*

INVITATION AND DENIAL

Each woman has within her a treasury of great riches. As children, we all have access to creativity's treasure, but usually only artists and creative people retain the golden thread that leads to it. Women can rediscover their own golden thread by watching their dreams, consulting their desires, asking their daimon.

Janet speaks about her own experience in terms of Persephone:

> ... where the maiden Kore leaves the upperworld to descend to the underworld to aid the dead in finding their way, to take from the riches of that realm and become impregnated with these riches which she returns to the upperworld in their rebirth. Going into my depths, into her realm, I see myself as reaping the riches of the unseen, the wisdom of the deities I meet there, the daimon within, bringing these riches back into everyday life to enrich it. For me Demeter and Persephone, the Kore, represent the two aspects of life: the seen and visible, and the unseen spiritual dimension beneath it. The daimon connects me to the unseen realms.

It is particularly within the creative process that we discover the daimon as regulator of the reservoir of passion. The sexual awakening of young womanhood is paralleled by another awakening in middle-life, or even earlier, when the daimon leads us to creativity. Passion becomes our pathway again, and the daimon leads us to the very doors of the treasury. It is passion that drives this relationship, the passion that pours out its bounty everywhere we look, whether it be the profligate seeding of flowers, trees, fish and insects which reproduce themselves in mind-staggering numbers or the generous outpouring of the loving heart which knows few boundaries.

Amanda speaks of creative daimonic relationship.

> We are all living a romance between our body and spirit. This is the love-affair between the inner male and female. As I clear and open the way for my intuition and trust it in action, there is balance. When I'm in balance, more and more energy flows through me. I become a channel for the divine universal source. This brings intense feelings of passion, creativity and awakening. As I follow my daimon, I deepen the experience of my relationship to the universe. This brings me real happiness in realizing and actualizing my potential. The daimon is letting me know what is needed and appropriate to intensively experience all of my being.
>
> This doesn't mean that I am doing it all myself. I have asked for help and received it from another being. Initially I saw only the reflection of what I wanted from him. To my amazement, as I became my inner male, I actually made way for someone more than my fantasy to emerge: from that something more came a living relationship with a non-physical entity.

It is passion that brings us down to drink from the springs of creation and know the beauty of the first day and the first night within that experience. The untouched and abiding temenos of delight beckons us closer, if we will but take the path towards it.

For Frances, the source of creative passion for her is

> ecstasy, life, living beings – particularly trees and water – laughter, song, dance, food, drink. Experiencing different realities at the same time. Drums, working, playing with others who are willing to let go and reach out. Writing and swimming, helping others help themselves, talking and telling stories.

For Anna it is 'the interaction of one's personal daimon and daimons that have been worshipped in the past, and the sacred places at which they still have tangible presence'. The pathways and thresholds vary for each of us, but we are led to the appropriate pathways by our sources of inspiration which come as invitations to the place of passion.

But it is not easy to accept these invitations or even recognize them as such. Our society has defined woman's creativity almost solely in terms of her biological function as child-bearer. In our own time, however, many women choose not to have children, or to limit their families with the help of birth control. The biological imperatives are not so severe, though the creative pressures upon women have risen: not only in terms of self-fulfilment, but also in terms of economic survival.

These new creative pressures have not yet been totally understood or assimilated in this century. At its onset, the twentieth century still saw women as predominantly mothers – only the poor or the single worked for their living, and unmarried well-to-do women were expected to live under the care of their families and keep up the appearances. As I write four years from its end, the twentieth century is struggling with new female roles, with women as workers and employers. Our perceptions of work, too, have varied according to world economics, ranging from mode of survival to creatively-satisfying and decently-renumerating career. But industrialization and mass-production together have robbed us of work as craft, and many traditional and professional skills are being lost, along with the creative satisfaction they once brought.

But we cannot define women's creativity solely by biological function or modes of employment: it spills beyond these narrow boundaries to embrace the full gamut of life. Our children and our work are part of a wider creative whole. The exploration and clarification of the daimon usually begins in women's middle years, which is when we also seek our creative roots. It is for this reason that so many of the respondents fall into this age-group.

Our roles as workers, wives, partners and mothers may distribute our resources in ways we cannot plan for, but the pursuit of our creative passion does not have to be deferred until after children are grown up, or to that mythic time when we will have enough money and time. I see many women who have denied or delayed their creative development in order to bring up families or support partners. In middle life, many find it hard to retune their creative frequency to their new circumstances: children may have grown up, partners may have remarried younger women, maybe the partnership is no longer dynamic or unified. Although there may be economic pressure to seek retraining or employment, I advise clients to allow opportunities to listen to the heart and seek the creative vocation patiently.

Historically, creativity has been associated with the production of great or significant works of art which accord to a standard of patriarchal pre-eminence. Women have not been major players in this field, or their achievement has been seen as deficient. Due to many changing factors, women today are feeling their way to new creative paradigms, to different roles. Jung noted that it is precisely in middle and later life that the habitual patterns of early female life change from nurturer and mediator to a more authoritative grasp of personal development.

Creative frustration among women has been accumulating for centuries. The urgent need for us to explore more authoritative modes has led us into a significant period of creative self-assessment. Many regard the female demand for 'space for self-exploration and expression' as a luxury. As Eve says,

> Women who step outside domestic duties for creative fulfilment are likely to suffer from extreme resentment and jealousy from their partners: even if they attend one of my evening classes once a week, they will often be made to feel as if it were an absence of days rather than two hours.

Creative self-assessment space is a very human need, for both men and women. In women, it is also the release of a creative dam some two or three millennia deep.

The legacy of female self-denial and creative frustration is still with us in the lives of our mothers and grandmothers; it is still part of our own feminine identity. The atrophy or repression of passion creates anger, jealousy, a dog-in-the-manger attitude that corrodes life, and a murderous fury that can be canalized into criminal acts of passion. Creative frustration is the source of much that is destructive in our world. It is the spilling over of wasted opportunity.

When the first liberating wave of feminism hit in the sixties, society as a whole responded with shock. Women were seen to be absconding from their 'rightful duties' left, right and centre. They had metaphorically 'downed tools' and gone on strike. Feminists everywhere engaged in the luxury of venting their ire at the general treatment of women: it was a long, hot blast and it hasn't yet stopped blowing.

The capacity for expressing rage also reveals the creative capacity to do something positive: it is certainly better than a meek settling down under the thumb of the projected daimon. When we hit anger, we also hit a vein of creativity. Venting anger may throw up rocks that hurt but, when they are blown out of the volcanic explosion, they are followed by the deep, pulsing magma which characterizes the earth's core. On finding the earth's core, we find our creativity. First clear the blockage, then access the power.

Taking out the dividing partitions which have contained and blocked our personal creative power is sometimes a painful process, bringing ideas, images, sensations and feelings into focus in ways that will refute what we have accepted as authoritative in our lives. Letting all the creative impressions mingle together like paint often feels too chaotic for those who have been used to control and neat borders.

Many women are unable to relinquish total control and so fail to loose the flow of creativity within them. If the critic or the authoritarian mask of the daimon sits at the floodgates, the waters of creativity can be dammed up. On the other hand, letting go control and allowing passion to motivate creativity is often a scary business. It feels dangerous and potentially self-exposing for the woman who has not discovered trust of her daimon and who is unused to acting powerfully.

In order to perform, speak publicly or create anything, I still have to formally relinquish control of myself and my fears. If I retain conscious control of myself and my fears, I cannot create. I know that, even to sit down to a blank screen or piece of paper, or to face a room full of strangers, I need to relinquish control and fear. It is necessary to sometimes say, 'It doesn't matter whether I write or say anything good today or not, I will let whatever is waiting within me, unknown, to appear.' I trust and it duly appears, wiser by far than I.

Releasing our creative springs is a task which goes hand in hand with making friends with our daimon. To deny the daimon is to uproot our creativity and deny our own passion and fulfilment. The respondents wrote about the times when they had purposely denied their daimon; most found that this simultaneously cut them off from their creativity. When Anna wanted a break from the intensity of her daimonic relationship and found that, though she 'was more grounded in the world', she was drained 'creatively and sexually'.

The price of giving up the authentic self to an inappropriate relationship is the loss of our creative and spiritual bridge to the soul's treasury, as Lairdearg discovered.

> I went to live with someone whom I knew was bad for me – but it got me away from home. The relationship with this man was very

intense and passionate, certainly sexual ecstasy was also spiritual ecstasy with him. During the first couple of years I virtually never saw the daimon. I realized this very suddenly one day and it really scared me – *I knew that if I lost him I would lose all my creativity, my connection to the innerworld and everything that was most important in my life.* I set about deliberately re-creating the link and after much hard work I regained what I had so nearly lost. It was a sobering experience.

Yet to accept and publicly own the daimon is sometimes beyond the ability of some women. Part of my own struggle for acceptance and understanding is revealed in the following poetic sequence:[38] the first part speaks of the confusion caused by the daimon's entry; the second part was written after a close friend suggested that my daimon ought perhaps to be 'killed-off' – a suggestion so horrific that it haunted my dreams for weeks and could only be exorcized by the second and third parts, which are a dwelling upon and a riposte to this suggestion; the fourth part speaks of the social and personal acceptance which I eventually found, of the recognition that there was both distance and erotic familiarity in our relationship, of the wider creative aspects which the daimon guards. The poets mentioned in this sequence are all significant correlatives of my own daimon-poet.

Daimonic Sequence

Four poems for my master-spirit

(i) Totemic Entry
There was no meaning of knowing,
Since he entered as a man,
How the room was filled with beasts –
Hocked, horned, feathered –
His breath like seraphims',
Gorgeously apparelled in glory.

Since his entering in,
There is no telling
This world from the other.
His teeming shapes turn,
– Hoof, paw, talon –
Since I entered into light,
The world is full of eyes,
As of eagles.

(ii) The Days of Darkness
My bright daimon dead,
And I despairing.
Quick-silvered spirit fled
And I preparing
His last memorial.

For he was Janus-headed,
Dream-herder
Of a thousand bedded
Sleeps. Murder
Of a matchless master.

He was my wholesome lord,
My making,
My bread, my board,
My own leave-taking,
And his end, my end.

This last beginning dark
Without fire.
These words a lightless mark,
A leaden gyre –
A life guttering out.

(iii) Spirit Harper
He dies not, but is changed –
I saw him in the prophet's chorus,
Singing, and my heart was glad.
Virgil, Dunbar, Abelard –
Master-makers, chorusing.
For you have harped and mastered me;
Strung me unprotesting to your mode.
I have died in your music, been rewoven
On the lyre of the world. Oh Master!
Make me virgin and restore the light!

(iv) Dawn Song
Dawn is fled.
On the steps of the walled garden
They sing your *alba* [dawn-song].
On the stepped fretwork,
Angelic notes ascending.

Notes spill from the *oud* [lute]
As the fountain gathers.
On the steps of the walled garden,
Where they come to draw water,
Women sing your *alba*
And sigh for envy.

You taught Areopagite and Abelard
Through the lute's discourse,
And – more subtle teaching –
Attic Eros, Ovidian Amor.

But to no earthly mistress
Are your musics made.
Nine brightnesses with nine lanterns
Light your way over the grey seas.

Denying the creative daimon is dangerous and potentially soul-wrecking. If we deny creative freedom, we dam up our power and can make ourselves ill. Repressing or ignoring creative vocation can result in bombardment by the daimon in a variety of fearsome or troublesome guises. Knowledge of the self and our deepest desires brings a strong torch into the dark corridor of the self.

Women often chose a mode of employment because it accords with one of their daimon's masks rather than with either the daimon or their feminine soul. This can become a strain, causing depersonalization and the creation of a cold, hard exterior which appears 'male and selfish' to others. We must honour the fact that our creative vocation is not a self-chosen pathway, although we may indeed be glad to walk along it; rather, *the creative vocation chooses us*. This may seem a contradiction for those who equate vocation with job. I am urging us to see creative vocation as a much wider and embracing mantle which covers our every action and which is coloured by our innate creative tincture. It extends to our whole life. That creative vocation remains an innate part of us whether we clean offices, direct high-powered businesses, nurse the sick, tend our children or deliver parcels for a living.

Here we come to the well-head of the creative daimon. Each of us is born with a guardian spirit, our daimon, who is tuned to a particular frequency; that frequency resonates to the frequency of our authentic female self. To purposely choose a different frequency is to do violence to our soul.

If we attempt to separate ourselves from the guiding frequency of our lives, our daimon immediately erupts with a warning that we are about to take a wrong step, as poet Kathleen Raine discovered when she decided to convert to Catholicism. Isolated in London in the middle of war, separated from her children, she made an intellectual decision to be a Catholic, a decision which her heart forbade. On the eve of her reception, her daimon visited her and told her that she was 'going against everything he and those greater ones who had at times visited me, had wished for me, demanded of me, given me ... I was about to separate myself from the inspirers...'.[59] He asked of her, 'Can you really form and fashion your imagination by those symbols to which you are about to bind yourself?' He continued to berate her for abandoning the elemental presences of her childhood and the precious gift of imaginative freedom; the daimon saw her act as an evasion of her creative duty.

Many people undergo a fresh religious dedication without such problems; it is only usurpation of the soul's role in creative commitment that the daimon objects to, not the act of conversion itself. Although Kathleen underwent reception into the Church, it was not the right direction for her and she has subsequently returned to her true devotion: 'All my attempts to exchange poetry for religion or to sacrifice it on the altar of human passion have proved in the end to be grandiose evasion'(*ibid*). Her poetry continues to flow, pure and strong, to this day.

Learning to be 'co-present' to our creative frequency and to the work of our hands, is a good way to describe our daimonic relationship. To be co-present to our authentic self and the daimon is to be simultaneously within the cauldron; the cauldron itself, and also, what comes out of the cauldron. This experience of non-duality is one of great power and presence. Just as we experience the ecstasy of sexual awakening through the daimon as young women, just as we are united in spiritual ecstasy in the mystical marriage, so too can we become infused with the passion of the creative process.

THE CREATIVE PROCESS

The reclamation of creativity from consumerist standards of

appreciation is essential; as artist Miranda Gray wisely says, 'creativity is not expressed in the product, but rather in the process of giving form'.[18] Thus creativity is not about continual manifestation, it is not about business and doing: it contains many equally important processes. Like the sevenfold alchemical process, creation has its own organic cycle or, rather, a cyclic spiral (figure 2).

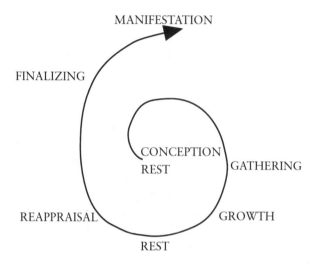

Figure 2 The creative process

The twofold resting period is important since everything proceeds from the brooding silence which waits receptively. The second rest during the creation is like the resting of dough, when it has to gather mass and stability, to 'prove'. In my writing, I always attempt to have this period of rest before I push on to the end of a project. If I omit it due to a tight schedule I know I have missed something essential that could have been included. I know now that what I am waiting for is the feminine input: that my initial creative effort always springs from my daimon. For a project to be fertile, it must have that union within it.

The period of conception is often doubtful as much as hopeful; conception occurs in the dark, in the depths of the unknown. It is only when we are sure that conception has taken place that we dare to announce pregnancy publicly. After the quickening comes the gathering, the nest-building period when we bring together the materials that will be needed. Creation enters its middle period of growth when we attend to feeding and nurturing our project. Then comes the first stage of rest; when it seems that little is happening, we often grow impatient to hurry things along, but the resting is essential.

The time of reappraisal now occurs – if we can stem our impatience and allow our project to resonate with its innate frequency rather than with our rational and pre-shrunk idea of it. When this has occurred, the project gathers the weight and momentum of a child about to be born: its head bears down and we scurry into the final stages of preparation wherein the project is completed and the way ahead made ready. Then the last stage of manifestation occurs and the project is no longer within us: it takes on its separate, independent life. This creative process has two parents, and, though the project will resemble them both, it will have its own frequency. Having given birth to the project, we return to the second period of rest.

This sevenfold process is an organic spiral of creation; none of its processes can be rushed or ignored without damage to the project, which may emerge misshapen or else be miscarried before its completion. Consumerist society doesn't understand or allow for this process in most areas of life; just as a cow's life is a perpetual cycle of pregnancy and birth in order to produce milk, so most employers milk their employees of their vitality by denying them the satisfaction of organic rhythms of work, by demanding over-time and stretching job descriptions to cover the work of two people instead of one.

The cycle of creation is identical in men and women, though each gender brings its own style to the process and it is this which is often held up as the difference between the sexes. It is the ability to draw upon the contrasexual other in creative projects that usually identifies people of sophisticated creative skill.

Writing or creating under the power of the daimon usually happens when it is performance-related, when it has to have clarity and direction, be of a professional standard and *for the benefit of others*. Writing or creating as a woman working from her female power is a different matter: there is no external demand upon the creation, only a flow of ideas, images and symbols that coalesce in self-pleasing and intimate ways. In writing from the female, the language is usually intimate or self-revelatory in some way. Daimonic writing is far more focused and precise.

This two-way method of creation has been part of preparing

this book. In the early stages, and at reflective intervals throughout the writing, I have gone deeply into my personal, female experience, writing from within and allowing thoughts to gel, and be nurtured and developed within the female matrix of creation. When I've needed to take a comprehensive overview, to collate and interrelate material, I've drawn upon my daimonic function to give me clarity and definition. This has been the only way of keeping the balance in such a complex and illusive subject: if I had written from a wholly feminine perspective, the material would have flowed off the page into a great puddle of incom prehensible liquesence; written from a wholly daimonic viewpoint, the material would have been cerebrally theoretical and dry as crispbread. Only an integrated balance has kept it afloat.

For women, the biological cycle interphases with any period of creative work. Allegra uses the language of the Tao – of the eternal feminine Yin and its counterpart the eternal masculine Yang – to express her own creative interphase: 'the menstrual phase is developing Yin; the post-menstrual is doing Yang'. And Pat writes:

> The powerful creative times have been when I'm bleeding: then I'm open to the innerworld and have had more mystical experiences which I've painted or written about ... I am also open to my deep inner wound, and, from experiencing it, paint or write to give expression and then evolve into an inner mystical experience of the Beloved consuming me.

Janet notes the importance of rest within the creative process: 'I feel non-creative at menstruation. It is a time for me to be quiet, to rest from working and to just be.' And Lauren takes 'silent, alone time during the bleeding days of my period, and that's when I allow myself more space and find room for a great deal of creative inspiration'.

The daimon keeps open the bridge to inspiration, and will emerge in playful forms to facilitate this process, coaxing us back into relating, as Frances describes here:

> He appears in dreams when I'm cut off. The more energized and whole I am, the easier it is for me to be in contact with him, to see, hear and experience him. He comments with an acerbic humour when I've been very reluctant to be in touch. In fact I've noticed recently that he and the Goddess are much at one on this. The ME makes it easy for me to get cut off and lose any sense of being in

life. He appears in whatever aspect seems appropriate. When I
need healing, he's Pan; if I need comfort and grounding, he will be
the Green Man. If I need knowledge, he is Merlin or Gandalf.
Plant lore and reflection bring him as Bear. If it's loving or dancing
that we're doing, then he's the Satyr. When I am emerging from
being very stuck or in a crisis, I'll be aware that he was there all
along.

Finding the sources of our inspiration and allowing them to nurture and enrich our experience is essential in the creative process.
We are aware of the way in which men have traditionally drawn
upon their muse for their work. Although men have frequently
projected the muse onto a living woman, as Dante did onto
Beatrice, the muse herself remains a spiritual rather than an incarnate inspirer. Just so, respondents have drawn upon their own
daimons as inspirers, sometimes seeing their reflections in living
artists and inspirers from many traditions.

These inspirers represent a more mature imaging of the daimon
within the soul than the teenage pin-up: these inspirers are evoked
because they mirror a woman's soul and the frequency of her creative vocation. They are not admired for their physical beauty but
because their voices speak resonantly of matters which are
attuned to our own passion. Significantly, they are not sought in
gods and archetypes so much as in human men who have themselves been inspired.

Hue is inspired by 'Peter Seeger's integrity, by Vincent van
Gogh's struggle against great inner demons, by the Forest Rangers
for their knowledge of the forest and their skill'. For Lauren,

> Kahlil Gibran and Ralph Waldo Emerson are two philosophers I
> find creatively, intellectually exciting. My attraction is in the com-
> passionate, eloquent and yet simple way of life seen through their
> eyes. I like Tom Robbins for his humorous biting critique of the
> hypocrisy and absurdities of Western societies. These writers com-
> bine my desire to see the beauty and simplicity of life and spirit,
> while also recognizing the need for realistic humour about where
> we are at really today.

Sheila is drawn to 'the great reformers of the past: Barnado,
Wilberforce, or men who sought to understand the human psyche
such as Freud and Jung. I'd like to have met Dickens or Pepys.'
Allegra is inspired by writer Lindsay Clarke, 'because he seems to
understand women', and by Jung 'because he is inspiring and I
dreamed of clambering on his old knee as a young child. I feel

that neither would reject me and would be on my wavelength.'

For Elizabeth it is 'the work of Dante Gabriel Rossetti: we share the same vision of beauty in woman-kind and goddess-kind, and express it in the same way'. Ioho ponders 'Thomas Hardy, who finds the intensity of the creative force, blends the power of the darkness and the light which is the magic of the natural world'.

Many of the respondents spoke of the way world leaders and humanitarian thinkers have inspired them, especially those who have been held under duress, like Brian Keenan, Terry Waite and John McCarthy, the hostages held in Lebanon for several years, yet who survived and endured. Pat writes, I feel these three touched their souls and looked deep within to their self.'

Fiona in particular wrote of a broader definition of creativity which encompassed social and political healing:

> M S Gorbachev, Nelson Mandela and Alexander Dubček, all of whom attempted to bridge, balance and reconcile. Even more than Mandela's release, I felt for Dubček that the years in the wilderness ended in the accomplishment of at least part of his vision. I wrote a poem about Dubček and Gorbachev in 1987:

> > They didn't turn him into a martyr,
> > A dead head or a quasi-saint.
> > No, they thought it much smarter
> > To let memory of him grow faint.
> > They gave him a job in lumber
> > And let the Prague spring slumber.
> > It slept, he worked, the nineteen years till now.
> > Strange news, good news, comes out from Moscow.

> > An old man, once demoted to the trees,
> > He reads the papers and reads between the lines
> > At least he's alive to witness these times.
> > He looks beyond the window and lets the memories unfreeze.
> > Back to those heady days when he believed
> > He really could amend the creed,
> > Let communism wear a human face,
> > Let all the changes come apace.

Here, Fiona movingly identifies herself with the archetype of the exiled inspirer, waiting to resume the power of the reconciler. This archetype of the peacemaker waiting to emerge is very clear in her own life and in the on-going evolution of her novel. Her sympathy for those under communist regimes is understandably personalized, since she herself has suffered 'the tyranny of critical judgement' from an earlier totalitarian form of her daimon since she was 13 years old. However, in awaiting the fullness of her own *perestroika*, she is forging the character of Nallikino, the warrior who wishes to be the peacemaker, allowing him to emerge from the creative process of her novel-writing with an extraordinary faithfulness.

The female psyche, like the land of Russia in 1996, seeks to throw off the legacy of totalitarianism but is sometimes still confused by the sudden freedom that results; there is still a great need for order and authority. This can only emerge from the shape of the creative process. We cannot hand over our creative projects to others and ask them to improve or finish them for us.

The creative process is not always fluidly easy. In discussing their own creative obstacles, people frequently remark to me that, 'it's all right for you, you just have the gift'. I point out that 'the gift' is merely a whole-hearted dedication to my passion, my creative frequency: to remain true to it is as challenging as staying in a difficult relationship or a demanding job. It is a matter of coming back day after day, faithfully returning to the bridge where creative passion and daimon meet. Some days, creative interphase will be impossible: communication lines may be bad due to my lack of respect for creation's organic dance, the materials at hand may be inadequate or cut the wrong way, unplanned interruptions may intervene. Some days, it will be a matter of going to weed the garden or cook instead, because the creative process is in its recessive phase; impatience and hustle will only delay its arrival. Being patient at these times requires ultimate trust, especially when deadlines snap their teeth menacingly from the kennel of next week. The mystery of 'the creative gift' is no more nor less than this faithful trust.

Creativity is not just about our hobbies and talents, although these may be primary expressions of our creative passion; it is also about finding resourceful ways of living, as Fiona states:

> Creative passion links into the state of the world. 'There is another way' is the cry that underlies a lot of what I create – even the needlepoint pictures can be colourful, not drab! My whole way of living, even not splitting up with my partner but instead moving into a different form of relationship to parent our son, is a

kind of search for another way. It is my animus who seeks all-round vision; it is equally my deep feminine, my experience of the Goddess that knows the present ways must change.

Following the frequency when creativity is in transitional phase is often a matter of good old human obstinacy.

Creation is not only about passive receptivity; it is also about active differentiation and choice:

> A woman feels the need to discriminate among the many seeds the animus inseminates, to know which ones to plant. Then she can nurture this inner nucleus until it is time to give birth to it in the outside world. She creates, then, out of the wholeness of being ... she can move to discover transcendence in immanence, spirit in everyday life.[69]

The process of creation is itself a mysterious coming together of male and female elements of ourselves: when creative and dai-monic frequencies resonate, we experience the cosmic music, as Janet reports:

> I feel I am merely the hands and voice of something that lies at my core, at the core of all being, the Beloved who wears different faces and transcends all form, time and place – he who has encoded my very genetic nature to move, think and act in accordance with the grand plan.

The creative process is dynamic and latent, skilfully unwoven and softly spun out of women's visceral, psychic and spiritual being. The daimon acts as a bridge to bring it forth in its own innate way (plate illustration 14). The moment when creativity is called forth is unforgettable:

> When things, a landscape or a work of art, come alive or 'grow transparent', this signifies that they are transformed into what we have called unitary reality ... There is nothing mystical about the symbolical unitary reality, and it is not beyond our experience; *it is the world that is always experienced when the polarization of inside and outside, resulting from the separation of the psychic systems, has not yet been effected or is no longer in force.* It is the authentic, total world of transformation as experienced by the creative [person].[52]

The environment of the creative life is important, and is frequently a significant feature in our daimonic journey. After a strong dream of union with her daimon, Valerie Harms made her 'bedroom a wedding bower with white lace canopy, satin sheets, white rose bouquet and ribbons in celebration of love, creation, dance, music, desire, and beauty'.[25] Other women create surroundings which harmonize with their creative purpose so that their genius is able to manifest: the nest, studio, inner garden, or laboratory for craft and creation are very important.

Becoming our authentic female selves takes organic time and space; it begins in the secret place of creation. For that we need a nest, a centring space, a place to call our own. We all need 'a room of our own' – one that doesn't have shared usage, a place in which to be still and quiet, contemplative, able to appreciate the deep creative gifts. For many women, this is their kitchen or garden, for few homes have spare rooms. Whether it be the kitchen table after the children are abed or the kitchen doorstep when the first blackbird sings at dawn, women are jealous of their private creative space.

Sometimes this externalization will be ritually formalized. An altar or shrine will be created to act as a seed or catalyst around which energy can build up. This magical action is a means of creatively constellating in outer form that which is awaiting manifestation in a woman's inner life. Altars and shrines bring focus to the creative process. They may consist of nothing more than a mantelpiece, shelf or low table on which are clustered objects which signify a woman's creative and spiritual focus. Conventional understanding sees altars merely as places of divine (and often passive) worship for the laity within the context of Western religious rites, but women's altars are far more aligned to the Hindu practice of shrine-making – an activity which happens as often in the kitchen as in the temple – where shrines are places of welcome for the divine action to manifest. In women's altars and shrines we see the focalization of their creative intention and spiritual frequency.[68]

Having a room of one's own is a great privilege, but any temenos of space which a woman can call her own is essential in order to call into being her creative self. Without it, we tend to hoard our treasure, never using it because we do not know its worth. If we create our own space, then our creative treasury can become our inexhaustible cruse of oil and grain which will sustain us whatever the circumstances. It is essential to substitute this self-created space for the enchanted tower in which Sleeping Beauty and the Lady of Shalott are enchanted.

Our own room or space is the place of self-expression wherein our experience of the outside world can coalesce into significant patterns that nourish our soul and assist in our work. Historically, this space has been a mantle which women assumed wherever they were in their house, and one which surrounded all 'women's work' – the daily, domestic acts which weave the fabric of life together. Felicity Wombwell writes of the need to

> establish our hearth within ourself and within our physical environment. We can then enter and leave this hearth as we please. The process of moving in and out then becomes like a spiralling as we move around the hearth.[78]

Let us allow ourselves the space and freedom to live creatively: to dream, wish, embroider, sing, paint, create, give space to whatever is within, for by giving rein to our innate womanhood, by teasing out the thread of ourselves, we may enter into dynamic relationship with the universe.

CREATIVE TENSIONS

By attuning to our feminine creative frequency we can pick up all the peripherals as essential clues to ways forward. But listening to the heart and obeying it requires great courage and fortitude since it will mean straying from the boundaries of conformity, going beyond what is 'normal', giving passion its head, in order to seek out our creative destiny.

As the poet Rilke wrote:

> the future enters into us in this way in order to transform itself in us long before it happens. And this is why is it so important to be lonely and attentive when one is sad: because the apparently uneventful and stark moment at which our future sets foot in us is so much closer to life than that other noisy and fortuitous point of time at which it happens to us as if from outside. The more still, more patient and more open we are when we are sad, so much the deeper and so much the more unswervingly does the new go into us, so much the better do we make it ours, so much the more will it be our destiny.[64]

Finding the strength to be able to step forward creatively may seem imperative, but most often, we have to 'await with deep humility and patience the birth-hour of a new clarity' (*ibid*). This deep inner listening is the first duty of all human beings: to spend time each day when we can attune to the universe as a whole rather than pursuing god-like, separated and increasingly isolated lives.

Being alone and comfortably at peace with the self fosters the creative process; avoiding solitude robs the daimonic relationship. But women often avoid this enclave of peace by putting the housework or tasks for others before their own creative genius. Poet Kathleen Raine recalls this subtle form of sloth, feeling compelled to darn the last pair of children's socks before allowing herself to write a poem. She acknowledges that 'I am wild and of the wilds, the inspirers meet me there'.[77] It is in the solitude of such wild places that many women currently wander, trying to reconcile the demands of their lives, dealing with the creative tensions of life.

Women question whether it is possible for them to combine the creative dynamic with a happy human partnership. Surely the pursuit of a creative vocation results in the 'spinster in the attic' syndrome? Women who pursued spiritual vocations were expected to remain celibate as priestesses, nuns and hermits: their sexual selves were committed to a deeper relationship, to their gods and spirits. Women who followed creative vocations in the past have similarly often found themselves isolated from the satisfactions and support of sexual partners: one of the most extreme examples of the 'spinster in the attic', is American poet Emily Dickinson. Not only was her tireless production of poetry unpublished in her own lifetime, but she also lived unpartnered and alone, never going out. Her repressive existence makes us both sad and angry to contemplate.

The message to blue-stockings, women who have been educated and who seek to live by their creativity, is one of lonely spinsterhood. And many women still believe that men don't like brainy women – a false message which has arisen over the last two hundred years as a reaction to women seeking to be better educated. The temptations not to engage our creativity are many-headed distractions.

Historically, many women have denied their personal creativity in order to underwrite the creative life of their husbands: Cosima Wagner became a virtual priestess at the shrine of Richard Wagner's every whim and fancy. The sublimation of passion is eventually paid for, however. Jacqueline Picasso sacrificed her life to Picasso's needs; at his death she found she had nothing else to live for.[25]

Subordination of female integrity to the masculine continues to be a critical factor in women's creative lives: a factor which may dismay those who view the daimon as yet another mode for diverting feminine creativity into masculine channels. It takes courage and stamina to access creativity in the face of over-whelming male output or presence. Miriam writes:

> The negative daimon is one aspect of my critic and can be destruc-tive. I find more inspiration in the concept of the Goddess. On the other hand, I'm far more creative because of my relationship with my husband: he's so overpowering in his macho-maleness that I retreat to my office to write, partly to demonstrate to him that I can do it and partly to escape from his assumptions about work that needs to be done. But he's very supportive of my work.

While women are entering their creative ground and redefining creativity in ways meaningful for them, they need to make their enclave of seclusion and trust the unfolding creative process. This may indeed involve some necessary friction within their relation-ships, especially if their partnership involves claiming creative ter-ritory.

Examples of women with a clearly delineated creative daimon are rare because of the social and historic burdens put upon women's behaviour. Most often, the daimon is safely identified with Christ or a saint, as in the case of Hildegard of Bingen who dialogued with her Saviour and with many saints, yet whose creative outpourings and mediation demonstrate a woman who was truly full of daimonic inspiration.

The love story of Abelard and Heloise yields the dichotomy of a mutually engaged relationship in which the brilliant teacher, Abelard, falls in love with the beauty and intelligence of young Heloise, who in turn falls in love with the personable and inspi-rational Abelard. After Abelard's castration by Heloise's jealous uncle, Heloise continued to draw upon him as a source of love and inspiration, even though she was engineered into a monastery and virtually abandoned by him. Although she was sworn to love Christ alone, it was Abelard who remained the subject of her veneration. In her years as Abbess of the Paraclite, they exchanged a brief and moving correspondence in which her faithful regard for him reveals Abelard as her daimon, although she was no longer his muse.

Clearer examples of daimonically-inspired women can be found in more recent times – in Mary Shelley's *Frankenstein*, for example, we see the exploration of the masculine in its many forms, from bestial to creative. Mary Shelley herself was the product of parents whose own creative outpourings represent the head-waters of the modern feminist movement. Her father, William Godwin, was a radical political theorist and her mother, Mary Wollstonecraft, was the author of *A Vindication of the Rights of Women* (1792).

But the obscure life of Emily Brontë still remains the model for the woman wrestling with her daimon and seeking to clarify it. In her depiction of Heathcliff we see a fusion of her dissolute brother, Patrick Branwell, and a far more chthonic figure whose wildness corresponds closely to her own tightly-reined soul. Like Emily Dickinson, Emily Brontë poured out her soul down the life-lines of poetry, in taut and mysterious ways which encode the daimonic message.

The manifestation of creativity is a requisite of female consciousness, as the diarist Anaïs Nin realized; while inspired by writers Henry Miller and Lawrence Durrell, she had to develop her own way:

> woman's creation far from being like man's must be exactly like her creation of children, that is, it must come quite of her own blood, englobed by her womb, nourished with her own milk. It must be a human creation, of flesh, it must be different from man's abstractions.[25]

To call formally upon our creative powers is to call upon the daimon to join with us and make 'a child' – this is the spousal dimension of creativity.

Women have been told that their creativity is akin to Pandora's Box: a receptacle for chaotic randomness whose contents sully the classical creative experience, and which cannot be judged as in any way beneficial or comparable to male and socially-acceptable forms of creativity. The matrix of female creation is stigmatized by those who fear the strange progeny which women bring forth: they are not always like 'normal' children.

In deciding what is creatively normal or acceptable, society has spun lofty definitions of 'creativity' from which many women feel excluded. Wider definitions of what is 'creative' are needed.

Creativity has become narrowly defined as 'artistic' creation. But whatever is spun out of our ideas, desires and passion is the stuff of creativity – not only paintings, plays, dances, books and music but also gardens, meals, clothes, surroundings and life-styles. By polarizing creativity as the preserve of the artistic alone, we disempower ourselves and our own creative ability. Being truly creative is to take charge of, refine and cultivate our own style rather than passively inhabit the ideas, styles and attitudes of others.

The work of our hands embodies our soul. The very physicality of creativity provides a centring activity which leaves our minds and hearts free as our hands are occupied. Creativity is not solely about producing 'fine art' – it means getting mud under our fingernails in the garden, staining the floor with varnish, following the thread through countless handicrafts of our creation, binding up the broken wing of a bird, finding resourceful ways to handle difficult encounters.

The separation of women's creative achievement from men's, and its judgement by two sets of criteria, can produce a subtly invasive form of feminine isolation if we allow it to. Ball-games are played between different groups over this: radical feminists decry sisters who 'sell-out to the establishment' and achieve in what they see as a 'male field', while the establishment neglects dyed-in-the-wool female creators. Some women never attempt to reach a general market, feeling that their feminine creative vocation is vulnerable to swingeing power-games. The creative field will undoubtedly broaden over the next few centuries as women begin to help the redefinition of creativity in our world. This can only come about if all women come into better alignment with their creative vocational frequency and honour that of others.

Women have to deal with the devalued image of womanhood as well as with the projections of female authority and the fear they invoke. Women who work closely with their daimon often demonstrate a natural ease and authority which is often resented by others – by women as well as men. Manifestations of female authority in our society are often accorded derision rather than respect. Men may register professional jealousy towards women who succeed in their field. But some women register levels of creative jealousy which can go off the scale, resulting in destructive behaviour towards other women. What emotions do creative achieving women provoke?

The level of freedom and easy control, the wide-ranging

overview and actual achievement often provoke response among women with unemergent daimons, turning them into destructive critics of their own gender. The poison of competitiveness often sours women's relations with each other. But that is a male game which women don't need to play.

The creative vocation transcends gender divisions, since it is a marriage between the daimon and the female authentic self, or between the muse and the male authentic self. This creative polarity is a dynamic one, creating the necessary tension by which life can be lived. Just as the warp and weft of good fabric are woven together to produce a garment of sufficient give to mould itself to our movements – neither too tight nor too loose – so the daimon's thread must be entwined with our authentic-self thread in a balanced weaving.

The life of the poet and Blake scholar, Kathleen Raine, is a model of how the creative woman's first duty is sometimes to the daimon alone. Her life-long pursuit of poetry was urged on by her daimon, to whom she finally dedicated herself, having learned that service to Eros was not her way. Despite her marriage and the kindling of her heart by men who were her kindred spirits, 'not Henry Moore, not Yeats himself could have come between me and that inner companion; no other person's inspiration, however strong, can take the place of our own inner light'.[60]

Kathleen Raine's dedication to the daimon is deeply moving, showing the depths of joy and anguish involved in loving a man from whom the light of the daimon shines. She regards her daimon as the well-spring of her work as a poet, as this part of her 'Northumbrian Sequence' demonstrates:

> Him I praise with my mute mouth of night
> Uttering silences until the stars
> Hang at the still nodes of my troubled waves.
> Into my dark I have drawn down his light
>
> I weave upon the empty floor of space
> The bridal dance, I dance the mysteries
> That set the house of Pentheus ablaze.
> His radiance shines into my darkest place.
>
> He lays in my deep grave his deathless fires,
> In me his flame springs fountain, tree and heart,
> Soars up from nature's bed in a bird's flight.
> Into my dark I have drawn down his light.

> My leaves draw down the sun with their green hands
> And bind his rays into the world's wild rose.
> I hold my mirroring seas before his face.
> His radiance shines into my darkest place.

She was a close friend of the writer Gavin Maxwell, famed for his series of books about his secluded life in the Highlands, where he kept otters. A complex and eccentric man, Maxwell was homosexual by inclination; throughout their tempestuous association, he was never her lover. Kathleen Raine writes of him: 'What drew me to him was nothing bodily, but rather the radiance his presence had for me always'.[60] He was always her 'man of light.' The bond between them was of the soul. For her, even staying at his Highland home was a participation in his numinous presence: 'seeing his sky over me, the spaces of his sea, those near hills and far mountains which were the regions of his imagination ... I lived like Psyche in the house of love, alone yet not alone.'

Her poem, 'The Marriage of Psyche',[58] encapsulates the charge that their association brought Kathleen:

> All this he has given me, whose face I have never seen,
> But into whose all-enfolding arms I sink in sleep.
> ... He has married me with a ring, a ring of bright water
>
> Whose ripples travel from the heart of the sea ...
> He has married me with the sun's circle
> Too dazzling to see, traced in summer sky ...
> He has married me with the orbit of the moon
> And with the boundless circle of the stars ...
> At the ring's centre
> Spirit, or angel troubling the still pool ...
> Transcendent touch of love summons my world to being.

Kathleen's love for Gavin Maxwell was so strong as to transcend the separation between human beings: 'I thought of him ... as part of myself; so accustomed was I to talking to him in my thought as if he were there, as if he were the daimon whose image I suppose some Jungian would say I projected on him ...'.[60] Their relationship was tempestuous, confused by this factor as well as doomed by Maxwell's contrary nature, which would have found fault with perfection itself.

After his death, Kathleen wrote her elegy 'On a Deserted

Shore',[58] asking:

> How many faces have you worn,
> Life after life,
> By human passion
> Obscured and torn? None
> So dear, my love,
> As I knew by your name ...
>
> Say I must recognize
> I but imagined love
> Where no love was,
> Say all is a dream
> In whose brief span
> Childhood, womanhood, the grave
> Where my love lies:
> That dream is all I am.

Although Maxwell was inextricably identified with her daimon, Kathleen continues to write poetry after his death, proving that the daimon, though sometimes reluctant as an errant lover, does still inspire. In Kathleen Raine's experience, we see the twofold relationship of poetic daimon and friendship with a man who reflects the daimonic other. Though she was not Maxwell's muse, Maxwell reflected her daimon, briefly and painfully incarnating him in a contradictory relationship.

The creative tension necessary to express our true frequency may be abrasive, but then the sculpting of our authentic self from the undisclosed rock of our being is never going to be a tame procedure. Nevertheless, we are rightly awed when daimon and authentic self draw closer to the marriage chamber, when creation hovers on the brink of manifestation.

The creative action of the daimon and muse are awesome for they attend the birth of universes:

> There is something mysterious about the presence of these *genii* at the wellhead of man's sensual soul ... they may be compared with the process by which they join form and matter and transmit them insensibly from generation to generation. Their generative function [can be] taken as ... a tutelary presence in the [soul]. An extraordinary degree of mental control and poetic insight is required to penetrate the mystery and its full significance is accessible only to the spiritually enlightened understanding.[76]

We naturally halt as we approach this holy ground, this inner garden wherein the daimon and muse or Jung's integrated anima and animus are to be found, since they hold the keys to the divine dimension of humanity in the natural world. Entry into the creative ground of our being does not come about by rational analysis, nor by wish-fulfilling dreams. Neither is it conferred by special status.

Polly Young-Eisendrath, writing in 1987, considered it 'a rare achievement among adult women' to achieve the full integration of the animus, where the daimon can be a creative partner.[83] It is true that the necessary tools to bring about this process – motivation, maturity and access to the imagination – are all important factors which arise from experience, but it is untrue to maintain that only a woman of certain background, income, skin coloration and educational standard can achieve it. The rich diversity of female experience of the daimon proves that, while communion with the daimon tends to be a feature of middle age, it is achievable by many. Whatever age we find ourselves at, it is never too late; there is always time to invite our creativity to percolate within us.

Our personal creative treasury is accessible, and the thread to the spiral centre of the creative process lies in our hands. How we are led to its centre can be an astonishing journey, for it is not solely about being passively inspired and receptive, it is also about the way our daimons find *us* inspirational. When we receive that accolade, we begin to believe in ourselves in a completely different way, following passion to its very core.

HOW THE DAIMON MUSES US

Irene Claremont de Castillejo writes, 'the animus is not a woman's inspiration' in the same way that a man's anima can be his muse.[10] Initially, I strongly disagreed with this statement, but then I read it again and changed my mind. The animus is truly not a woman's inspirer because *the daimon* is.

The daimon who is still masked by accumulations of masculine images from a woman's upbringing does not inspire; the animus may repel, excite and offend, but he is composed of masks. The respondents have used the terms daimon and animus to mean roughly the same thing, but here we must distinguish. The Jungian animus as a complex is unrefined and suspect; it is only at his Jungian archetypal level, as a universal appreciation of the masculine, that he begins to approach what I have striven to reveal as the personal daimon of women.

The daimon as guardian spirit, as masculine counterpart, as soul-image, emerges fully only when a woman attunes to her creative frequency, when she attunes to her authentic self. This may not be a clear and continuous experience; she may sense intermittent union within herself, days when she feels immensely empowered and confident, days when all is obscured again. However, as in all creative endeavour, practice makes perfect.

Even though the true daimon, the inspirer of the soul, may be likewise obscured, we may hear his voice, sense his light-shedding focus. Like any migrational bird, we will steer towards the land of our home, despite wind and weather, in hope and trust.

Significantly, when the respondents have spoken of their inspirers, they have singled out those who have deep or resonant voices which remind them of their daimon: these voices resonate to the frequency which is emitted from the soul.

Meg recalls:

> I used to try and write songs which came very much from inside but my creative talents have never been with words, so I found it very hard. Often when I sing, I can feel the male inside become a focus, something to sing to if you like. I suppose the reason for being so attracted to song-writers is that they are creating something I can't create myself, but which I can express myself through anyway ... Sometimes we make music together. Sometimes we just sit in silence staring into each other's eyes above a vast scenic expanse and knowing that nothing can touch us. He doesn't always have a human form – sometimes we fly together over the earth as spirits or stars.

Whichever of our senses, or combination of senses, is most acute, tends also to be the major pathway of inspiration for us, the path that leads to the daimon. Sound appears to be the most common pathway at the stage when a woman is seeking her authentic self. This is significant but hardly surprising when one the earliest creative channels of the senses to become blocked is often that of the voice. The repression of the singing-voice or the expressive voice has a profound effect upon a child: it grows up with a lack of confidence in self-expression on all levels. Women are particularly prone to self-chosen forms of vocal manipulation in order to survive, 'disguises of "niceness", "vulnerability", the "look after me I can't cope" voice'.[65]

The finding and empowering of our own female voice is one of the means to contact our authentic self. In my shamanic practice, I take great care to listen to the timbre of the voice as well as the verbal content of a client's relation. Since I work predominantly with sound and resonance, the voice is a primal revealer of the soul's constitution. The person who is holding on to fear speaks with restriction, with a tinny timbre that sounds hollow. When she expresses those fears through anger or sorrow, the timbre is briefly liberated in an extraordinary vocal release which affects her whole body. When long-seated blockage is shifted, vocal release becomes habitual.

Women are prone to 'de-voice' or excise robust tones from their natural timbre in order to appear softer or conciliatory: a technique infamously used by Tory prime minister Margaret Thatcher in order to appease and control her electorate. Vocal therapist, Paul Newham, writes of the way in which women avoid the natural lower registers of their voices, for

> to sing bass is to confront all that is 'base' in us ... to sing bass a woman must make contact with part of herself that is the most secure and possesses a sense of stillness and authority. It is a regal sound ... with a paternal warmth to it.[53]

The daimon speaks with that timbre, reminding women that this is their true expressive frequency: to sing or speak from our lower depths is to bring up the deep authentic voice which comes from our womb and our womanliness.

The daimon also uses the other pathways of our senses to awaken us. We may be initially enraptured with those who are in the train of Dionysos, the singers, actors and dancers who reflect our daimonic frequency with such ease and beauty, but we will seek these qualities more often within ourselves as we mature.

Several respondents have written about the physicality of the daimon, or his embodiment within their own body. For Amanda, an important mode is that of touch:

> Whatever the creative medium, my companion always gets involved. One good method for communication with him is through clay. I turn my attention inward and call out to him

mentally; after a moment I can feel his presence near me. I then relax my mind and ask him to let the energy flow through to my hands. Together, we create wonderfully surprising forms that tell the story of our contact at that unique moment. I find this a good way of exploring the hidden meanings that my logical thinking doesn't encompass.

One of the foremost channels for direct embodiment of the daimon is dance. The adult woman who is out of her twenties rarely dances in our culture, as opposed to people in traditional cultures world-wide. But it is traditionally in the ecstasy of dance that creative passion is accessed and the authentic self liberated to appear, if only briefly. Finding our authentic selves takes organic, unhurried time and it is here that the daimon can help us. By taking long walks, or by performing household tasks, the body rhythmically allows the soul to enter the deep hallowing of nurture. Interrelation with the way we move and the process of breathing can itself prove a liberating pathway.

In suggesting these methods, I am hoping to enable those women with deep creative blockages to look beyond classical psychotherapy towards creative therapies of many kinds – especially dance, drama, art and voice therapies – for more supportive and interactive methods of self-discovery.

In *Troytown Dances,*[43] Miranda's creative direction receives fresh impetus and authority from the identification of her daimon with the maze-maker, Daedalus:

> The presence of Daedalus suddenly helps. No longer caught in the webs of Minos' weaving, Miranda is able to plumb the depths of her necessity. She feels disentangled through the mediation of this clever man. Like a smith, he has melted down her desires and made them into a useful tool.
>
> After these blunt years of indescribable confusion, she holds in her hands a blade that will pare and shape. No more fruitless shuttling between this and that task, hiding from her joy. Now she takes up her pen with the vibrant ease of a craftswoman. This task transcends the political correctnesses of feminism and socialism – she has entered into the way of the craft of life and like all artists knows the fierce joy and privilege of practice. Now she knows that to avoid writing in her book is to court death of the soul. She runs to it, as to a lover.

The thread which marks the way through our own creative processes leads to the heart of the labyrinth: not to a fearsome minotaur, but to the daimon. The story of Ariadne reveals the pattern by which our maze is threaded. Ariadne is given a sacred light-bestowing wreath or diadem from Dionysos in return for acting as his nurse. When her half-brother the Minotaur – product of the union between her mother, Pasiphae and the Sea-Bull, Poseidon – begins to demand sacrificial victims, she aids the hero, Theseus, to find and kill the Minotaur, by giving him her sacred Dionysian wreath to light his way through the Labyrinth. Theseus takes Ariadne and her sister Phaedra away from their home, but chooses to abandon Ariadne on a small island. Here, Ariadne laments her bad decision to follow Theseus and berates herself for forsaking her motherland and her parents. As she reaches the depths of despair, Dionysos comes to her while she is alone and marries her. Her light-bestowing wreath or diadem becomes immortalized as the Corona Borealis, the constellation of the Crown of the North.

Ariadne's progress reveals a pattern common to all women striving to make sense of their daimonic relationship:

- She has a symbiotic bond with Dionysos in her youth which she neglects.
- She seeks the destruction of the Minotaur, symbol of bestial masculinity and of wild, horrific nightmare.
- She choses the likeliest man to be her rescuer – Theseus – but fails to consult her authentic self as to his suitability as a partner.
- When Theseus abandons her, she is consoled by Dionysos, who honours their childhood symbiotic relationship by a marriage between equals.

Ariadne's weaving progress, shuttling between different masculine images, reveals hope for all who are far from the centre of their creative treasury at the heart of the maze. Even though she has neglected her true daimon, in the person of Dionysos, he does not forget her, but comes bearing the diadem of light which is her authentic self. The Daimon remains faithful and marries the Authentic Self in a wonderful way.

This is how the daimon muses us, seeing us as beautiful and desirable in our own right. He does not judge us by the standards of human men or by the distorting projections of patriarchal culture. To the daimon, the authentic self is intrinsically good, true and beautiful. This loving appreciation restores to us the diadem of our female sovereignty, recognizing us as queens of our own realm, powerful and creatively authoritative. With such a diadem we need no longer crave authoritarian approval, but are ready to relate to the masculine in a more honest way. So adorned, we may at last consider how the masculine can be encountered with more balanced understanding.

Questions

1 Where is creative passion manifest in your life?
2 At what stages are your plans and projects in terms of the creative process?

Actions

1 Begin to see all your actions – hobbies, skills, talents, your job, daily tasks – as creative.
2 While walking outdoors, meditate upon your creative vocation. If blockages (the 'oughts', 'shoulds' and 'can'ts') are thrown up, sing them out, allowing your body to express their restriction for a brief moment: then experience the release of letting them go.

Reflections

Reflect upon your creative vocation and the daimon as torch-bearer through this 14th-century prayer:

> Give then yourself to me, O best of givers and giver of the best; for, as for yourself, you are mine, and nothing can be mine nor can I be my own, unless you be mine first. Be mine, be mine, therefore; for so long shall I be mine, and yours; but if you are not mine, nothing is mine.[69]

CHAPTER 8

What Women Most Desire

The only beloved is the living mystery itself.
Kathleen Raine, *The Lion's Mouth*

DISENCHANTING THE HAG

The 14th-century English story entitled *The Wedding of Sir Gawain and Dame Ragnell*, tells how King Arthur is challenged by an otherworldly being of great power – Sir Gromer Somer Joure (the Man of Summer's Day) – to find out 'what it is that women most desire'. Gromer challenges Arthur because he has given Gromer's lands to Arthur's nephew, Sir Gawain. Arthur must find the answer within a year and a day or suffer beheading, he enlists Gawain to help him. They make a book of the responses they receive from women, but there is no one clear answer. Then Arthur encounter a fiercesomely ugly women in the forest, Dame Ragnell, who promises to give him the answer if, in return, she may marry Sir Gawain. Arthur readily assents and produces the answer for Gromer, who retires, much peeved that Dame Ragnell, who is his sister, has obviously been aiding his enemy. The answer given by Arthur is:

> All women, both free women and those in bondage ... desire power, for that is their pleasure and their greatest wish. To have the rule of the manliest man, then are they happy, and thus they gave me the knowledge to rule you.[21]

Ragnell then requires her bargain to be ratified and, ugly though she is, Ragnell is betrothed to Gawain and the wedding takes place, to the dismay of the ladies of the court who bewail the loss of one of their handsomest knights. After the wedding breakfast, the couple retire to their chamber, and the hideous

Ragnell demands a kiss from her husband. 'I will do more than kiss you,' replies the ever courteous Gawain. As they embrace, Ragnell becomes the most beautiful woman he has ever seen. But this is not the fairy-tale end of the matter. Ragnell sets a riddle for Gawain: shall he choose to have her fair by day and foul by night to his public honour, or foul by day and fair at night for his delight?

Gawain responds:

> Although I would be glad to choose best, still I do not know what in the world I can say. So do as you wish, my lady dear. The choice I put in your hands. Do with me as you wish, for I am bound to you ... Both my body and my goods, my heart and all parts of me are all yours, to buy and sell.

Ragnell blesses him,

> for now you honor me. You shall have me beautiful both day and night and I will be fair and attractive as long as I live ... I would have been enchanted until the best man in England married me and give me sovereignty over his body and his goods ... You have given me sovereignty.

They are acclaimed by an astonished court the next morning, and remain faithfully married as long as they both live.

The impact of this story when it was first told would have been far greater than now, when Gawain seems to be just a nice, considerate guy. In medieval terms, 'women's freedom to choose' didn't exist: her whole life was lived in terms of her father, husband and sons. This story is most often quoted because of its central mystery question – 'What do women most desire?' – and its answer. As we see in this story, the answer is experienced on several levels.

- the general answers given by individual women
- the version given by Arthur to Gromer – 'women desire power and to rule over men'
- the core answer – unwittingly revealed in Gawain's behaviour – which is about women's freedom to choose and sovereignty

The first answers do not bear fruit; many are born of wish-fulfilment which will never be actively pursued or are the kinds of answers that are given when any national survey is done, when the respondents give the answers the survey wants to hear. The second answer solves a personal crisis for King Arthur, and also rectifies an injustice to a particular family: as he has been responsible for giving Gromer's lands to Gawain, so he unknowingly restores those lands Gromer's sister when he grants Gawain in marriage to Ragnell. This is the reverse of the normal medieval dowry where a bride's goods are handed over to her husband.

The third answer lies between Ragnell and Gawain themselves, and here the true and personal answer is achieved. Ragnell tests Gawain by asking him to choose between her being fair by day and foul at night, or foul by day and fair by night. If Gawain chooses the first, he puts his social kudos before his pleasure; if he chooses the latter, he puts pleasure ahead of kudos at court. What of Ragnell? If Gawain makes either of these decisions, she will suffer for ever after the consequences of his judgement. It is a big risk that Ragnell takes in setting this question at all.

Despite the changing mores of society, the situation of any woman today is much the same as Ragnell's at this point. A woman is still judged in society by her relationship with men at large – in what manner she is the daughter, mother or partner of a man. Her true nature can be obscured by all manner of pre-judgements about her femininity, her appearance, background and education. Her authentic self is rarely given rein or recognized by society.

But a woman's true nature *is* her beauty – a beauty which is not just 'inner', for her whole being is illuminated and ensouled by her self-respect, her compassion for others, her truth and integrity.

In this rich story, Ragnell is the representative of the Celtic Goddess of Sovereignty, she who bestows the stewardship of the land upon the most worthy ruler, but she is also all women.[47] Likewise, Gawain is both the champion of the Goddess of Sovereignty and all men. Gawain 'relinquishes sovereignty' over the question 'what do women most desire?', having already observed that no man and even most women do not know the answer to this. In Jungian terms, Gawain allows the eros of his anima to answer, not his innate male logic.

Just as Gawain refuses to dictate an answer to Ragnell, so too will the daimon allow woman's authentic self to furnish the answer, without any male games. This is the gift that all women may receive from their damon: the gift of being themselves on their own, not others', terms. Amanda's dream of a Gawain-like knight reveals that the daimon does not usurp women's right to choose, that he is not a dictator:

> The first time he appeared in dream, a multi-coloured light approached whom I recognized as my guide; he then transformed into an angelic knight. Opening my arms to receive him I exclaimed: 'At last you've come to me! Tell me, what is my higher purpose? What should I do with my life?' He opened his arms, took me by the shoulders and shook me up like a rag-doll, saying, 'It doesn't matter what you choose. Just CHOOSE! Any path will do'

Similarly, in Cocteau's film *La Belle et Le Bête*,[86] the Beast asks Belle if he may watch her dine every night. She submissively responds, like a daughter to a father, 'You are the master.' But he refutes any such title, 'No! Only you may command here.' It is no use our giving away power to the daimon in such ways: he will not make our decisions for us, he will not be vaunted into positions of supreme power. This relationship is an equal partnership and women must be responsible for their share. Our daimon, like the Beast, will seek to encourage us to greater self-motivation, with less reliance on the opinions about us. *Gawain and Ragnell* is the folk-story counterpart of *Beauty and the Beast*, for it discusses the disenchantment of the hag, just as *Beauty and the Beast* deals with the disenchantment of the beast. Being oneself is one of the hardest things for any human being. For women, it is perhaps *the* hardest thing, since her whole life is lived at the behest of others or as *the reflection* of others' projections. It is only when a level of maturity is achieved, when our female acceptance of projections is laid aside, that the daimon can hold up the mirror of truth and reveal our true inner nature and beauty, that the misshapen and socially-distorted view of ourselves as women can be dispelled and the centuries-old enchantment undone.

The medieval model of sovereignty was about dominance and submission. Sovereignty in a partnership is not about the dominance of one partner over another but about finding mutuality and respect for the sovereignty of the other. Personal sovereignty is about finding the authentic self and acting with integrity and passion from that sovereign ground of our being.

But the process of disenchanting the hag or beast requires the wisdom of the opposite sex to be effective ultimately. Until we are able to recognize each other's authentic self as the true face, rather than relating to the masks of projected femininity and masculinity, how are we to proceed?

In the context of the story, Ragnell's question and its true answer are addressed to men but, it must be said, women now need to ask this question of themselves if their passion is to serve them in the 21st century. What do women most desire? Indeed, most women have so skilfully covered over their needs, never mind the desires, of their inmost heart, that many no longer know. It is often assumed that 'women want what men have because it is intrinsically better'. Consequently, women's needs are very often formulated 'not as actual desires for sovereignty over their own lives, but as compensatory desires in reaction to men'.[82]

Many women have been in a state of stasis, so frozen into a mode of service that they no longer recognize their own needs and desires. Of the many clients I've seen in my shamanic practice, a predominance of women have come to rekindle their vocational pathway. I always ask them, 'What do you want in your heart of hearts?' The vocalization of secret or suppressed desires opens the road for passion to come in and lead the way forward. For a woman to express her desire is like sending out a golden pathway of song before her.

I believe that in the question 'what do women most desire?' we have a powerful way to open up the pathways of the soul: for when we contact the roots of our passion, the daimon will gladly hold open the door that has been closed too long. But in order to approach the big question, we must answer the little one first: 'what do I, as a woman, most desire?'

Like Arthur and Gawain's survey, the questionnaire I sent out for this book contained the big question. Here are some of the answers I received: some express personal desires, some speak for all of us.

Lauren speaks for many when she says,

> I most desire a monogamous, committed, passionate relationship with a man who is intellectually compatible and adventurous. It would be a relationship that offered freedom to pursue individual goals, yet that has stable foundation to raise a family.

Annie most desires 'the meeting of desire', a feeling reciprocated by Janet: 'Women most desire to love and to be loved back.'

Meg doesn't think that

any two women desire the same thing. For men and women: companionship with a member of either sex. Someone you can trust as well as yourself. Someone who can share everything with you, with no shame or embarrassment. I think that, sadly, this rarely happens. Chaucer was wrong when he said in the Wife of Bath's tale that what women desire is dominion over their men – a relationship cannot work as a fight for supremacy; it has to be a partnership on equal footing.

Anna longs for 'Perfect love and perfect trust'. For Elizabeth, it is 'Respect, love, honour, to become queen of our own realms – to find my queendom!'

Eve needs 'a relationship in which physical, psychic and spiritual reciprocation are possible'. Frances most desires

life, love, laughter and lots of light – when the dark clouds are there, I desire to be myself, rather than the image of myself that I think will most please others. I desire courage and support to do what it is I most need to do now and then go on to whatever is next. I most desire acceptance of my self as a complete being who is in partnership with other beings – a small lifetime's quest!

Pat believes that women desire

to be who they really are. To be passionate, sexual without abuse, recrimination or victimization. To be able to freely express themselves and be equal and accepted in society. To be accepted and love unconditionally for who they are, especially as a woman ... But I think collectively women don't know what they desire as they've been so corrupted and distorted from their true selves.

Sheila speaks personally, 'A private income. The freedom to be myself, to make my own decisions, to be "on top".'

Allegra's desires are passionately expressed:

> To be adored by a man I adore,
> To meet with shared magic,
> To laugh until we drop,
> To reach ecstasy and beyond,
> To live, die and live again,
> Dancing through and around
> each other without suffocation
> To be free together, but with no desire
> to be anywhere else but joined in the
> rhythm of our dance.

Melissa says, 'regardless of sex, gender, race and species, we all need and want Sovereignty – inner and outer – a space of our own so that we can realize our dreams, expectations and be/become doers, lovers, beloveds and parents of our deeds and future generations in all worlds.' For Hue it is 'respect'; for Fiona, 'to become whole'. Lairdearg lists 'respect, love and fulfilment: the three desires of the woman who has embraced her daimon'.

We can see the loving respect of the daimon in Gawain when he refuses to answer the question 'how would you like me to be?' which Ragnell poses. This is a woman's trick question to a man, implying 'what projection would you like me to fulfil?'. Had Ragnell been the kind of woman who ducks back behind the screen of the animus when confronting men, she might have immediately answered her question with a, 'Well, I suppose you'd like me fair at night because sex is all you think of!' or a 'Well, I suppose you'd like me fair by day because you only care about what others think.' These are analytical animus answers. But Ragnell does not answer this way, rather she stands firmly on the ground of her feminine self and meets Gawain as an equal, without any attempt at feminine manipulation or animus aggression (animosity). She doesn't mix levels.

But some men do indeed project their anima upon their wife's public face and desire her to be the ideal woman, but at night, when she returns to her own nature, they may not find her so sexually exciting. Similarly, those who project their anima upon their wife's sexual function may have to bear the stigma of her ungraceful behaviour during the day and the public taunts of 'what does he see in her?'.

If we as women feed back into this question – to ascertain the issue of being 'fair by day and foul by night, or foul by day and fair at night' – we miss the whole issue of women's disenchantment and what it is that we most desire. We will never discover the power of women's sovereignty by answering with 'what will other people think?' or 'who cares what they think?'. Only by personally answering the question will we access the passion that will empower change. If we continually engage the lesser question – 'how do you want me to be?' – we are just passing the buck.

Meeting the masculine on an equal footing is essential for relationships of integrity. In order to do this we need to be aware of and distinguish between the levels – to bring the daimon out of the theoretical realms into the realm of human relatedness with men and the masculine. This lack of acknowledgement of the daimon is one of the hidden agendas of spiritual and political feminism. He is not here, it is said, but then he rather obviously turns up in a prime piece of feminist action when the woman identifies with the obstructive or patriarchal masks of her daimon and allows them to function through her.

True feminism works from the ground of the creative and passionate feminine, to which the daimon gives access. False feminism is fuelled both by the denied feminine and by the reflected authority of the unintegrated and neglected masculine, which then become daimonic masks. This is one of the reasons why false feminism provokes such a knee-jerk reaction in men and women, because it pushes complex buttons concerning gender roles and projections given and received. It must also be said that the male projection of the excluded feminine as hag upon the whole women's movement casts a giant sorceress shadow. But within feminism itself there is a huge denial of the masculine which can surely only serve to further disempower women.

My questionnaire asked how lack of information or understanding about the daimon impacted on women's lives. The respondents were refreshingly frank on this subject.

Amanda thinks that

> lack of information is leaving us to seek by trial and error for our whole-self in the world around us. Women are manipulated by the fashion industry, magazines, beauty product firms and masculine concepts of society into thinking that we have to find our happiness by pleasing others, being beautiful but not self-loving. The biggest heart-breaker of all is women's search in our relationships for that special someone who will come and make us whole again. And when we aren't happy, we go shopping to fix things up – another way that men problem-solve.
>
> If women and children are assisted in honouring the inner voices, to look fearlessly without for wisdom and help, we would have a powerful evolution as emergent spiritual beings. Men have had their chance ... our only hope is that women will show the way to our wholeness, compassion and wisdom. I have found through listening to my daimon, an incredible doorway to my stength as a harmonious loving being!

Frances responds:

> Not being encouraged to meet with and know our daimon, women

will stumble about for much longer than they need to. However, this is changing all the time and perhaps the next generation of women will not feel and experience such harsh criticism for simply being women who choose not to accept a stereotypical role. However, with the imbalance still so strong in our culture here in the West, I am sure that women, particularly young girls, would benefit hugely from learning early about their daimon. Most women I know, of all ages, feel a great empty loneliness until they find or are in relationship with their inner selves and many take years and years to experience that wholeness. I have found in relationship to my own daimon that I am a lot more complete than I ever thought possible.

Gwen puts another view:

Everyone has to work out their own relationships with their daimon themselves. The lack of information means that each individual comes to her own way of handling the relationship as best suits her ... If women are afraid of their daimon, maybe its nature's way of telling them to leave well alone. That sounds a bit hard, but I think it's like a test, a test which wouldn't count if you already knew the answers. Even in folk tales, the naive blunder through by simple kindness much of the time, just doing what they have to.

This permission to 'do what we have to do' needs to be heeded by women who have poor self-motivation. Janet gives them encouragement:

People cannot really be told about the daimon, they can learn only so much from reading about it. I think they need to experience it and allow themselves to be open to it. If they allow themselves to be open, the daimon will reveal the truth they need to know.

It is clear that the confusion, shame and fear of self-delusion which denial of our daimons brings us needs to be addressed. As Anne says:

I've thought I was set apart in some way because I didn't know other people experienced this. Not as shameful as masturbation is thought of, but still rather odd.

Elizabeth instances feelings of

guilt, sexual guilt, fear of men and masculinity within us. So many people have this relationship but don't understand it or can't accept it.

Miriam feels that

> we have lost a valuable resource that could perhaps make us more
> allowing of the failures and foibles of the other men in our lives. If
> we have an active relationship with our daimon we are not asking
> a human male to take on the huge role. The ignoring of the
> daimon may be that some of us remain suspicious of the male,
> believing that he's always out to denigrate us, put one over on us,
> use us, not give us the consideration and validation we deserve, not
> *hear* us. We women become shadows.

But Hue's response to the conspiracy of silence is frank:

> It's part of the male attempt to beat anything competitive out of us
> and leave the way clear for themselves. As long as we are willing
> to languish in the castle, as long as we are willing to settle for the
> poor specimens that many men allow themselves to be, they don't
> have to try very hard at all. I think of the bumper sticker which
> says 'Men of Quality are not threatened by Women of Power'.

However, it must be said that women have also colluded in the
silent conspiracy. Lairdearg says:

> It means we don't know who we are, and we become afraid of
> ourselves. Without his strength, we are easily manipulated and
> overcome by men and the masculine world-view. We become
> victims. A woman without her daimon is an overly-feminine
> stereotype – at her worst, a homebody/Barbie Doll, helpless
> without a 'big strong man' to look after her. She doesn't grow up.
> Fortunately though, life has a way of creating doorways through
> which it is possible for the woman and her daimon to connect, any
> shock severe enough to crack the veneer can do it. One's husband
> leaving one for a younger woman is a classic example.

Amanda concludes:

> I think the daimon fulfils a genuine need that women are not
> finding satisfied in their lives. Throughout history, women have
> demonstrated resourcefulness and responsibility to the most
> oppressive circumstances. It's only logical to me that, in a time
> when we are under pressure to balance an increasingly male-
> dominated world with lowly-regarded female energy, we begin to
> go within for our own masculine energies. Just as the lies with
> which we have been raised have brainwashed men, women have
> ironically begun to emerge as messengers from the creative and
> spiritual reservoirs where we have been seeking our sanity all
> along. As we bring forth our wisdom, it's no surprise that we are

reshaping masculine energy to match the power and intensity of our conceiving abilities.

The disenchantment of the fearful masculine has to proceed at the same time as the disenchantment of the hag for the story to come true. The excluded masculine becomes a wanderer, looking for home, recognition and return. Elizabeth recognizes this aspect in her own daimon in the figure of 'Odysseus, searching for home. I strongly identify with his wife, Penelope'.

It is possible for the masculine and feminine to return home and be together? Can we relate in true partnership and friendship, no more passing each other by?

THE DANCE OF YIN AND YANG

The polarization of masculine and feminine, or male and female, of man and woman, creates an energy distortion affecting the whole world. Where one pole is a focus of achievement and satisfaction and the other is a focus of repression and dissatisfaction, there will be massive fluctuations of energy in which fear/appeasement, power/repression, anger/avoidance patterns are played out between men and women.

The misapprehension of one sex about the other is usually based on contraries rather than polarities. Men and women each represent a pole of the universal experience of humanness. Finding the complementaries rather than the contraries is now the challenge. This is the dance of Yin and Yang, of eternal feminine and masculine qualities, of which Katya Walter writes:

> Seeking to hold both poles without your attention will allow you to identify with more than half of an issue. You transcend the two attractor points that pull at you willy-nilly, each demanding loyalty for only its side. In psychological terms, if you can hold both sides of an issue in your mind, seeing ill and benefit rather than labelling one pole as automatically good and the other as therefore evil, then somehow this balance allows you to move calmly past a linear label of good and evil, demons and exorcists, saints and sinners ... so we can seek wholeness, learning to *befriend rather than be-fiend the shadow*. [my italics][72]

One of the first tasks is for women to acknowledge the feminine, but within the initial experience of feminism is a deep desire 'to avenge the mother', a volcanic rage which is triggered by the realization of all that women have been denied, by the waste of female potential, by the abuse of our mothers. In this phase of reaction, it is easy to allow the animus to arise as a feminist champion, to kick ass and put paid to the demonic masculine that caused all this. However, in doing this we but raise up another projection which blocks the way to progress and harmony within feminism.

Many women have been touched by their daimon, but all that they have been able to bequeath to their daughters of this intimate experience are 'all the things she felt and could not say, all the stored honey, the black hatred, the wistful homesickness for the unfenced wild – all that other women would have put into their prayers ...'.[74] This incoherent and sometimes rambling exploration of daimonic experience can be aided by the friendship of other women.

Some women act as initiating priestesses of the daimon by virtue of their lives, example or thoughts; when these are perceived or shared with other women, a line of wisdom extends and something precious is passed on. Women learn from each other far more than is realized: this is one of the reasons why female friends are so necessary. When women talk together – in what seems, to men, to be long conversations about nothing much – they are actually expressing a need to reality-check, to inspire and support, to reinforce the daimonic creative instinct. The co-operation between women is often baffling to men. The loss of the positive masculine in our society is a loss for all of society. Its recovery requires a reappraisal of the masculine on all levels of life, in its fresh, not its outworn, patterns. It is not currently politically correct for women to admit to any taint of masculine influence but I hope that the evidence presented here reveals another part of the picture. Marion Woodman writes:

> The Berlin Wall is down. The Wall of Mirrors through which men and women fail to see each other is still up. It stands invisible in the streets, in our institutions and in personal relationships.[79]

Men and women have become separated from each other by a series of projected images. We no longer respond personally and uniquely to the opposite sex, but via a series of filters. We look at the other person but see only a video playing there which tells us facts and builds up our expectations in ways that falsify or muddle our real experience of the other. To switch off that video is exceedingly difficult, for if a woman succeeds in ceasing to project expectations upon her partner, the man may go on watching his own video.

The torture-racks of political correctness bind and disempower us with each other, we need something more fluid than tolerance, more hopeful than good intentions. We need to give space and allowance for the authentic soul of both men and women to be expressed. It requires a patience that I fear most people nowadays seldom reach for. It may mean going and standing patiently day after day with that fluid and hopeful allowance in our hearts to whatever relationships are unproductive and unsatisfactory, whether at home, at work or in the world at large.

It requires that women begin to speak to men from their authentic soul rather than telling them what men want or expect to hear. This may require an emotional honesty and spiritual courage that is also hard to summon up. To attempt to answer the question of what women most desire may be the beginning of mutual understanding for, unless women speak up and state what they do want from the core of their authentic soul, no man will ever know.

Many men whom I've spoken to while working on this book have expressed their disquiet about the way they are treated by some women: that is, not as an individual, but as the representative of an insensitive male tribe, one to be castigated for monstrous crimes against womankind. The rules of the baiting game of the sexes have to change. It is certainly no use women mocking 'the mother-bound sons of the patriarchy all the while using the wily feminine intrigues that make men pageboys rather than kings'.[79] The alienation and affront is palpable on both sides, creating a wall through which no meaningful communication can take place. Perhaps all of us, women and men, need to call upon our daimon or muse to act as ambassador to the other side of that wall.

Jocelyn writes.

> Most modern feminists are neither anti individual men because they're men or against male images and energies: what we recognize is that we all live in a profoundly patriarchal society, speaking and even dreaming within a male symbolic order. To transform an

uncontrollable, invasive and external male dream image into a
controllable, supportive and internal one is a deeply empowering
and feminist act.

And for Elizabeth:

> I feel that masculine and feminine are meant to be different, and
> equal within that difference. Denying one of these qualities doesn't
> strengthen the other. At times when my daimon was absent from
> my life, I felt weaker, not stronger. I love being a woman and have
> never understood why being equal to men needs to mean being as
> like a man as possible. The daimon gives us nothing to fear if we
> believe that [women] have no need to change. I've observed that
> women who don't live with the daimon take on masculine quali-
> ties outwardly, as they are not accepted inwardly. Like all aspects
> of the psyche, the daimon will always out somehow!

Diana also adds, 'When men feel free to accept the goddess within without feeling diminished, women will be free to acknowledge
the god within.'

Let us all acknowledge that the imbalances that have come
about affect all people, whether female or male. The intelligent
view is to seek to rectify this and realize that several hundred
years' of imbalance cannot be changed overnight, and that the
processes of anger, disillusion, of drawing up fresh expectations,
of learning how to re-relate, must necessarily be undergone first.
Women must change, as well as men.

> Negotiations between the sexes are bound to collapse into misun-
> derstandings or remain suspended in compromise that satisfy
> neither, so, long as men and women remain strangers to their inner
> reality.[79]

In our understanding of women's role, we have seen a trend away
from demands for equality to an urgent call for complementarity.
How we arrive at complementarity of the sexes very much
depends on the steps that we take to achieve it. One of the
greatest needs is for mutual respect between men and women: a
respect which discerns the soul of each individual, which
comprehends how the pathways of soul have been muddied by
deeds, assumptions and neglects.

Let us remember that women's rights have been neglected to the
same degree as men's.

The oppression of the feminine within a patriarchal tradition renders the masculine shaped by that tradition its natural enemy. It is therefore also necessary to disarm the feminine of its fear of the patriarchal masculine in order to release the dynamics of the new realtionship.[79]

The release from fear can come in two ways: by seeking the authentic self and its spiritual landscape, and by exploring our relationship with the daimon. When the daimon comes clear and shining from the river-bed of the soul like a nugget of gold, free of the shale and gravel of projection, then our relationship with men can become correspondingly clearer.

THE CONSUMMATION

Passion is fuel. It runs through all kinds of women, whether they be sexually active or celibate. It brings erotic, creative and spiritual freedom, for this is the frequency of what women most desire – making eros and passion manifest in our lives.

As the faculty of the female soul, the daimon awakens love and points the way, he reveals pathways to ecstasy; he encourages creative fulfilment; he is the psychopompus, the leader of the soul; he is the chorus-master who stirs up our passion so that we step confidently into the dance of life.

Many respondents speak of this experience of continual support as one which does not finish at this life's end. As Lairdearg says:

> All that I know of him, I've learned directly from him. I know that I am part of him and that, when I die, he will be there to welcome me home.

The daimon does not die, nor fade or grow old, as Kathleen Raine's poem, 'Falling Leaves'[58] promises:

> Long ago I thought you young, bright daimon,
> Whisperer in my ear
> Of springs of water, leaves and song of birds,
> By all time younger
> Than I, who from the day of my conception
> Began to age into experience and pain;
> But now life in its cycle swings out of time again
> I see how old you were,

Older by eternity than I, who, my hair gray,
Eyes dim with reading books,
Can never fathom those grave deep memories
Whose messenger you are,
Day-spring to the young, and to the old, ancient of days.

As Diotima, the Mantinian sibyl said to Socrates, 'the greatest of the daimons is Love', and love is ageless. The daimon accompanies us to the ends of this life and beyond.

Psyche falls in love with Love himself, patiently and lovingly following his steps until she wins the highest prize: immortality. Partnership with the daimon defines our soul's pathway through this life: a pathway that leads between the worlds of physical and subtle reality, beyond this present life. The bridge is built of loving trust.

Where our love is given, there also is our passion to be found: whether that love and passion are sexual, creative or spiritually dedicated does not matter. The fact that we have loved and have been loved in whatever field of life we have walked is what matters most, for love confers its own shining immortality to our souls.

Ubi caritas et amor Deus ibi est: 'wherever loving-kindness and love are, there is God also.' Whether we speak of God, Goddess or Spirit, the Divine manifests in many forms, but the touch-point of that manifestation is always the passionate spark of love: whether it be for a lover, a child, a place, a craft or a cause. Spirit does not spark in cold, shuttered hearts or in unkind, blinkered institutions. Spirit is not cosy and amenable, capable of being wheedled into uneasy compromises: Spirit is ever true to its nature, lightning-quick, revealing, ecstatic and compassionate.

The word 'compassion' says it all: the creative friction between ourselves and the Divine is passion, a like-heartedness which bridges all separations and leads us into the unity of love. The male and the female are the two hands of the Divine, which combines both genders and may express itself as God or goddess, Yin and Yang.

The guardian of that bridge for women is the daimon who summons us to passion and invites us to cross the bridge of separation to find the consummation. Divine messengers do the bidding of the gods, leading us along the road of sacred duty to our soul's vocation. If we refuse to walk that road, we will never realize our soul's vocation and begin to detest the messenger's insistent appearance in our lives and dreams. It may grow monstrous in our eyes, a premonition of deeply-buried fear of our potential. But if we take the daimon's hand and explore the road to our soul's vocation, we are sure of being accompanied by a wise companion who knows our soul's needs and who will be adept at dealing with our fears and anxieties along the way.

Finding our soul's vocation is about becoming authentic, about discovering our own task, not about following someone else's. Becoming authentic is to arrive finally at the destination of the self and find welcome there. This means being comfortable about ourselves and being true to the soul's task. This is not necessarily a religious destiny; it may manifest in a number of ways – by learning and achieving, by no longer avoiding the soul's desire but engaging passionately in what the soul is leading us towards.

Denise Levertov's poem 'The Spirits Appeased',[49] speaks with the daimon's voice of recognition:

> *now she is looking*, you say to each other,
> *now she begins to see.*

How long has the daimon sought you and waited for you to enter into the country of your own soul and take possession? By what attractions and allurements has he besought you to even look in his direction? How often have you looked with longing down that soul-road?

But what lies at the end of that road? For each of us it is a different, wondrous story. Its mystery is not normally discussed, but rather, closed by a folk-story 'they all lived happily ever after' ending, or by the saint's nirvanic departure from the physical world.

The idea of a final ending or a satisfactory conclusion appeals to us, but the reality needs to be discussed here. After any experience of mystical or passionate union, a deeper consummation is achieved and the previous sense of separation from the object of union is never again so separating. Once non-duality has been experienced, the possibility of sequential ecstasy accompanies all of life's duties – for the simple reason that the object of our love lends its shine to everything we do, think and feel.

The entering into daily and ordinary consummation of spirit is what follows the taking up of our soul's vocation. We then come daily to the meeting place of human and spirit in commonplace ways that would once have bored or distracted us. In short, we continue to live our lives, *but with the dimension of love ever present* – and that is what makes all the difference. Whether we are poor, rich, healthy, ill, old or young, our circumstances themselves do not miraculously improve after the consummation of the spirit, but our hearts, souls and minds perceive our lives to be true stories in which we have engagement, and to which we bring a real service.

Love and service are inextricably linked. As we receive, so can we give. Once this circuit of spiritual consummation has been set up, the sheer generosity that wells up in our hearts cannot be retained only for our own use. By our service – whether through work, relating to others, or being true to our spiritual vocation – we lubricate the universe with the superabundance of the love we have entered into.

The consummation is the true meeting with daimon and fulfils his purposes. But what happens, how does the daimon change when that moment of consummation has taken place? For each woman it will be a different experience. From my years in shamanic practice I know how spiritual allies transform when the subject undergoes great changes. The sense of a spirit outside of us fades, the sense of self-identification with the spirit grows. In Denise Levertov's poem 'Matins' (*ibid*) we catch a sense of this:

> Speak to me, little horse, beloved,
> tell me
> how to follow the iron ball,
> how to follow through to the country
> beneath the waves
> to the place where I must kill you and you step out
> of your bones and flystrewn meat
> tall, smiling, renewed,
> formed in your own likeness.

This seemingly harsh image of 'slaying what we love' is commonplace in shamanic experience. What happens here is really *a releasing of loving power*, not a murder. As I have written in my poem 'Releasing the Daimon':[38]

> I have stood with upraised knife
> At your command. An Abraham
> consumed with panic terror,
> I've wavered and refused the task.
> Yet you returned, more needful than before:

> 'Kill me and release me!
> Take heart and love and all.'
> I hesitated. Still you come again.
> Last time you bade me bury you
> In a dark hollow, my tears as gravegoods
> To guard you. Yet you rise again
> Through the deep rocks,
> A man in hawthorn like Merlin.
> Love is not locked out of me
> Only now your images float free
> To inspire me where they will.

The masks of the messenger change, but the love between us and the daimonic never dies. We must trust that

> When you are self-gathered in the purity of your being, nothing now remaining that can shatter that inner unity, nothing from without clinging to [you], when you find yourself wholly true to your essential nature ... call upon all your confidence, strike forward yet a step – you need a guide no longer – strain and see.[57]

LEAVING THE ENCHANTED TOWER

The recurrent theme of the human quest for energy balance between men and women is one of dominant and recessive patterns or modes of awareness. This is seen in the symbol of the tower. For women, the tower is the place of imprisonment or enchantment from which they must escape: Sleeping Beauty lies asleep while Rapunzel is imprisoned within hers. Both await the Prince who will bring her forth into the daily world. For women, the Tower is a place to be shunned and escaped from.

But for men of mature spirit, the Tower is a place of retreat and study, as in Milton's thoughtful prayer in 'Il Penseroso':[48]

> Let my lamp at midnight hour
> Be seen in some high lonely tower,
> Where I may oft outwatch the Bear
> With thrice great Hermes.

Two men in our century physically built or restored such towers and then retired to them. In order to help with the process of their re-mythication and to make a creative enclave for the alchemical work of soul-making, both psychoanalyst C G Jung and poet W B Yeats retreated, respectively, to their towers at Bollingen and Thoor Ballylee with a will. Yeats wrote of the winding stair and the gyres or cyclic corridors of time, space and resonance into which our life-experience evolves: images which come directly from his tower.[81] Jung meditated upon the alchemical mysteries of integration within his.[71]

Why is it that, for women, the tower is a place of terror and restriction when, for men it is a place numinous enlightenment? The answer lies in the nature of the soul-quest of men and women.

For women and men, the world of the opposite sex is an otherworld to which they seek entry and understanding. As we mature, we move from innate models of understanding into more sophisticated realms which balance out the inequities of maleness and femaleness we have derived from society.

The soul-realm of women is bounded by the tower, the dimension wherein they explore the feminine and psychic frequencies of early womanhood. For them, the masculine realm lies outside the tower. The soul-realm of men is the wide world wherein they explore the masculine and active qualities of early manhood.

Women's necessary initiation involves how to relate their female qualities to the realm of the wide world that lies outside the tower. The initiation for men is to learn how their male qualities relate to the subtle, hidden queendom of the tower. Both sexes seek the initiation of the contrasexual otherworld which is a mystery to them.

The initiators in this process of balance and maturation are the contrasexual figures who inhabit the soul. This process is apparent in myths world-wide, where the contrasexual other appears as a saviour or initiator. Myths tend to focus upon the male quest. The many folk-stories which deal with the female quest are rarely recognized as such because they seem to be about women's victimizations and suppression rather than active searches for glorious and exciting goals. We have been short-sighted. The female quest is invariably about leaving the enchanted Tower and attaining competence in the wide world.

We find that the male quest in myth and story is facilitated by magical and powerful female figures, as we can see in the Arthurian and Celtic legends.[47] The female quest in myth and story is facilitated by helpful and heroic male figures. The quest for wholeness, healing and transformation is facilitated by representatives of the contrasexual other who initiate men and women into the realm of the opposite sex. These quests invariably concern the transmission of the secrets of life and how we live it, as well as of deeper mysteries concerning the potent core of masculinity and femininity.

Men's stories relate the journey into the place within; women's stories relate the journey into the place without. Men meet sibyls, priestesses, witches and ladies who endow them with powers which are beyond male accomplishment. Women meet heroes, princes, kings and magicians who give them help or gifts which enable their integrated return to a life of wholeness and completion.

The helpful contrasexual figure is an enabler with the power to grant gifts which enhance our innate powers. Our innate soul-frequency is not denied or ignored; thus, men and women must demonstrate their innate courage, strength, virtue, beauty, gift or ability *before* other gifts are granted. The gift which women are offered is the secret of the Sacred Masculine.

If we attempt to engage the contrasexual other before we have clarified the innate qualities that define our authentic self, we risk identifying with and embodying qualities of the masks which are often worn by the contrasexual other. These masks are, I believe, the warning face of the threshold guardian with whom we must struggle before we pass within or without. This Janus-headed one is encountered by all human beings: for men seeking the realm of subtle reality and maturing soul, the face of the threshold guardian will be the terrifying feminine; after the essential period of struggle, answering riddles or performing impossible tasks, the face will change to that of the initiator. If men neglect this primary task – identifying the anima – the masked muse will surface and they will take on the excluded feminine aspects of their background, becoming a very non-heroic, whining and self-pitying crew.

Women likewise must face the masked daimon who, as challenging threshold guardian, will ask difficult questions and set impossible tasks. It seems a characteristic of the female quest that for women to find their way through to the ordinary world of physical reality and be effective therein, they must cast off the enchantments and projections which bind them. If they attempt to do so without drawing upon their innate authentic qualities, they risk identification with the excluded masculine elements of their upbringing, becoming a strident and opinionated crew with little of the heroic feminine.

The Janus-headed contrasexual figure has another face, however. Men and women who accept their own authentic qualities come into relationship with the transcendent and initiatory face of the muse or daimon. After this encounter, there is no longer a frantic shuttling between male and female modes, no more headlong quest into the other realm from which they have been excluded. The tides and rhythms of self with contrasexual other will be established, and that will affect the way in which we all live.

This is the work of maturity: to arrive at a state wherein we no longer play the silly games which prolong the gender wars. Here we arrive at a true understanding of complementarity wherein the poles of gender come together in a dance of Yin and Yang (plate illustration 15). Within the symbol of the Tao, the black fish has a white eye and the white fish a black eye. The male sees with a female awareness, and the female with a male awareness.

The place of the Tower is dramatically demonstrated in the powerful story of the withdrawal of Merlin. In the primal story told by Geoffrey of Monmouth in the 12th century, we find a Merlin who is both dynamic and unpredictable – a far cry from the decrepit old sorcerer of later medieval story who is incarcerated in a tower by virtue of his own lust for Nimue. The proto-Celtic story restores to us a pattern which has long since been overlaid – a pattern of rhythmic dance between dominant and recessive, of the antiphonal chorus of male and female.

In this story, Merlin enters a period of madness after his horrific exposure to the carnage of war. He abandons his wife, Guendolena, who later remarries, and lives wild in the forest. Merlin's sister Ganeida builds him a house of 70 doors and windows from whence he can see over the land and watch the changing heavens, for Merlin's time of withdrawal is nigh. Although she frequently mediates on her brother's behalf, Ganeida's life up until this point has been primarily bound up with her husband, King Rhydderch. On his death, she declares, 'In company with my brother I shall dwell in the woods and shall worship God with a joyful heart, clothed in a black mantle'.[47]

After his restoration to sanity by the poet Taliesin, Merlin asks

Ganeida to visit him often. As he retires into his tower, he becomes absorbed in his observations and Ganeida takes prominence and becomes the one active in prophecy. Merlin says to her, 'Sister, is it you the spirit has willed to foretell the future? He has curbed my tongue and closed my book. Then this task is given to you. Be glad of it, and under my authority declare everything faithfully.'

Merlin's instruction to Ganeida to, 'declare everything faithfully' is the daimon's exortation to us to be authentic and true to our visions, to tell it like it is! Ganeida does not usurp the prophetic task of Merlin: he willingly acknowledges it as her true task and she assumes it naturally as something within her competency and vocation. As Merlin retires to his tower, Ganeida confidently emerges.

Ganeida instructs us to 'arise from prison and open the books of inspiration without fear', as the earliest Celtic dialogue between Merlin and his sister relates. We women can leave the enchanted Tower and enter the wide world secure in the knowledge that the task of our dear brother, the daimon, is done. Thenceforward, it is our task to speak with the prophetic voice which combines our female wisdom with the knowledge of the masculine.

The last thing we can do with and for our daimon is to release him from all imprisoning projections and images. Just as Shakespeare's Prospero relinquishes his book of art and releases Ariel from the imprisoning cask of the tree, letting him free to be spirit and leaving Miranda free to return to life outside the enchanted island of *The Tempest*, so too can we release our own aerial spirit from the imprisoning masks of Tyrant, Critic and Patriarch and allow our feminine authentic self to return home.

This doesn't mean that our daimon will necessarily disappear, become invisible or never take another form, but that Love cannot be bound. Love is a Spirit and its nature is unconditional surrender and commitment at the same time. Once we enter the ground of our own female soul by the bridge of loving trust, the daimon is no longer janitor and messenger to it, but is free.

As Plato records in the *Symposeum*:

> Nor will [our] vision of the beautiful take the form of a face, or of hands, or of anything that is of the flesh. It will be neither words, nor knowledge, nor a something that exists in something else, such as a living creature, or the earth, or the heavens ... but subsisting

of itself and by itself in an eternal oneness, while every lovely thing partakes of it in such sort that, however much the parts may wax and wane, it will be neither more nor less, but still the same inviolable whole.[56]

When the authentic self and the daimon emerge unmasked, from their wrappings, and meet, then we experience a deep communion in the soul. Because there is no more clinging, obsession, argument or berating – only love – the soul becomes a place where we can use, not neglect, our passion. As Sheila says,

When the potential of the daimon is harnessed, then our dreams can live in the everyday world. The daimon brings focus and passion to our work.

We may leave the tower at last, no more enchanted.

No relationship is more lasting than that between human soul and guiding daimon. This is why Psyche gains immortality. It is why I have written this book. For the daimon comes to enable and make possible that which lies beyond our capacity to ignite. The passion of a woman's viscera, soul and mind are the tinder: the daimon is the lightning flash which makes us incandescent.

Women in all situations, whether single or partnered, need to find their authentic self. No woman wishes autonomous independence which separates her from all other human alliances. Relationship with the daimon will not isolate a woman; although she may indeed seek purposeful periods of seclusion to comprehend her experience, she will also seek her peers' advice and mutual support. Correct identification of the daimon under his animus masks will bring us into good relationship with the whole universe.

It is the nature of Spirit to take human forms, but Spirit can only incarnate through receptive love. The return of the daimon to Spirit is a cause of human sadness, but at the same time it is conveyed by an act of willing and human love: Christ is crucified, Dionysos is torn in pieces. Only the fragrance of the Beloved is left. No longer a vessel of projection, no longer imprisoned within the contraints of one image, Love is then free to invade the universe with its uncompromising ecstasy. As the 14th-century anonymous poem says:

> His love is fresh and ever green,
> And ever full without waning;

His love sweetens without paining,
His love is endless to world's rim.

We are each a filament in the web of life. By our thoughts, actions, meditations and understandings, by our rejection of gender projections, we take responsibility for mending the web of universal relationship between human beings.

May you discover your authentic self by the light of the daimon's illumination.

Questions

1 What is your heart's desire?
2 What do women most desire?

Actions

1 Put your answers to the above into practice.
2 Reconsider your attitudes to the masculine – in men, the masculine within your own life, the Divine Masculine. Make any changes in the light of your authentic self.

Reflection

Reflect upon the wisdom of your own life experience and the ways in which your passionate nature has been revealed.

Afterword

We have followed the daimon through a variety of guises and transformations, in unlikely places and by unorthodox routes of investigation. It may all seem rather strange, scary or overwhelming, but I hope that you have also discovered encouragement and fresh heart from the respondents' generous sharing of their experience.

Always remember that each woman's experience is unique. The clues and suggestions which have been scattered throughout this book do not represent the 'one right method' to hasten the arrival of the authentic self at the platform of the true daimon. There are many pathways and variations on this daimonic quest. Some women will require the help of professionals to clarify confusions, but many will find their own way on intelligent and playful quest. Remember that the daimon cannot be sorted out in a few short weeks, months or even years. Like any relationship, it takes time and effort, as well as love and understanding.

Finding a framework of life that suits you is a task only you can begin – at this moment, now. Maintaining such a framework is hard but rewarding work which must have regular input. Those who are addicted to perfection need to realize that all women commonly experience failure in minor or major ways, that we all have 'off-days' when nothing goes right. Clear some reflective and creative space for yourself so that you are not harried into self-forgetfulness by the pressures of the world. The rhythms of your own body and the times and seasons of the natural world are your allies: listen to and play with them.

Make friends with your daimon, allow him to show you the passionate roads that lead to your soul, playfully explore the creative possibilities, and allow him to lead you to your authentic self by the winding roads of self-discovery.

> Hand in hand we shall us take
> And joy and bliss shall we make.

Glossary

This short glossary lists words used in specific ways in this book: they may differ from received usage.

Anima Jungian term for the *soul-image* of a man, appearing in female guise. In this book, the unemergent or masked *muse*. The anima may be *projected* upon a living woman.

Animus Jungian term for the *soul-image* of a woman, appearing in male guise. In this book, the unemergent or masked *daimon*. The animus may be *projected* upon a living man.

Authentic Self The true self, often hidden by projections which have been received and accepted.

Contrasexual other The indwelling *soul-image* of a person, revealed itself in heterosexual people as of the opposite sex; among homosexual people, it may be of the same sex.

Creativity The mode by which the *soul* expresses its *genius*; frequently guided, inspired and supported by the *daimon* or *muse*.

Daimon (pronounced dy-mone) The indwelling companion, inspirer and spirit-guardian of a woman, who illuminates her soul; often shrouded by the *projections* of the *animus*. The daimon is never a human man but a spirit although it may be *projected* onto a man.

Demon Lover Name given to ghostly or spirit lovers of human beings who have no physical manifest reality.

Divine The Spirit, neither male nor female, which may appear as God or Goddess.

Feminism The movement which restates and seeks to establish women and the role of women as significant in their own right. It promotes viewpoints which disentangle women from patriarchal expectations and *projections*.

Genius (pronounced gay-neus) The indwelling potential and creative quality with which human beings are gifted.

God The Divine Masculine appearance of *Spirit*.

Goddess The Divine Feminine appearance of *Spirit*.

Hierodule Hierodules were dedicated at temple sites to embody the Divine Feminine; worshippers came to engage in sexual congress with the hierodules as an act of sacred veneration.

Imagination The faculty of the soul which enables us to view and participate in the life of our sacred *symbolic landscape*.

Incubus The medieval term for the male *demon lover* of women.

Individuation Jungian term for the clarification between *authentic self* and *projections* and the integration of the *contrasexual other*.

Love That uncompromising passion which cares for the beloved with equal or better care than that given to the self; Love is also manifest as an appearance of Spirit in all cultures.

Mediation The ability to be a go-between, medium or ambassador between physical and subtle reality, and vice versa.

Muse The indwelling inspirer, companion and spirit-guardian of a man, and illuminator of his soul; often shrouded by the projections of the *anima*. The muse is never a living woman but a spirit although it may be *projected* on to a woman.

Myth A story told out of the personal or collective to demonstrate the truths arising from the interrelationship of *physical and subtle realities*.

Passion The innate fire of life which permeates all beings; underlying and manifesting in physical vigour, sexual ardour, creative aspiration and spiritual service.

Patriarchy The prevalent cultural life-style in which everything is determined from a male viewpoint and to the benefit of men, and in which women, children and the feminine aspects of manhood are spurned or neglected.

Physical reality The realm of the apparent, everyday world which, with subtle reality, makes up a greater universal reality.

Power The dynamic energy or fuel of the universe which permeates all beings; in women, the authority to act and think in accordance with personal integrity. Loss of power may result the blockage of *passion*.

Priestess A woman who exercises the role of spiritual *mediation* in her community.

Projections The tagging or assumption of presumed qualities upon other people or upon ourselves; projections mask the *authentic self* and play a large part in the lack of comprehension between the sexes.

Psyche The soul; hence **psychic**: of or belonging to the *soul*.

Sacred symbolic landscape The territory of the individual *soul* which shows itself to us in dreams, reflections and creativity.

Shadow In Jungian terms, the submerged part of the self which remains hidden, elusive or unconscious.

Shamanism The practice of spiritual *mediation* by which a shaman purposefully visits the worlds of *subtle reality* for the purpose of obtaining healing, information and wisdom from *Spirit* for people in his or her community.

Soul The spiritual correlative of the physical body which interacts with both *physical* and *subtle reality*, as well as between the events of daily and psychic life.

Soul-image The indwelling image within the soul of the *contrasexual other*; soul-images reveal themselves in many symbolic ways and are indicators of how we experience *subtle reality*.

Spirit The Divine, which may take any form apprehensible by the individual soul.

Subtle reality The realm of the unseen, spiritual world which, with physical reality, makes up a greater universal reality.

Succubus The medieval term for the female *demon lover* of men.

Temenos A holy place or sacred enclave.

Unemergent daimon or muse The indwelling inspirer who is not free to help or companion because it is still masked by projections.

List of Respondents

The respondents to the questionnaire whose work has been used in this book are listed here. Their material remains copyrighted to them under the term of this book's contract and should not be quoted without their express permission: this should be sought via Caitlín Matthews, BCM Hallowquest, London WC1N 3XX. Respondents are listed below in alphabetical order of pseudonym, some with their ages; their descriptions are self-chosen.

Allegra 53, artist and counsellor, divorced.
Amanda 31, cook and yoga teacher.
Anna creative artist.
Anne 43, writer.
Annie welfare rights adviser.
Diana novelist and priestess.
Elizabeth 32, artist and priestess.
Eve 48, painter and teacher.
Fiona 42, single mother, artist and emerging priestess.
Frances 45, writer, mother, facilitator and healer.
Gwen 45, artist.
Hue 46, music and conversation-loving painter.
Ioho Druid priestess.
Janet herbal and shamanic practitioner.
Jocelyn Jungian psychotherapist and artist.
Karen 30, management consultant and shamanic student.
Lairdearg community priestess.
Lauren 31, graduate student.
Meg 29, musician.
Melissa 35, PhD, information scientist.
Miriam 48, writer, priestess, tarot consultant, farmer and college professor.
Moyra 52, teacher and poet.
Myra 43, counsellor and healer.
Pat, an ex-nurse.
Sheila 50, mature student.
Susanna 44, writer and teacher.
Suzanne 50, photographer, poet and creative writer.

Sources

The following sources are listed numerically and are cross-referenced in the text.

BIBLIOGRAPHY

Unless stated otherwise, all books were published in London.

1 Albery, Nicholas, *Poem for the Day*, London, Natural Death Centre, 1994

2 Allione, Tsultrum, *Women of Wisdom*, London, Routledge & Kegan Paul, 1984

3 Amberston, Celu, *Deepening the Power: Community and Sacred Theatre*, Beach Holme Publishers, Victoria, BC, 1995

4 Andersen, Hans Christian, *The Complete Fairy Stories*, trans Erik C Haugaard, London, Gollancz, 1974

5 Brontë, Emily, *Wuthering Heights*, London, J M Dent, 1993

6 Brown, Karen McCarthy, *Mama Lola: A Vodou Priestess in Brooklyn*, University of California Press, Berkeley, 1991

7 Carter, Angela, *The Bloody Chamber*, London, Vintage, 1995

8 Carter, Angela, *The Magic Toyshop*, London, Virago, 1981

9 Chaplin, Jocelyn, *Love in an Age of Uncertainty*, London, Aquarian Press, 1993

10 Claremont de Castillejo, Irene, *Knowing Woman: A Feminine Psychology*, New York, Harper & Row, 1974

11 Dalai Lama, Tsong-ka-pa, and Hopkins, Jeffrey, *Deity Yoga*, Ithaca, NY, Snow Lion Publications, 1981

12 De Pizan, Christine, *The Book of the City of Ladies*, London, Picador, 1983

13 Dowman, Keith, *Sky Dancer: the Secret Life and Songs of the Lady Yeshe Tsogyel*, London, Routledge & Kegan Paul, 1984

14 Eliot, George, *Middlemarch*, Oxford, Oxford University Press, 1988

15 Fortune, Dion, *The Esoteric Philosophy of Love and Marriage*, London, Aquarian Press, 1970

16 Fortune, Dion, *Moon Magic,* London, Aquarian Press, 1956

17 Fortune, Dion, *The Sea Priestess*, London, Aquarian Press, 1957

18 Gray, Miranda, *Red Moon: Understanding and Using the Gifts of the Menstrual Cycle*, Shaftesbury, Element, 1994

19 Greer, Mary K, *Women of the Golden Dawn*, Park Street Press, Rochester, VT, 1995

20 Grimm Brothers, *Tales for Young and Old*, trans, Ralph Mannheim, London, Gollancz, 1979

21 Hall, Louis, *The Knightly Tales of Sir Gawain,* Chicago, Nelson-Hall, 1976

22 Hannah, Barbara, *The Problem of Contact with Animus*, Guild of Pastoral Psychology Lecture 70, 1962

23 Harding, M Esther, *The Way of All Women*, New York, Harper & Row, 1975

24 Harding, M Esther, *Women's Mysteries: Ancient and Modern*, New York, Harper & Row, 1976

25 Harms, Valerie, *The Inner Lover*, Boston, Shambhala, 1992

26 Herodotus, *The Histories*, Harmondsworth, Penguin, 1972

27 Hoban, Russell, *The Moment Under the Moment*, London, Jonathan Cape, 1992

28 Jung, C G, *The Archetypes and the Collective Unconscious*, trans. R F C Hull, London, Routledge & Kegan Paul, 1959

29 Jung, C G, 'The Syzygy: Anima and Animus' in *Collected Works*, vol 9, part II: 'Aion, Researches into the Phenomenology of the Self' trans R F C Hull, London, Routledge & Kegan Paul, 1967

30 Kerenyi, C, *The Gods of the Greeks*, London, Thames & Hudson, 1951

31 Leader, Darian, *Why Do Women Write More Letters Than They Post?*, London, Faber, 1996

32 Leonard, Linda Schierse, *On the Way to the Wedding: Transforming the Love Relationship*, Boston, Shambhala, 1986

33 Lewis, C S, *That Hideous Strength*, London, Bodley Head, 1945

34 Lucius Apuleius, *The Tale of Cupid and Psyche,* trans Robert Graves, Boston, Shambhala, 1992

35 Matthews, Caitlín, *The Books of Glass,* (unpublished journals 1965–96)

36 — *The Celtic Devotional*, Alresford, Godsfield Press, 1996

37 — *The Celtic Tradition*, Shaftesbury, Element, 1995

38 — *Dancing with Daimons* (unpublished poetry)

39 — *Elements of the Goddess*, Shaftesbury, Element, 1989

40 — *The Search for Rhiannon*, Frome, Bran's Head Press, 1981

41 — *Singing the Soul Back Home*, Shaftesbury, Element, 1995

42 — *Sophia, Goddess of Wisdom*, London, Harper Collins, 1996

43 — *Troytown Dances* (unpublished novel)

44 — *Voices of the Goddess*, London, Aquarian Press, 1989

45 — and Matthews, John, *The Arthurian Tarot*, London, Aquarian Press, 1990

46 — and Matthews, John, *The Encyclopaedia of Celtic Wisdom*, Shaftesbury, Element, 1995

47 — and Matthews, John, *Ladies of the Lake,* London, Harper Collins, 1996

48 — and Matthews, John, *The Western Way*, Harmondsworth, Arkana, 1994

49 McNeely, Deldon Anne, *Animus Aeternus*, Toronto, Inner City Books, 1991

50 Meldman, Louis William, *Mystical Sex*, Tucson, Harbinger House, 1990

51 Nelson, Gertrud Mueller, *Here All Dwell Free: Stories to Heal the Wounded Feminine*, New York, Fawcett Columbine, 1991

52 Neumann, Erich, *Creative Man and Transformation*, New York, Pantheon Books, Bollinger Foundation Inc, 1948

53 Newman, Paul, *The Singing Cure: an Introduction to Voice Movement Therapy*, London, Routledge, 1993

54 Ovid, *Metamorphoses*, Harmondsworth, Penguin, 1955

55 Piercy, Marge, *Eight Chambers of the Heart*, Harmondsworth, Penguin, 1995

56 Plato, *The Complete Dialogues*, eds. Edith Hamilton and Huntington Cairns, Princeton, Princeton University Press, 1961

57 Plotinus, *Collected Works*, London, Faber, 1956

58 Raine, Kathleen, *Collected Poems*, London, Hamish Hamilton, 1981

59 — *The Land Unknown*, London, Hamish Hamilton, 1975

60 — *The Lion's Mouth*, London, Hamish Hamilton, 1977

61 Rice, Anne, *Lasher*, Harmondsworth, Penguin, 1993

62 — *Taltos*, London, Arrow, 1994

63 — *The Witching Hour*, Harmondsworth, Penguin, 1990

64 Rilke, Rainer Maria, *Letters to a Young Poet*, trans Joan M Burnham, San Rafael, CA, Classic Wisdom Collection, 1992

65 Rodenburg, Patsy *The Right to Speak: Working with the Voice*, London, Methuen, 1992

66 Sanford, John A, *Fate, Love and Ecstasy: Wisdom from the Lesser-Known Goddesses of the Greeks*, Wilmette, Ill, Chiron Publications, 1995

67 Shuttle, Penelope, and Redgrove, Peter, *Alchemy for Women: Personal Transformation Through Dreams and the Female Cycle*, London, Routledge, 1995

68 Suthrell, Charlotte, *Domestic Shrines*, PhD thesis (forthcoming)

69 Ulanov, Ann and Barry, *Transforming Sexuality: The Archetypal World of Anima and Animus*, Boston, Shambhala, 1994

70 Von der Heydt, Vera, *On the Animus*, Guild of Pastoral Psychology Lecture 126, 1964.

71 Von Franz, Marie-Louise, *C G Jung: His Myth in Our Time*, London, Hodder & Stoughton, 1975

72 Walter, Katya, *Tao of Chaos*, Shaftesbury, Element, 1996

73 Webb, Mary, *The Golden Arrow*, 1916

74 — *Gone to Earth*, London, Virago, 1979

75 — *Precious Bane*, London, Virago, 1978

76 Wetherbee, Winthrop, *Platonism and Poetry in the Twelfth Century*, Princeton, Princeton University Press, 1972

77 Wolkstein, Diana, and Kramer, S N, *Innana*, London, Rider, 1984

78 Wombwell, Felicity, *The Goddess Changes*, London, Mandala, 1991

79 Woodman, Marion, *The Ravaged Bridegroom: Masculinity in Women*, Toronto, Inner City Books, 1990

80 Yeats, W B, *Collected Plays*, London, Macmillan, 1934

81 — *Collected Poems*, London, Macmillan, 1950

82 Young-Eisendrath, Polly, *Hags and Heroes: A Feminist Approach to Jungian Psychotherapy with Couples*, Toronto, Inner City Books, 1984

83 — and Wiedemann, Florence, *Female Authority: Empowering Women Through Psychotherapy*, New York, Guildford Press, 1987

DISCOGRAPHY

84 Lister, Anne, *A Flame in Avalon*, Hearthfire, 34 Nightingale House, Thomas More Street, London E1 9UA

85 — *Spreading Rings*, as above

CINEMATOGRAPHY

The following titles are available on video. The reference numbers given are for PAL format only, except for no 90.

86 *La Belle et la Bête*, Jean Cocteau, Conoisseur Video CR018 (screened 1946)

87 *Beauty and the Beast*, Ron Koslow, Braveworld STV 2131 (screened 1987 onwards)

88 *Dracula*, Francis Ford Coppola, 20-20 Vision, NVT 14590 (screened 1992)

89 'Sub Rosa', *Star Trek Next Generation*, episode 165, Brannon Braga, CIC VHR 2862 (screened 1993 in USA, 1994 in UK)

90 *Truly, Madly, Deeply*, Anthony Minghella, Touchstone 1353 (screened 1990)

READER RESPONSE

While the author cannot enter into personal correspondence, she would welcome reader's responses to this book. Readers who would like a copy of the original questionnaire should send a medium-sized self-addressed envelope with six first class stamps *inside it* (within Britain) or eight international reply-paid coupons (outside Britain) – no foreign stamps – to the address below.

To receive one issue of Caitlín Matthews' quarterly newsletter, detailing events, books and courses, send eight first-class stamps (within Britain) or eight international reply-paid coupons or four US dollars in cash (outside Britain) to:

Caitlín Matthews, BCM Hallowquest, London WC1N 3XX, Britain

Index